THE CATHOLIC UNIVERSITY OF AMERICA
CANON LAW STUDIES
Number 112

THE VISITATION OF RELIGIOUS

A DISSERTATION

Submitted to the Faculty of Canon Law of the Catholic University of America in Partial Fulfillment of the Requirements for the Degree of

DOCTORATE OF CANON LAW

BY

THOMAS FRANCIS REILLY, C.SS.R., J.C.L.
of the Baltimore Province

THE CATHOLIC UNIVERSITY OF AMERICA
Washington, D. C.
1938

Imprimatur:

ANDREAS B. KUHN, C.SS.R.,
Superior Provincialis.
Brooklynii, die II Iunii, 1937.

Nihil Obstat:

HUBERTUS L. MOTRY,
Censor Deputatus.
Washingtonii, D. C., die XXV Ianuarii, 1938.

Imprimatur:

✠ MICHAEL J. CURLEY,
Archiepiscopus Baltimorensis.
Baltimorae, die XXV Ianuarii, 1938.

Printed by
THE PAULIST PRESS
New York, N. Y.

TO

THE MEMORY

OF

MY FATHER

TABLE OF CONTENTS

CHAPTER V

CHAPTER VI

CHAPTER VII

CHAPTER VIII

CHAPTER IX

CHAPTER X

FOREWORD

THE purpose of this study is both to set forth, in outline, the development of the law on the visitation of religious, their houses, and their churches from the earliest years of monasticism and to present an adequate commentary on the legislation which under the present Code of Canon Law regulates such visitations. Canonical visitation for centuries has occupied an important position as an instrument of ecclesiastical government and today all persons within the Church are, and must remain, subject to the visitation of some prelate.[1] For superiors, ecclesiastical and religious, entrusted with the care of a number of religious communities, visitation has furnished a sound and effective method of suppressing abuses and maintaining the ideals of the religious life in their purity. Visitation, as the term indicates, is a visit which a superior pays to persons or places subject to him with the purpose of conducting an inquiry into the condition of affairs in general or of investigating into the observance of certain laws which bind such persons or places. It is a fairly obvious idea and in its elements may be traced back to apostolic times. St. Paul after a missionary tour suggested to Barnabas: "'Let us return and visit our brethren in all the cities wherein we have preached the word of God, to see how they do. . . .' And he [Paul] went through Syria and Cilicia, confirming the churches, commanding them to keep the precepts of the apostles and ancients."[2] Visitation, however, did not develop into a legal institution until after some centuries.

Systematic visitation offers the superior an opportunity to collect information more reliable than might otherwise be obtained. As a consequence, he is enabled to encourage a spirit of good observance, to punish excesses and defects with justice and to provide remedies which will be well adapted to the concrete situation. The scope of a visitor's investigation into a religious community may

[1] *Cf.* Canon 1509, 7°.

[2] Acts XV, 36, 41.

cover a wide variety of topics: the observance of the rule, obedience to canonical laws, the studies which are pursued, the pastoral, missionary or teaching activities of the religious, the relations between the local superior and his subjects, the financial status of the house or of the church, and such other matters as may in particular instances require attention.

Visitation has been throughout its history and is in the present law primarily an administrative proceeding. The older canonists were fond of saying that by visitations a superior fulfilled the scriptural prescript: *Diligenter agnosce vultum pecoris tui, tuosque greges considera.*[3] Ordinarily, the visitor's inquiry and corrections were to be paternal in form, dispensing with the technical rules of judicial proceedings. However, if a visitor possessed judicial powers, he also assumed on visitation the character of a circuit judge. As he went upon his rounds, he might be confronted with cases which required that he hold court in a religious house and carry through a complete judicial trial. Yet judicial duties were and are today a secondary aspect of the visitor's office; in the present law a number of visitors are entirely lacking in judicial authority.

The course of history shows that religious have been visited chiefly by the local ordinaries and their own higher superiors. Under episcopal visitation those laws of the past, which delegated to the bishops in a permanent manner the right to proceed as apostolic visitors, have been included. Many instances might be collected in which popes commissioned extraordinary visitors to inquire into religious institutes or individual monasteries for particular cases. No attempt has been made to discuss the activities of such apostolic visitors; for, although the papacy by possessing supreme jurisdiction over all religious has of course the power to send forth visitors at any time, this form of visitation remains unusual and is not the subject of general laws.

The history of visitation, whether by bishops or by religious officials, cannot be considered as an isolated legal institution. In connection with episcopal visitation the wider questions of the extent of the bishop's jurisdiction over religious, his general duty of vigilance and the long and often confused history of exemptions, are

[3] Prov., XXVII, 23.

inevitably drawn into the discussion. In treating of the visitation by religious superiors, it is necessary to touch upon the development of the higher forms of monastic organization and the machinery of monastic government of which visitation became an integral part.

The writer wishes to express his gratitude to his Redemptorist superiors for the opportunity of advanced studies and to the Faculty of the School of Canon Law for their invaluable supervision. He is likewise appreciative of the gracious assistance given by the librarians of the University Library.

LIST OF ABBREVIATIONS

AAS—Acta Apostolicae Sedis.
ACII—Acta Congressus Iuridici Internationalis.
AKKR—Archiv für katholisches Kirchenrecht.
Ap—Apollinaris.
ASS—Acta Sanctae Sedis.
BZ—Byzantinische Zeitschrift.
C—Codex (Justinianus).
CpR—Commentarium pro Religiosis.
CR—Clergy Review.
DACL—Dictionnaire d'archéologie chrétienne et de liturgie.
Fontes—Codicis Iuris Canonici Fontes.
JP—Jus Pontificium.
JThSt—Journal of Theological Studies.
MGH—Monumenta Germaniae Historica.
MPG—Migne, Jacques Paul, Patrologiae Cursus Completus—Series Graeca.
MPL—Migne, Jacques Paul, Patrologiae Cursus Completus—Series Latina.
N—Novella.
NRT—Nouvelle Revue Théologique.
Periodica—Periodica de Re Canonica et Morali Utili praesertim Religiosis et Missionariis.
ThPrQS—Theologisch-prakitische Quartalschrift.

Part One
HISTORICAL SYNOPSIS

CHAPTER I

THE DEVELOPMENT OF VISITATION WITHIN RELIGIOUS ORDERS

SECTION 1

PRIOR TO THE FOURTH LATERAN COUNCIL (1215)

THE religious life, in the technical sense which that term has acquired in the Catholic Church, implies a withdrawal from ordinary social life and the pursuit of evangelical perfection to which aspirants obligate themselves by the vows of poverty, chastity, and obedience. Those who assume this life must separate themselves to some extent even from the general body of the faithful. They form a distinct class; they acquire a special status. Visitation by religious superiors as a means of controlling and promoting the religious life could evidently develop only when the religious life had been well established. The existence of a visitatorial system clearly presupposes the existence of communities of men or women organized for the attainment of the religious ideal. It further presupposes some sort of union among several religious communities and the creation of an official whose authority extends over more than one community. History shows two main types of religious unions. In the one the houses (or monasteries) form a federation; they are bound together in subordination to a central government with authority lodged in a superior general or a general assembly. In the other type of union, independent houses (or monasteries) meet and by common agreement pass laws and pledge themselves to maintain a uniform discipline. In either situation a visitatorial system is a fairly obvious development as a means to ensure the observance of one standard mode of life. But until one or the other situation is found it is clearly useless to seek traces of visitation by religious superiors.

From the earliest days of the Church the effort to carry out the teachings of Christ in their fullness and to observe His counsels as well as His commands was vigorous and widespread, but it is only late in the second or early in the third century that one hears of

"ascetics" and "virgins" as a distinct type of Christians, who were somewhat set apart from the rest of the Christian community and who no longer mingled freely in the general social activities about them. The ascetics and virgins had no well defined status; they remained in the cities and towns, living in their own homes or in the neighborhood with other kindred spirits, and were distinguished chiefly by their more intense preoccupation with prayer and ascetical practices. Yet to the ascetics and virgins may be traced the first discernible division between the general body of the faithful and a type distinctively religious.

The monastic movement, which had its beginnings in the early years of the fourth century, does not differ essentially in its aims from the earlier asceticism. Monasticism may be said to have begun with St. Anthony. In the year 285 Anthony shut himself up in a deserted fort at Pispir, on the Nile, and endeavored with great single-mindedness to achieve perfect mastery over himself and union with God. The force of his example brought from the cities and towns enthusiastic souls who took up their abode in the neighborhood of his retreat and sought to imitate his rigorous mode of life. Overcome by their urgings, he emerged from solitude and undertook to direct them and an ever increasing number of ascetics scattered through the desert of lower Egypt. Evidently a sharp line of demarcation set off the monks from other Christians. The monks had broken with the world; they had renounced home and friends and had fled to the deserts of Egypt where as poor and celibate men they strove for holiness alone. Thus the earliest monasticism shows the religious life as something unmistakably different from the ordinary Christian life.

While the great St. Anthony inspired the monastic movement and his luminous teaching remained a source of guidance throughout the centuries, he contributed little to its organization. He continued to live as a hermit and his followers remained hermits or, at most, settled in loose communities and adopted a semi-eremitical mode of life.[1] St. Anthony and his famous disciple, St. Hilarion, the

[1] Cuthbert Butler, O.S.B. *The Lausiac History of Pelladius* (Texts and Studies, VI, Cambridge, 1898-1904) I, 232-235; W. H. MacKean, *Christian Monasticism in Egypt* (New York, 1920), pp. 69-75.

leader of the Palestinian monks, were content to maintain a certain unity of spirit by informal instructions and admonitions to those who professed to be their disciples.[2] It remained for the monk Pachomius to organize religious communities, to bind them into a union, and to initiate the first visitatorial system.

The Pachomian Order

Pachomius, a monk of southern Egypt, whose career is contemporaneous with Anthony's, not only developed the cenobitic form of religious life, but also founded the first monastic order. A convert to Christianity he first took up the eremitical life, attaching himself to the venerated monk Paelmon. Then, with the latter's consent, he established a community of monks at Tabennisi, near the eastern bank of the upper Nile, sometime about the years 315-320.[3] The number of monks increased rapidly and another monastery was built at Pabau, a few miles to the north. Pachomius supervised both houses for a time and in later life transferred his residence to Pabau, appointing the monk Theodore as superior of Tabennisi. Eventually there arose nine monasteries for men and through Mary, the sister of Pachomius, two monasteries for women. Over these monasteries Pachomius ruled as superior general till his death about the year 346.[4]

The Pachomian rule [5] contains most of the features of later monastic discipline. Poverty, chastity, and obedience are insisted on;[6] regulations were laid down for common prayer, religious instruction, work, dress, the hours of sleep, the punishment for

[2] *Cf. Vita Antonii Abbatis,* cap. 53, 55—*MPL,* LXXIII, 165 (for the historical value of this life—*cf.* Butler, *Lausiac History,* I, 215-228); *Vita S. Hilarionis Eremitae,* nn. 24, 25—*MPL,* XXIII, 41; Cabrol, "Monasticism," *Encyclopedia of Religion and Ethics,* VIII, 785.

[3] Butler, *Lausiac History,* II, 206; MacKean, *Christian Monasticism in Egypt,* p. 92; Schiwietz, "Geschichte und Organisation der Pachomianischen Klöster," *AKKR,* LXXXI (1901), 630-638.

[4] Schiwietz, *loc. cit.,* 638-640.

[5] *Cf. MPL,* XXIII, 61-87. Cabrol states: "The rule attributed to Pachomius is substantially his work despite later retouchings and additions."—"Monasticism," *Encyclopedia of Religion and Ethics,* VIII, 785.

[6] Paulin Ladeuze, *Etude sur le cénobitisme Pakhomien* (Louvain, 1898), pp. 282-285.

transgressions, the visits of relatives, the treatment of sick confrères, and so forth. The number of monks in each monastery was large [7] and according to their trade they were subdivided into houses, each containing about thirty to forty monks, who were assigned to cultivating the fields or to the workshops as smiths, carpenters, bakers, fullers, and tailors.[8] The superiors of the houses were ruled by the superior of the monastery and all the monasteries were subject to the superior general (the archimandrate).[9]

The two most important devices for preserving this union of monasteries were the general assembly held twice a year and the visitations of the superior general. The visitations appear to be one point of which the recession of the Pachomian rule as translated by St. Jerome, makes no explicit mention. Such authorities on the Pachomian order as Ladeuze [10] and Schiwietz [11] state that visitations were conducted regularly by Pachomius, who laid down rules and made such corrections as were necessary. The *Vita Pachomii*, which seems to be the principal source on this point, gives very incomplete descriptions of Pachomius's visitatorial activities.[12] Visitation, however, became part of the established duties of the general and when Theodore succeeded to the generalship, shortly after Pachomius's death, he went about interviewing the brethren, privately, one by one, reproving and correcting whenever it proved necessary and always offering spiritual direction.[13]

From the Fifth to the Ninth Century

Monasticism as it developed elsewhere during the next centuries, both in the East and in the West, did not become so highly organized.

[7] Palladius states that Pachomius was the superior, in all, of three thousand monks (Butler, *Lausiac History*, II, 26).

[8] *Praefatio* [*S. Hieronymi*] *in Regulam Pachomii*, *MPL*, XXIII, 63.

[9] MacKean, *Christian Monasticism in Egypt*, p. 99.

[10] *Le Cénobitisme Pakhomien*, pp. 173, 186.

[11] "Geschichte und Organisation der Pachomianischen Klöster," *AKKR*, LXXXI (1901), 640.

[12] *Cf. Acta Sanctorum Maii*, III, 310, 316.

[13] *Cf.* François Kozman, *Textes Législatifs touchant le Cénobitisme Egyptien*, nn. 134, 163, *Codificazione Canonica Orientale*, Fonti—Serie II, Fasc. I, Vaticane: 1935.

The monasticism of the Greek Church was shaped according to the views of St. Basil (331-379). He and his followers were content to let each monastery exist as a self-sufficient and independent community. The longer Basilian rule speaks of the amalgamation of small communities into a single strong monastery, but does not seem to contemplate bonds between separate monasteries or one superior general.[14]

The archimandrate of Constantinople as a visitor was an external, ecclesiastical superior rather than a religious superior, for he enjoyed supervisory powers only as a delegate of the metropolitan. Similarly the two archimandrates of Palestine were representatives of the patriarch of Jerusalem and derived their visitatorial authority from him. Hence the visitations conducted by these monks (through delegated authority) are examples of episcopal visitation rather than instances of visitation which developed within the monastic order.[15]

Monasticism in the West was propagated by St. Martin of Tours, St. Caesarius of Arles, John Cassian, Eusebius of Vercelli, St. Paulinus of Nola, and others. Although some of these leaders founded more than one monastery, they made no attempt to unite their foundations.[16] The coming of St. Benedict of Nursia and his rule made no change in this regard. In writing his rule Benedict merely intended to propose what he considered essential for a well-regulated life in any monastic community.[17] The rules were concerned only with the interior discipline of each individual monastery and each abbot

[14] *Cf.* Margaret G. Murphy, *St. Basil and Monasticism* (Washington, D. C., 1930), p. 46, note 86. For the two rules of St. Basil, *Cf. MPG*, XXXI, 889-1052.

[15] *Cf.* Granic, "Die Rechtliche Stellung und Organisation der Griechischen Klöster nach Justinianischem Recht," *BZ*, XXIX, 30-32. *Cf. infra*, p. 36.

[16] *Cf.* Count de Montalembert, *The Monks of the West* (New York, 1896), I, 285-385; Herbert B. Workman, *The Evolution of the Monastic Ideal* (London, 1913), pp. 101-124.

[17] "The clerical order of the Church was regarded as one. . . . In the same way the monks of the West were one body, though following different rules and there was no thought of the followers of St. Benedict of forming an exclusive congregation or order in the modern signification of those words."—F. A. Gasquet, Introduction to Montalembert's *Monks of the West*, I, xx. *Cf.* John Chapman, *St. Benedict and the Sixth Century* (London: Sheed and Ward, 1929), pp. 28, 29, 203, 204.

was the father superior who bore the ultimate responsibility for their observance. Benedict had no thought of creating a federation of monasteries by erecting a governing superstructure over the individual houses [18] and for three centuries after his death (547) autonomous isolated monasteries were the rule everywhere.

With the beginning of the ninth century Western monasticism entered a new period. A tendency to create certain bonds between groups of monasteries was in evidence and this eventually culminated in the building of international monastic corporations under centralized control. This involved far-reaching changes in the constitutional law of Western monasticism and introduced systematized visitation by religious superiors. The first manifestation of this trend to unite the monasteries appeared in the efforts of St. Benedict of Aniane and King Louis the Pious.

St. Benedict of Aniane

St. Benedict of Aniane, in Aquitaine, had at the end of the eighth century embraced the monastic life with great earnestness and sought among the rules of the past for the best manner of living this life.[19] Inclined at first to an austere monasticism of the Egyptian type, he came to appreciate that the rule of St. Benedict of Nursia presented a standard of life possible to the many.[20] The Benedictine rule by that time had become almost the common law of Western monasticism and had supplanted the rules of St. Caesarius of Arles, of St. Columban and others.[21] In writing the rule the first St. Benedict had purposely refrained from complete and detailed regulation of every point in the daily order; it was left to the

[18] Cuthbert Butler, *Benedictine Monachism* (New York, 1919), pp. 28, 29.

[19] *Vita S. Benedicti Anianensis auctore Ardone seu Smaragdo eius discipulo*, n. 18—*MGH, Scriptores,* XV, I, 206, 207. Benedict later edited a compilation of monastic rules. *(Codex Regularum—MPL,* CIII, 423-702).

[20] L. M. Smith, *The Early History of Cluny* (Oxford, 1920), p. 5.

[21] Fernand Cabrol, *St. Benedict* (London, 1934), pp. 56, 131. The triumph of the Benedictine rule was assisted by counciliar legislation.—*Cf.* Hefele, *Conciliengeschichte,* III, 501, 502, 744. The Council of Chalons-sur-Saone (813) mentioned that practically all the monasteries of that region professed to follow the Bendictine rule (C. 22).—*Mansi,* XIV, 98.

good judgment of each abbot to supplement the broad prescriptions of the rule and to make the adaptation required for different times and circumstances. These additions to the rule peculiar to each monastery tended to become customs (*consuetudines*, or later *constitutiones*) and even in the eighth century they were in some places written down and took on a quality of permanence.[22]

Benedict of Aniane saw many serious disorders in the monasteries of his time and believed that the way to reform lay in imposing a uniform set of customs upon the Benedictine rule. He brought his own monastery at Aniane to a high level of observance and with the support of Louis the Pious, then king of Aquitaine (until 814), he diffused throughout the kingdom his interpretations of, and his additions to, the Benedictine rule. The life by his disciple Ardo relates that Benedict was given charge of the monasteries and at the command of Louis visited them not once or twice but many times, showing the monks each ordinance, confirming what was clear and explaining what was obscure so that almost all the monasteries of Aquitaine came to live according to a uniform discipline.[23]

When Louis became emperor in 814, the way was open for Benedict to extend his activities over a wider sphere. In the year 816 the Council of Aix-la-Chapelle decreed that the Benedictine rule was obligatory on all monks and in 817 the emperor summoned all the abbots to a conference with Benedict. The rule was thoroughly discussed; conflicting interpretations were cleared up and useful customs were confirmed. Uniform regulations in regard to food, drink, the chanting of office were agreed upon. Louis ratified the result of the conference and to ensure compliance with its regulations placed Benedict in charge of all the monasteries. Benedict continued his visitations and from his own monastery dispatched monks to other monasteries to serve as models of the reformed observance. Inspectors were also sent by the emperor to further the reform.[24]

This venture of Louis and Benedict constituted the first union among the monasteries of the West but it never passed beyond the

[22] Raphael Molitor, *Aus der Rechtsgeschichte benedictinischer Verbände* (Münster, 1928-1934), I, 39.

[23] *Vita S. Benedicti Anianensis*, nn. 29-31—*MGH, Scriptores*, XV, I, 211-214.

[24] *Op. cit.*, n. 36—*MGH, Scriptores*, XV, I, 215.

rudimentary stage. Benedict's right did not belong to him by reason of a permanent office, but was due rather to his personal influence and the commission derived from the assembly of 817 and the emperor. Upon Benedict's death in 824 the visitations ended and the reform collapsed. His work, however, did not utterly perish for the monks who founded Cluny a century later had been trained at Baume, one of the few monasteries to maintain the customs of Benedict of Aniane.[25]

The Cluniac Order

The Cluniac Order, composed of Benedictine monks, was the first order in the West with a centralized government.[26] It marked the full transition from autonomous, unrelated monasteries to a thoroughly unified system and yet there was continuity of development; for Cluny represented, in a highly accentuated form, tendencies which had already made their appearance in Benedictine history. As has been seen, under Benedict of Aniane a number of monasteries were drawn together for a reform that was to be attained by observing the same customs. With a similar aim Cluny established relationships with other monasteries. It had also happened before the founding of Cluny that colonies of monks sent from an abbey to make new foundations, would remain united to the parent community at least until the new foundation had sufficient resources and numbers to stand alone.[27] Cluny developed the full possibilities of this idea, and carried it to lengths before unknown by insisting on the continued subordination of its colonies

[25] Cabrol, "Zum Millenium von Cluny," *Studien und Mitteilungen zur Geschichte des Benedictiner-Ordens,* XII (1911), 54.

[26] Cluny was founded in 909 and by 937 seventeen monasteries acknowledged its authority. In its most glorious era, under the abbot Hugh the Great (1049-1109) Cluny ruled over two hundred monasteries, which had in turn a number of dependent priories. These were not all new foundations; many were older monasteries which, having been reformed by Cluniac monks, were drawn into the system. *Cf.* Graham, "The Relation of Cluny to Some Other Movements of Monastic Reform," *JThSt,* XV (1914), 183; Max Heimbucher, *Die Orden und Kongregationen der Katholischen Kirche* (3 ed., Paderborn, 1933), I, 184, 185.

[27] Molitor, *Rechtsgeschichte benediktinischer Verbände,* I, 86-110.

and only rarely permitting them to rise from the ranks of priories to abbeys.[28] Another factor in Benedictinism that might lead to a certain overlordship of one abbey was the personal prestige or ambition of an individual abbot.[29] For two hundred years Cluny was ruled by a series of statesmanlike abbots of astounding energy and breadth of outlook. The combination of these factors resulted in the growth of an order—"a vast feudal hierarchy,"[30]—that was one of the most powerful and influential institutions of the Middle Ages.

The abbot of Cluny was *pater et iudex totius ordinis* and upon his authority there were no restrictions. From time to time the abbots of Cluny drew up new customs or statutes supplementary to the Benedictine rule.[31] For the most part these customs or statutes were concerned with the liturgical service or the daily order[32] and there is little concerning the machinery of government and, until the year 1202, nothing on the subject of visitation. Yet, the chief reason for the success of the Cluniac enterprise was the practice of visitation.

In the first three centuries of Cluniac history chapters were held rarely and irregularly. Still, in order to preserve unity, contact between Cluny and its dependencies had to be frequent and regular. This was accomplished by the extraordinary activity of the abbots who traveled through France and to other countries in which Cluny had houses, visiting everywhere and overseeing everything. It has been said by Lavisse that the abbots Odo, Mayeul, Odilo and Hugh, who built up and maintained the far-flung realms of Cluny, appear to have been endowed with the gift of ubiquity.[33]

Not till the thirteenth century were the abbot and abbey of Cluny made subect to visitation. When visitation of Cluny as well

[28] Molitor, *op. cit.*, I, 120.

[29] Molitor, *op. cit.*, I, 43.

[30] Gasquet, Introduction to Montalembert's *Monks of the West*, I, xxxii.

[31] *Cf.* Peter the Venerable's prefatory statement to his constitutions.—*MPL*, CLXXXIX, 1025.

[32] Graham, "The Relation of Cluny to Some Other Movements of Monastic Reform," *JThSt*, XV (1914), 184-187.

[33] *Histoire de France*, II, Part II, 127, 128.

as of the whole order became legally regulated, the prescription was due to a borrowing from the practice of the Cistercians, who in the twelfth century initiated a model visitatorial plan. To fit this plan into the Cluniac government involved drastic changes. Before discussing the plan it is necessary to consider the Cistercian Order.

The Cistercian Order

The Cistercian contribution to the development of visitation as a monastic institution can hardly be exaggerated. Their system of visiting was adopted with modifications by most of the later orders and many features of the system passed into the canon law at the Fourth Lateran Council.

The Cistercian Order was another reform movement of Benedictines and began with the foundation of Citeaux (1098) by Robert of Molesme. The stark simplicity of the New Monastery, as Citeaux was called, led the youthful St. Bernard to apply for admission. Largely through his efforts the Cistercians spread rapidly and became the foremost order of the twelfth century. The great legislator for the Cistercians was Stephan Harding, the third abbot of Citeaux, who by the *Carta Caritatis* determined the structure of the order. The *Carta Caritatis* was drawn up as a compact among the Cistercian abbots and, upon ratification by them, received the approbation of Pope Callixtus II in the year 1119.[34] The Charter[35] is divided into five chapters, of which the second is devoted to the system of visiting. The relationship of mother abbeys to daughter abbeys—the latter, the abbeys which the former had founded directly—was the basis for associating the monasteries into groups for the purpose of visitation.[36] The Charter determined that once a year the abbot of each mother abbey shall visit personally or through one of the abbots of his group, all the daughter abbeys and "if he visit them more often let them rejoice the more" (§ VIII). There is some obscurity in the Charter on the right of the abbot of Citeaux to visit any house of the order

[34] *Cf.* Molitor, *Rechtsgeschichte benediktinischer Verbände,* I, 166-170.

[35] *MPL,* CLXVI, 1378-1383.

[36] The annual general chapter (*Carta Caritatis,* § § xii-xvii—*MPL,* CLXVI, 1380, 1381) served to bind all the monasteries together and to offset any possible tendency to break down the order into entirely separate groups.

(§ IV). Certainly he is obliged to conduct an annual visitation only of the houses immediately founded by Citeaux. Citeaux itself is visited each year by the abbots of La Ferté, Pontigny, Clairveaux, and Morimond (§ IX). When the abbot visitor is on his rounds, he presides (except at Citeaux), but has no right to prescribe any changes apart from correcting neglect of the rules. If the abbot of the house is present, the visitor shall consult him before making corrections; if the abbot is absent, the visitor may proceed alone (§§ VI, VII, X).[37]

Diffusion of the Cistercian Plan

With the swift advance of the Cistercians to a position of the highest prominence their fundamental law became widely known and found ready imitators. The Premonstratensian Order was the first to adopt the innovations of the *Carta Caritatis.* At Magdeburg in 1120, St. Norbert founded the Premonstratensians as canons regular and, using the 211th (109th) epistle of St. Augustine as his basic rule, added statutes of his own which obtained in 1126 the approval of Honorius II.[38] Yet, within a few years the Premonstratensian abbots had agreed upon constitutions which conformed closely to the *Carta Caritatis.*[39] Visitation, as prescribed in the sixth chapter of the fourth distinction of these early constitutions, was directly copied from that source.[40] There is the same relationship between mother and daughter abbeys. The abbot visitor may make no changes unless there are abuses against the rule. The abbot of the daughter abbey shall show every sign of respect and cede his place to the visitor. The subsequent chapter reveals an important difference which, incidentally, led to the widely adopted practice of forming provinces as administrative divisions within the orders. The chapter begins by stating that because of the large number of foundations and

[37] The Cistercian statutes, as they existed by the year 1256, show that the scope of the visitor's powers were later defined with more precision and detail. *Cf.* "Cistercian Statutes *(De Forma Visitationis),*" *Yorkshire Archeological Journal,* X (1889), 223-225.

[38] Heimbucher, *Die Orden und Kongregationem,* I, 434.

[39] Graham, "The Relation of Cluny to Some Other Movements of Monastic Reform," *JThSt,* XV (1914), 191.

[40] E. Martène, "Primaria Instituta Canonicorum Premonstratensium," *De Antiquis Ecclesiae Ritibus* (Antwerpiae, 1739), III, 922.

their distance from one another the abbots find it impossible to visit the daughter abbeys. Therefore, it is determined that there shall be a division into regions and that two *circatores* will visit the abbeys of each circuit or region. They are to make the corrections themselves or refer the matter to the general chapter. In case certain monks are refractory and refuse to accept the corrections of the visitor, the abbot of the parent abbey may be called in.

In Cluny the visitatorial plan of the *Carta Caritatis* as modified by the Premonstratensians was introduced by the Statutes of Abbot Hugh V and promulgated in the year 1202. The legislation of Hugh involved a revolution in the Cluniac government, for Hugh abdicated the unlimited powers enjoyed by the former abbots of Cluny and allowed the heads of the subordinate houses a voice in the government.[41] The general chapters were to be convoked annually.[42] The general definitors of the chapter were to elect a committee composed of two abbots and two priors, who would visit the abbey of Cluny during the octave of the feast of SS. Peter and Paul. The power of the visitors extended over the abbot himself and over the spiritual and temporal affairs of the abbey.[43] The visitors were to make the necessary corrections and notify the general chapter of their findings. Further, the order was divided into ten provinces. For each province one or two procurators or *camerarii* were to be appointed who would visit and correct as seemed necessary. They were to report to the definitors of the general chapter on the condition of the houses and the conduct of the monks. The chief duty of the *camerarii* was to supervise the proper administration of temporalities and they were under oath to the abbot of Cluny not to authorize any substantial alienation of monastic goods without his consent. The *camerarii* might have three or four horses and should receive nothing from the houses which they visited except food and lodging.[44]

[41] *Hugonis V Abbatis Cluniacensis Statuta,* praefatio et cap. 59—*MPL,* CCIX, 882, 896. *Cf.* Molitor, *Rechtsgeschichte Benediktinischer Verbände,* I, 126.

[42] *Op. cit.,* cap. 58—*MPL,* CCIX, 894, 895.

[43] *Op. cit.,* cap. 1—*MPL,* CCIX, 883.

[44] *Op. cit.,* cap. 56—*MPL,* CCIX, 893, 894.

The diffusion of Cistercian ideas is also seen in the Order of the Canons Regular of Arrouaise (diocese of Arras) [45] and, more important, in the Military Orders. Several of the military orders in Spain borrowed their statutes from the Cistercians or subjected themselves to the jurisdiction and visitation of Cistercian abbots.[46] St. Bernard was closely associated with the Order of Knights Templar. Due in great part to his efforts the order was confirmed at the Council of Troyes (1128). The rule was drawn from the Benedictine rule and the Cistercian customs and St. Bernard, if not the author, was at least the editor. The rule however is not concerned with the structure of government,[47] and in that the Templars seem to have departed widely from the Cistercians. Yet, visitations are part of the governing machinery. Pope Alexander III had commanded that the mother house should be established at Jerusalem and from there the Grand Master sent out visitors with plenary authority to all provinces.[48] Moreover, the general and provincial chapters sent out their own visitors to examine into disorders, to restore observance and to punish delinquents.[49]

The twelfth century saw the rise of several other centralized orders of men. Unfortunately their constitutions, as they existed in that century, are not accessible. Yet it seems that by the beginning of the thirteenth century visitation, if not legally prescribed in every cenralized order, was nevertheless a practice and was well on its way to becoming an integral part of their constitutions. Outside these centralized orders were a number of monasteries which stood alone and those, chiefly Benedictine and Augustinian houses, were still unprovided with religious visitors.

[45] Through St. Bernard's influence, this order (founded in 1097) took over the Cistercian system of filiation and visitation.—Graham *English Ecclesiastical Studies* (London, 1929), p. 17.

[46] Heimbucher, *Die Orden und Kongregationen,* I, 339; Thompson, "Monastic Orders," *Cambridge Medieval History,* V, 682, 683.

[47] *Cf. Regula Templariorum—MPL,* CLXVI, 855-874.

[48] D. Frederick Münter, *Statutenbuch des Ordens der Tempelherren* (Berlin, 1794), pp. 450, 454.

[49] *Op. cit.,* 452, 456.

Visitation of Nuns

The history of the visitation of monasteries of nuns requires no extended treatment. The greater number of nuns were immediately subject to the bishop and were visited only by him. Other nuns were under regular superiors of centralized orders and were visited by male visitors in the same manner as the order of men with which they were affiliated. In two orders, the Order of Gilbertines and the Order of Fontevrault, which were composed of double monasteries, nuns were sent forth as visitors.

The Gilbertines, an English order, founded in the early twelfth century by St. Gilbert of Selpringham, relied to a large extent for their rules upon the *Carta Caritatis* and the *Liber Usuum* of the Cistercians.[50] The nuns as well as the male religious (the men of this order were canons regular) attended the general chapter. At first the general superior, the Prior of All, was the sole visitor. He examined into the spiritual condition of each house, heard all the confessions, and regulated the sale and purchase of land and goods over the value of three marks.[51] As the order grew the task became too much for any one man. The Prior of All was then permitted to appoint certain canons and nuns to go about to all the houses and granges to correct and instruct the members of the order.[52] These canons (*scrutatores* or *circatores*), two in number and attended by a lay brother, visited the men; two choir nuns (*scrutatrices* or *circatrices*) and one lay nun visited the women. The visitations by the *scrutatores* were frequent; the *scrutatrices* made their rounds only once or twice a year for they had to be drawn in a cart and were attended by a canon and a lay brother. The Gilbertine rules cover to the minutest details the entire visitation, the proper safeguards for the *scrutatrices,* the examination of the accounts and the enclosure, the report that must be submitted to the Prior of All, and the penances for the abuse of visitatorial powers.[53]

[50] Graham, *St. Gilbert of Selpringham and the Gilbertines,* pp. 48, 49.

[51] Graham, *op. cit.,* pp. 52, 53.

[52] Holsten-Brockie, "Regulae Ordinis Sempringensis," *Codex Regularum* (Augsburg, 1759), II, 473, 474, i, ii.

[53] Holsten-Brockie, *op. cit.,* II, 274-276, iii-xii.

The Order of Fontevrault, which was also established in the beginning of the twelfth century, spread swiftly through France and into Spain and England. The founder, Robert of Abrissel, appointed a woman to rule after his death.[54] The property and the books were in the hands of women [55] and the men occupied a very subordinate position.[56] The enclosure did not exclude the possibility of journeys by the nuns [57] and therefore visitation naturally became the duty of the superioress general, who rode about to the monasteries attended by two nuns, two monks, and two servants.[58]

Such orders of double monasteries were few [59] and centralized orders of nuns were never formed. The nearest approach to a centralized order of nuns was the union of Cistercian nuns in Spain at the end of the twelfth century. These nuns held their own general chapter under the abbess of Burgos and the abbess and abbey of Burgos were visited by four abbesses after the manner in which Citeaux was visited by four abbots.[60] The constitution "*Periculoso*" of Boniface VIII in 1298,[61] which prohibited nuns to

[54] Heimbucher, *Die Orden und Kongregationen,* I, 327-330.

[55] *Regulae Sanctimonialium Fontis Ebraldi,* xliii, xliv—*MPL,* CLXII, 1082.

[56] *Regulae Sanctimonialium Fontis Ebraldi (Praecepta Recte Vivendi),* viii, xvii, xix, xx, xxiv, xxv—*MPL,* CLXII, 1083, 1084.

[57] *Regulae Sanctimonialium Fontis Ebraldi (De Itinere Faciendo)—MPL,* CLXII, 1082.

[58] Graham, *English Ecclesiastical Studies,* pp. 21, 22.

[59] There were only two other centralized orders, the *Humiliati* and the Brigittines, in which double monasteries existed by rule.—*Cf.* P. Stephanus Hilpisch, *Die Doppelklöster* (Münster: Aschendorffsche Verlagsbuchhandlung: 1928), pp. 70-77. In the Order of the *Humiliati,* the offices including that of visitor were held by men. *Cf.* Hieronymus Tiraboschius, *Vetera Humiliatorum Monumenta,* (Mediolani, 1768), III, 125, 128, 195. In the Brigittine Order the women governed the houses, but as the order was founded in the fourteenth century (after the legislation of Boniface VIII on the enclosure), the only visitors were the bishops of the places where their houses were situated.—*Cf. Regula S. Salvatoris sive Constitutiones S. Birgittae,* cap. 23—Holsten-Brockie, *Codex Regularum,* III, 115.

[60] Ludovicus Thomassinus, *Vetus et Nova Ecclesiae Disciplina* (Venetiis, 1730), part. I, lib. III, cap. 68, n. 12; Graham, *English Ecclesiastical Studies,* pp. 21, 22.

[61] C. un., *de statu regularium,* III, 16, in VI°. *Cf.* Valentine T. Schaaf, *The Cloister* (Cincinnati, 1921), pp. 40-44.

leave the enclosure, was followed by similar legislation in particular councils and put a stop to any possible development along such lines. There is no further history of visitation by female religious until the rise of congregations of simple vows in the eighteenth century, wherein the enclosure did not prohibit the egress of the sisters and hence opened the way to a union of religious houses and the consequent visitations conducted by the sisters.

Section 2

From the Fourth Lateran Council (1215) to the Council of Trent (1545)

The Benedictine and Augustinian Houses

While the religious of the centralized orders had generally developed visitatorial systems by the beginning of the thirteenth century, a large number of religious were living in autonomous monasteries which were in no juridical way related to other monasteries and were subject exclusively to the local abbot or prior. These autonomous monasteries were almost all Benedictine or Augustinian houses. It has been seen that the establishment of autonomous Benedictine houses antedated the growth of centralized orders in the West. After Cluny led the way, there were other efforts to form unions among the Black Benedictines, but the great majority of Benedictine communities remained separate families. Communities of Canons Regular arose in great numbers during the latter half of the eleventh century and adapted a rule from the famous 211th epistle of St. Augustine.[62] Throughout the twelfth century they continued to multiply rapidly and like the Black Benedictines they existed as separate communities related to one another only by the observance of the same basic rule.[63] Up to the time of the Fourth Lateran Council neither the Canons Regular of

[62] *MPL*, XXXIII, 958-965.

[63] *Cf.* W. H. Frere, "The Early History of Canons Regular as illustrated by the foundation of Barnwell Priory," *Fasciculus Joanni Willis Clarke dicatus* (Cambridge, 1909).

St. Augustine nor the Black Benedictines, outside the Cluniac Order, were visited by religious officials.

The Constitutions "In Singulis" and "Ea Quae"

The Fourth Lateran Council (1215) furnished the first example of universal legislation on visitation by religious officials. The constitution *"In Singulis"* (the twelfth canon of this council) outlined a scheme of triennial chapters and visitations which, while departing in several respects from the Cistercian plan, is yet an official recognition of the value of these two instruments of monastic government for which the Cistercians are above all responsible. However, the constitution *"In Singulis"* did not disturb the visitatorial systems already in existence, for it was concerned only with such monasteries as had not been accustomed to meet in chapter and were not visited by regular superiors. Thus it had application chiefly to the Benedictines and Canons Regular. This constitution was inserted into the Decretals of Gregory IX and stands with the constitution *"Ea Quae"* of Honorius III.[64] The latter, originally addressed to the abbots and monks of Lombardy, became universal law by being incorporated into the Gregorian Decretals and served to amplify and clarify the provisions of the constitution *"In Singulis."* These constitutions deserve to be considered in some detail for they contain essentially all the law for the visitation of autonomous houses and have made their influence felt even down to the present.

The constitution *"In Singulis"* decreed that triennial chapters should be held in every kingdom or province. The chapter was to be attended by all the abbots and by the priors of those houses which had no abbots. To facilitate the procedure of the first chapters, two Cistercian abbots were to be invited since they were well acquainted with the workings of such assemblies. The Cistercian abbots were to preside with two members of the chapter whom they might freely select and none of the four presidents was to arrogate to himself the power of a superior. The proceedings of the chapter followed the Cistercian model. Among the several duties of

[64] C. 7, 8, X, *de statu monachorum et canonicorum regularium,* III, 35.

the chapter was the appointment of the visitors. Certain prudent and religious men were to be selected to visit each monastery of monks and nuns to make such corrections and reforms as were needed. Thus if they learned that the superior of a place should be removed from administration, they were to denounce him to the local bishop, who was to take steps to remove him; if the bishop did not act they were to refer the matter to the Holy See. The chapter laid down the manner in which the visitors should make the visitation, but the visitors were sent forth in the name of the Pope. It was expressly mentioned that the bishops were not relieved by these provisions of their obligation to care for the discipline in the monasteries subject to them and they were admonished to maintain the non-exempt monasteries in such order that the visitors from the chapter might find the monasteries deserving of praise rather than correction.

The constitution *"In Singulis"* was supplemented by the constitution *"Ea Quae"* which outlined in more detail the scope of the visitation. The latter granted the visitor power of reform in spiritual and temporal matters; the correction and the punishment of delinquent monks were to be effected through the abbots in accordance with the visitor's mandate and the rules of the institute. If the abbots failed so to act, they were to be punished publicly in the general chapter. Upon contumacious and rebellious monks the visitors might inflict censures as delegates of the Holy See. Non-exempt abbots who failed notably in their duties were to be denounced to the bishop who would provide a trustworthy coadjutor until the time of the next chapter. The visitor might even call for the removal of an abbot who was wasting the goods of the monastery or was otherwise deserving of removal and, if the abbot was not exempt, the bishop was to remove him summarily and then appoint a temporary administrator. If the bishop was unwilling or neglected to act, the visitors or the presidents of the chapter were to inform the Holy See. The visitors themselves or the presidents of the chapter might suspend exempt abbots from administrative duties and appoint other administrators in their place. Deposition, however, was reserved to the Holy See. The visitors themselves did not escape supervision, for if they were guilty of any abuse of au-

thority the visitors appointed at the next chapter to succeed them were to make mention of this in their reports. The male visitors appointed by the chapter were also to visit abbesses and nuns in the same manner.

To the Benedictines the plan of the Fourth Lateran Council and of Honorius III gave that measure of support and supervision which was needful and at the same time did no violence to the Benedictine principle of autonomous monasteries. When tried this system of visitation proved sound and effective, but unfortunately it was not adopted universally.[65]

In England, in the two provinces of Canterbury and York, the Black Benedictines instituted chapters and visitations almost immediately after the Fourth Lateran Council and continued them with great regularity down to the time of the dissolution of the monasteries under Henry VIII. As most of the English Benedictines were not exempt, their houses were subject to a twofold visitation.[66] On the continent several provinces held the chapters and sent forth visitors, but, faced with difficulties, few kept up the practice regularly.[67]

By the Augustinian Canons the provisions of the Fourth Lateran Council were even more generally disregarded. Several provinces endeavored to put the plan into execution, but soon allowed it to lapse. A few popes granted dispensations from the constitution "*In Singulis,*" but more often the Papacy urged the necessity of the triennal chapters and visitations to both the Benedictines and Augustinians. At the Council of Vienne (1312) Clement V renewed the legislation of the Fourth Lateran Council on this sub-

[65] *Cf.* Heimbucher, *Die Orden und Kongregationem,* I, 210.

[66] *Cf.* Butler, *Benedictine Monachism,* pp. 221, 240, 241. Gasquet, writing of the Lateran scheme, states: "The system complex, as it may appear to the theorist, in practice worked thoroughly well. In England, under its influence, the monasteries maintained their prestige and secured in general good discipline. . . . To the last not a single English Benedictine house ever even thought of secularization. If this be so it is simply owing to the fact that the monasteries of England accepted and loyally carried out, the system proposed to them by the Lateran Council."—Introduction to Montalembert's *Monks of the West,* I, xliii, xliv.

[67] *Cf.* Heimbucher, *op. cit.,* I, 210, 200, 402; Gasquet, *op. cit.,* I, xlv.

ject.[68] The most serious efforts to secure compliance were made by the Cistercian Pope Benedict XII.

The Legislation of Benedict XII

In his bull *"Summi Magistri"* (July 12, 1336), popularly known as the *Benedictina,* Benedict XII divided the Black Benedictines into thirty-six provinces.[69] Reenacting the laws of the Fourth Lateran Council and of Honorius III on a visitation, he added a number of prohibitions to ensure that visitation might not be used as a source of illicit revenue for those who conducted it. The visitors were not to remain in any one place more than two days and should not ask for sumptuous fare. Visitors who received money or gifts of any kind were obliged to restore twice the value within a month, or otherwise be suspended *ab officio et beneficio.* Three years later this same pope in his bull *"Ad Decorem,"* [70] made similar provisions for the Canons Regular of St. Augustine. They were divided into twenty-two provinces and were commanded to hold annual chapters and elect visitors. Provisions similar to those in Benedict XII's bull *"Vas Electionis"* prevented the visitors from receiving gifts.[71] However, if the visitors had to travel some distance, the house which they were visiting might be asked to defray their traveling expenses. If the house visited was without adequate resources, the traveling expenses were to be supplied from the fund contributed to the provincial chapters for this purpose (§ 20).

The efforts of Benedict XII were attended with no more success than the endeavors of his predecessors. Obstacles were many and, while chapters and visitations were maintained for a time, they gradually ceased. To the neglect of these laws Gasquet and Heimbucher ascribe the subsequent misfortunes of the Benedictines and Augustinians.[72]

[68] C. 1, *de statu monachorum vel canonicorum regularium,* III, 10, in Clem.

[69] *Bullarium Magnum,* I, 218-237.

[70] *Bullarium Magnum,* I, 237-253.

[71] *Cf. infra,* p. 56.

[72] Gasquet, Introduction to Montalembert's *Monks of the West,* I, xlv; Heimbucher, *Die Orden und Kongregationen,* I, 402.

Efforts in the Fifteenth Century to Promote Visitation

The Council of Constance (1414-1417) stimulated a movement for monastic reform. The Benedictine abbots of Germany were ordered to assemble and to put into practice the injunctions of the bull *"Summi Magistri,"* with the result that visitations were held regularly in the Province of Mainz, which covered the greater part of the present Germany.[73] Pope Martin V made a further attempt at enforcement and in the year 1422 fifty-seven abbots of the Province of Cologne-Treves assembled and elected visitors.[74] Later in the century the Bursfeld Congregation of German Benedictines arose and besides providing visitors according to the constitution *"In Singulis"* also instituted the president of the congregation as general visitor with the right to appoint annual visitors.[75]

During the same century the Cassinese Congregation was formed by a union of the Italian Benedictines and this congregation was ruled by an annual chapter which appointed all the officials including the visitors.[76]

Among the Augustinians a similar congregational movement provided visitors for some of the houses and in the middle of the fifteenth century the papal legate, Cardinal Nicholas of Cusa, was active in Germany. He managed to revive the practice of annual chapters and visitations in several Augustinian provinces.[77] Yet, up to the time of the Council of Trent, a number of Augustinian and Benedictine houses remained without the benefit of regular visitation by monastic officials.[78]

[73] Butler, *Benedictine Monachism*, p. 241.

[74] *Cf.* Martene, *De Antiquis Ecclesiae Ritibus*, IV, 861-866.

[75] Butler, *op. cit.*, pp. 242, 243.

[76] *Cf.* Butler, *op. cit.*, pp. 243-245.

[77] Heimbucher, *Die Orden und Kongregationen*, I, 424-428; 402, 403.

[78] There is no need to discuss visitation in the centralized orders during this period. As has been mentioned, most of the orders in existence before the Fourth Lateran Council had initiated the chapters and visitations and therefore were not bound by the constitutions *In Singulis* and *Ea Quae*. The orders which were founded after the Fourth Lateran Council provided for chapters and visitations, with certain divergencies in detail and the

The Visitation of Nuns

The visitation of nuns subject to regulars of centralized orders was regulated entirely by the constitutions of each order up to the fourteenth century. Nuns who were subject to regulars of the Benedictine and Augustinian houses were visited—if at all—by religious officials, in conformity with the constitutions *"In Singulis"* and *"Ea Quae"*; for, as has been mentioned, the male visitors sent from the chapters were to visit both monasteries of men and of women.

In the year 1312, with the approval of the Council of Vienne, Clement V enacted a special law *"Attendentes"* [79] on the visitation of nuns. Exempt nuns subject to regular superiors were to be visited annually by the latter. The visitors should not permit the nuns to use silks or such styles of dress and coiffure as might be considered unsuitable to their state; the visitors should see that the nuns did not attend dances or secular activities, that they did not go through the towns or the streets either in the daytime or at night, and that they did not in any way lead a life of pleasure, but rather that they devoted themselves to the cultivation of virtue within their monasteries. The visitors were to be satisfied to have as companions two notaries, two persons from their own church, and four other upright and mature men. Those who dared to hinder the visitors in carrying out the aforesaid ordinance incurred, *ipso facto,* excommunication if after having been admonished they did not repent.

Holy See approved of the constitutions and, so long as these features were present, made no attempt to impose complete uniformity in the systems. The Dominicans instituted an excellent visitatorial plan, with several innovations which were in harmony with their democratic constitutions.—*Cf.* Galbraith, G. R., *The Constitution of the Dominican Order (1216 to 1360)* (London: Longmans, 1925), pp. 155-162, 246, 247. For visitation in the Franciscan Order, *cf.* H. Holzapfel, *Manuale Historiae Ordinis Fratrum Minorum* (Fribourg, 1909), pp. 24, 156. A number of rules and statutes of other orders on visitation, as they were during this period, may be found in the valuable collection edited by Holsten-Brockie, *Codex Regularum.*

[79] C. 2, *de statu monachorum vel canonicorum regularium,* III, 10, in Clem.

Section 3

From the Council of Trent (1545-1563) to the Code of Canon Law (1918)

Legislation of the Council of Trent

In its twenty-fifth session the Council of Trent devoted twenty-two chapters to the reformation of monasticism. In its earlier sessions the council had somewhat increased the power of the bishops over regulars in order that they might thereby aid in this reform, yet the council would have the revival of monastic discipline proceed as far as possible from within and built its hopes particularly upon the chapters, provincial and general, and upon visitation conducted by regulars themselves.[80]

The first chapter of the twenty-fifth session enjoined religious, in general terms, to live according to the rule they had professed, to observe their vows and to live the common life. The superiors were urged to use all care and diligence in the chapters and visitations, which they should not neglect to undertake at the proper seasons, that in these matters there be no relaxation.[81]

The chapter on the visitation of exempt monasteries of all orders organized under central governments decreed:

> Abbots, who are the heads of orders, and other superiors of the aforesaid orders, who are not subject to bishops, but have a lawful jurisdiction over other inferior monasteries or priories, shall, each in his own place and order, visit officially the said monasteries and priories that are subject to them, even though held *in commendam:* . . . and those who preside over monasteries of the orders aforesaid shall be bound to receive the above named visitors and to execute their orders. Also, those monasteries themselves, which are the heads of orders, shall be visited conformably to the constitutions of the Holy Apostolic See and of each several order . . . [82]

80 *Cf.* Molitor, *Rechtsgeschichte benediktinischer Verbände,* I, 319.

81 Council of Trent, sess. XXV, *de regularibus,* c. 1.

82 Council of Trent, sess. XXV, *de regularibus,* c. 20. Translation from Waterworth, *Canons and Decrees of the Council of Trent,* p. 250.

It seems that at the time of the Council of Trent all the centralized orders were exempt from episcopal visitation and jurisdiction and hence were comprised under this decree. The law did nothing more than call for the enforcement of what the constitutions of the several orders had long prescribed. The frequency, the scope and the procedure of visitation remained as theretofore determined in the various statutes and rules of each particular order. In the centuries between the Council of Trent and the Code no further ecclesiastical legislation was issued to regulate the visitation in the orders under central control.

The eighth chapter of the twenty-fifth session of the council undertook to deal with monasteries which existed without juridical ties to one another. As the meaning of this eighth chapter was the subject of prolonged debate, in the years after the council, it may be well to reproduce the pertinent part.

> All monasteries, which are not subject to general chapters or to bishops, and which have not their own ordinary regular visitors, but have been accustomed to be governed under the immediate protection and direction of the Apostolic See, shall be bound within a year from the end of the present council and thenceforth every third year, to form themselves into congregations, according to the reform of the constitution of Innocent III beginning *"In Singulis"* published in a general council; and shall depute certain regulars to deliberate and ordain as to the mode and order of establishing the congregations aforesaid and touching the statutes to be therein observed. But should they be negligent in these matters, it shall be lawful for the metropolitan, in whose province the aforesaid monasteries are situated, to convoke them for the above named purposes as delegate of the Holy See.[83]

The council then goes on to say, in the same chapter, that if the number of monasteries within the limits of a single ecclesiastical province be too few, then the monasteries of two or three ecclesiastical provinces may combine to establish a congregation and to appoint visitors; but if at the instance of the metropolitan the

[83] Council of Trent, sess. XXV, *de regularibus*, c. 8. Translation from Waterworth, *Canons and Decrees of the Council of Trent*, pp. 242, 243.

monasteries do not take steps to execute this decree, they are made subject to the bishops as delegates of the Apostolic See.

The Benedictines

This decree was important because of its influence upon the Black Benedictines, who seem to have been the only large group of regulars who were still not visited at stated intervals by religious officials. The decree, however, was directed, as is evident from its text, to exempt monasteries and many of the monasteries of the Black Benedictines were under the jurisdiction of the bishops. Thus this decree seemed to have a more restricted application to the Benedictines than did the constitution *"In Singulis"* which sought to provide chapters and visitors for exempt and non-exempt monasteries; but, in one way the Tridentine decree appeared to go much further in so far as it commanded the exempt houses of each province to form a congregation (*se redigere in congregationem*). By many of the Black Benedictines of the following century this was interpreted to mean that exempt monasteries were authorized to attach themselves to a Benedictine congregation already in existence or to create once and for all a congregation which would exist as a moral person.[84]

Whatever may have been the intent of this decree of the council, its principal effect was to bring about the formation of perpetual congregations and only thereby to establish visitatorial systems. In the seventeenth century some twelve congregations, composed of both exempt and non-exempt Benedictine houses, came into being and received papal confirmation and exemption.[85]

[84] Molitor, *Rechtsgeschichte benediktinischer Verbände,* I, 319, 320. Fagnanus, carefully interpreting this passage of the Council of Trent and citing a decision of the Congregation of the Consistory, concludes that the council merely intended to bring the monasteries together every three years for the purpose of holding chapters wherein visitors would be appointed and statutes passed, but did not intend to grant the right to create perpetual congregations in the form of juridical persons. *Commentarium in quinque libros decretalium,* lib. III, de statu monachorum, cap. 7, nn. 8, 10. In certain places the Benedictines did make efforts to hold the triennial chapters and to send forth visitors. *Cf.* Molitor, *op. cit.,* I, 326; Fagnanus, *op. cit.,* p. 482, n. 11.

[85] Molitor, *Rechtsgeschichte benediktinischer Verbände,* I, 325, 384; Heimbucher, *Die Orden und Kongregationen,* I, 230-235.

Through this congregational movement all the Benedictine monasteries were at last provided with regular visitors.

The civil laws to secularize religious which were passed during the period of the Enlightenment and the French Revolution accomplished the destruction of these congregations,[86] but in the nineteenth century a revival of Benedictine life brought new congregations into being and reestablished some of the old congregations. In all of them systematic visitation was assured.[87]

Leo XIII determined to unite these congregations in some manner and by the brief *"Summum semper,"* [88] created the abbot primate. Butler has discussed thoroughly the position of the primate and the independence which remained to the congregations.[89] The only point relevant here is that the abbot primate received a certain right of visitation when the extent of his jurisdiction was determined by the decree *"Inestimabilis"* of the Congregation of Bishops and Regulars.[90] The decree stated that in cases of urgent necessity the abbot primate had the right of visiting any of the federated Black Benedictine Congregations; if there were questions which could not be settled peaceably and without delay and yet called for immediate adjustment, he might then and there decide such questions and thereupon was to refer the matter to the Holy See.

Visitation of Nuns

Where monasteries of nuns were subject to the jurisdiction of regulars, the Council of Trent did not disturb this relationship.[91] Indeed, when urging upon regulars the duty of visiting the various houses subject to them, the council made no distinction between the monasteries of men and the monasteries of women.[92] Regular

[86] "Von mehr als 1500 Benediktinerklöster, welche zur Zeit des Konstanzer Konzils bestanden, überdauerten kaum 30 den Sturz Napoleons."—Heimbucher, *op. cit.*, I, 251.

[87] *Cf.* Butler, *Benedictine Monachism*, pp. 248-257.

[88] 12 Iul. 1893—*Fontes*, n. 619.

[89] *Op. cit.*, pp. 263-265.

[90] 16 Sept. 1893—*Fontes*, n. 2022.

[91] Sess. XXV, *de regularibus*, c. 9.

[92] Sess. XXV, *de regularibus*, c. 20.

superiors thus retained their position as visitors in spiritual and temporal matters in accordance with the law *"Attendentes"* of Clement V and the prescriptions of their own particular rules. Thus, up to and after the Council of Trent they were obliged, but not limited, to an annual visitation.[93]

The law on the visitation of nuns by the regular superiors did however undergo a few changes during the post-Tridentine period. Gregory XIII in his constitution *"Dubiis"*[94] forbade regular superiors to enter the cloister of nuns subject to them, except in cases of necessity and then only when attended by a few religious and rather elderly persons.[95]

Alexander VII, by his constitution *"Felici,"*[96] for Italy and the adjacent islands, regulated in detail the visitation by regular superiors. The following points were determined: (a) Regular superiors could not enter the enclosure except for the purpose of local visitation; (b) there was to be only one visitation a year by the regular superiors; (c) if it were necessary to visit more frequently, the regular superior had to be accompanied by the bishop or an ecclesiastic of mature age deputed by the bishop; (d) the regular superior could not delegate to another the task of visiting the interior of the monastery and thus the visitation had to be postponed if he was unable to visit in person; (e) the regular superior was to

[93] The visitatorial rights granted to bishops in regard to the enclosure and administration of temporalities (*cfr. infra,* p. 63) did not deprive the regular superiors of their right to an independent visitation in these matters.—*Cf.* S. Pius V, const. *Circa Pastoralis,* 29 Maii, 1566, § § 2, 8—*Fontes,* n. 112; Angelus Lucidi, *De Visitatione Sacrorum Liminum,* (3 ed., Romae, 1883), II, p. 220, n. 219.

[94] 23 Dec. 1581—*Fontes,* n. 148.

[95] The question was raised by canonists whether this limited the regular superior to the annual visitation to which he was obliged by law. Gaudentius de Janua *(De Visitatione Cuiuscumque Praelati Ecclesiastici et Regularis* [Romae, 1748], dub. XXI, n. 5) was of the opinion that no such restriction resulted from Gregory's constitution. The Roman Congregations interpreting the phrase of the above constitution, *in casibus necessariis,* decided that it did not limit the bishops to the annual visitation to which they were obliged by law (*cf. infra,* p. 63), but there appears to be no decision or declaration in regard to regular visitors.

[96] 20 Oct. 1664—*Fontes,* n. 240.

hold the personal visitation of the nuns at the grille outside the enclosure and, as in the previous point, he could not delegate to another this duty; (f) the general superior could bring two companions into the enclosure; other superiors, one companion; (g) refreshments were not to be taken by the visitors while within the enclosure; (h) four of the older nuns were to attend the visitor and his companion while the latter were within the enclosure; (i) those who violated the aforesaid provisions *ipso facto* incurred excommunication, privation of all offices, were incapable of holding office in the future, and lost the active and the passive voice. The bishop might correct and punish violations in these matters despite privileges and exemptions.[97]

The only other legislation on the visitation of nuns came from the Sacred Congregation of the Council, which demanded that the bishop of the diocese be informed of the day and the hour when the regular superior intended to make his visitation of monasteries of nuns.[98]

[97] Ferraris ("Moniales," art. III, nn. 74-77), Lucidi *(De Visitatione,* II, 221, n. 221), and Benedict XIV *(De Synodo Dioecesana,* lib. IX, cap. 15, n. 6) write as though this constitution had later become universal law. Bouix *(Tractatus de Jure Regularium,* I, 139) states that he knows of no legislation which thus extended the binding force of the above constitution.

[98] S. C. C., 22 Sept., 1742, ad 5—*Fontes,* n. 3543; S. C. C., 13 Mart., 24 Apr., 8 Maii, 1751—*Fontes,* n. 3613.

CHAPTER II

EPISCOPAL VISITATION OF REGULARS

Section I

Prior to the Fourth Lateran Council (1215)

Conciliar Law and Monastic Rules Before Gregory the Great

There does not appear to be any evidence that bishops conducted formal visitations of the ascetics and virgins of the second and third centuries. It can hardly be expected that a legal institution for the control of the religious life would go back to the first small beginnings, when religious were not even a class clearly marked off from the rest of the Christian community.

There is no difficulty after the beginning of the fourth century in distinguishing the religious class; the rise of monasticism, as has been mentioned, created not only a clear distinction, but a sharp cleavage, between the religious life and the life of the ordinary Christian. But the relationship between the monks and the episcopate was decidedly indefinite up to the time of the Council of Chalcedon in the year 451. Monasticism began as a private venture of Christian laymen and laywomen who separated themselves from the general body of the faithful. For a century and a half it remained of a strictly private character and was not the specific object of ecclesiastical legislation. In three general councils of this period and in the many particular councils no laws appeared to determine the extent of the bishop's jurisdiction over the monks and the monasteries. In the most famous and complete rules of this time—the rule of Pachomius,[1] the two rules of St. Basil[2] and the institutes of Cassian[3]—there do not seem to be any statements on

[1] *Cf. MPL,* XXIII, 61-87.

[2] *Cf. Regulae fusius tractatae—MPG,* XXXI, 889-1052; *Regulae brevius tractatae—MPG,* XXXI, 1051-1306.

[3] *Cf. De Coenobiorum institutis libris duodecim—MPG,* XLIX, 53-475.

what was conceived to be the proper relationship between the monks and the episcopate. From a legal point of view no more can be said than that the men and women who withdrew from the general body of the faithful and entered the monastic state put themselves in a position in relation to the episcopate which was not defined until the Council of Chalcedon.[4]

The Council of Chalcedon (451) determined this relationship in no ambiguous terms. The fourth canon of the council decreed that no one should establish a monastery contrary to the will of the bishop and that the monks in every city and place should be subject to the bishop and not leave their monasteries without episcopal permission. The eighth canon stated that the clergy of the poor-houses, the monasteries, and the martyries were to remain under the authority of the bishops, according to the tradition of the holy Fathers; they were not to remove themselves from the rule of their own bishops. Those who dared to overturn this canon and did not submit to the bishop, were to undergo canonical penalties, if clerics, or excommunication, if monks or laymen.[5]

[4] The monasticism of the fourth century was not, however, as it sometimes has been represented, a movement which in its early stages developed outside the Church. The tendency seen in certain hermits to consider their mode of life so excellent as to render unnecessary episcopal supervision and the ordinary means of sanctification along with the evidences of hostility between the monks and the clergy, cannot obscure the fact that the ideals of this monastic movement were derived from the ascetic teachings of Christ and that the great leaders of the monks, such as St. Anthony, St. Basil, Pachomius, and Schenoudi, were highly esteemed by various bishops, which could hardly have been the case had there been the slightest suspicion that these men were heading a separatist movement. On this question, *cf.* Workman, *The Evolution of the Monastic Ideal,* pp. 16-20; Hannay, *The Spirit and Origin of Christian Monasticism,* passim; Johannes Leipoldt, *Schenute von Atripe und die Entstehung des National—Aegyptischen Christentums* (Texte und Untersuchungen zur Geschichte der Altchristlichen Literatur, N. F. Bd. X., Hft, I, Leipzig: 1903), pp. 52, 90, 159, 160; *Vita Antonii Abbatis, Athanasii Praefatio—MPL,* LXXIII, 127; MacKean, *Christian Monasticism in Egypt,* passim; Butler, *Lausiac History,* I, 233-251; P. Pourrat, *Christian Spirituality* (Burns, Oates and Washburne, London: 1922), I, 74-110.

[5] *Mansi,* VII, 359, 362. Other canons of the council served, though less directly to uphold episcopal authority over monasticism. *Cf.* cc. 16, 18, 23, 24—*Mansi,* VII, 364-367.

During the next century and a half several particular councils issued laws, framed in rather general terms, which placed the monks under the jurisdiction of the bishops and put no limitations on the exercise of the episcopal authority over them.[6] In effect, the laws constituted each monastery as a separate diocesan institute. The bishop had an unrestricted right of vigilance over the abbot and monks, yet little was said on the manner in which this right was to be exercised. The obvious courses, which the bishop might adopt, were to visit the monasteries, personally or through a delegate,[7] or to summon the abbots to himself in order to be informed of the state of each monastery. The latter expedient was urged in the Council of Orleans (511); [8] but, though the bishops had the right to visit as often as they desired, there is no evidence in the conciliar legislation of this time that visitation was a duty which had to be undertaken at stated intervals.

The rule of St. Benedict (480-547), which came to have such an immense influence on the monastic life of the West, took for granted a certain amount of episcopal vigilance over the monasteries. Thus the Benedictine rule requested the bishop of the diocese to overthrow the election of an abbot who was unworthy and

[6] The Council of Orleans (511) stated that abbots were under the authority of the bishop and that the latter should convoke them for an annual meeting at a place which he had selected (c. 19—*MGH, Leges,* III, I, 7). The Council of Epaon (517) gave the bishop power to punish and even remove delinquent abbots, though in case of removal the abbot might appeal the case to the metropolitan (c. 19—*MGH, Leges,* III, I, 24). The same law was passed by the Second Council of Orleans (553) (c. 21—*MGH, Leges,* III, I, 64). The Fifth Council of Arles (554) asserted that the discipline of the monastery was under the care of the bishop in whose territory the monastery was situated (c. 2); the bishop should watch over the monasteries of women (c. 5—*MGH, Leges,* III, I, 119). *Cf.* also Council of Agde (506, cc. 27, 38, 58—Hefele, *Conciliengeschichte,* II, 654, 656, 659); Council of Vannes (465, cc. 6, 8—Hefele, *op. cit.,* II, 594); Council of Lerida (524 or 546, c. 3—Hefele, *op. cit.,* II, 746).

[7] The right of general vigilance certainly included the right of visitation and there is evidence that episcopal visitation was practiced, though the term visitation was not in common use at this early period. *Cf. infra,* pp. 35, 37.

[8] C. 19—*MGH, Leges,* III, I, 7.

to appoint a suitable superior[9] and, in the case of the presence of a contumacious priest in the order, the rule again asked for episcopal intervention.[10] In these provisions of the rule Butler sees a basis of visitation, for it would be a natural extension of such episcopal intervention to recognize that the bishop had the right and duty to visit in order to correct scandals, disorders and abuses which arose in the monasteries.[11]

Against the unlimited jurisdiction and the right of visitation which the bishops generally possessed from the Council of Chalcedon to the pontificate of Gregory the Great certain exceptions have been urged.

Thus, in 455 the metropolitan of Arles summoned a council to settle the quarrel which had arisen between Faustus, abbot of the famous monastery of Lerins, and Theodore, a bishop whose territory embraced the island of Lerins. The council decided that the clergy remained under the power of the bishop, but that the bishop had no rights over the lay monks and that he could not raise them to the clerical state except upon the request of the abbot.[12] The statement, however, is so vague that it is not clear whether this was an exemption and deprived the bishop of his right to visit or whether it merely guaranteed the limited autonomy which is essential to any monastic community that it may follow the rule and be governed in its internal affairs by its own superior.[13] In any event, the decision concerned only the monastery of Lerins.

In Africa it appears that many of the monasteries were never

[9] Linderbauer, *S. Benedicti Regula,* p. 78, cap. lxiv.

[10] Linderbauer, *op. cit.,* p. 76, cap. lxii.

[11] Butler, *Benedictine Monachism,* p. 218. *Cf.* Leclercq, "Exemption Monastique," *DACL,* V, I, 980. The rules of St. Caesarius of Arles (+ 543) were in use in many of the monasteries from the sixth to the eighth century, but they shed no light on the powers of the bishop over the monks and nuns. *Cf. Regula ad Monachos—MPL,* LXVII, 1098-1103; *Regula ad Virgines—MPL,* LXVII, 1107-1121.

[12] *In Causa Fausti Abbatis Lirinensis—Mansi,* VII, 908; Hefele, *Conciliengeschichte,* II, 583.

[13] *Cf.* Hüfner, "Das Rechtsinstitut der klösterlichen Exemption," *AKKR,* LXXXVI (1906), 305; Thomassinus, *Vetus et Nova Ecclesiae Disciplina,* part. I, lib. III, cap. 26, n. 16.

subject to the local bishops. There is record of a dispute between the abbot Peter, of the province of Byzacena, and his bishop, Liberatus, the primate of the province. The dispute was brought before the Council of Carthage (525). The abbot protested that, as the monks in his monastery were drawn from all parts, they should not be brought under the authority of Liberatus in the same way as the clergy of the diocese. He emphasized the freedom which the monks had traditionally enjoyed in Africa and cited St. Augustine and the decision of the Council of Arles in 455, as he argued that the monasteries should be maintained in their former state. The council resolved: *Erunt igitur omnia omnino monasteria sicut semper fuerunt, a conditione clericorum modis omnibus libera; sibi tantum et Deo placentia.*[14]

There is only one case on record of papal exemption in this period. Pope Hormisdas (514-523) approved of the monastery of women established by St. Caesarius of Arles and upon the latter's request exempted it from the power of St. Caesarius's successors. However, the future bishops of Arles were to be allowed in the exercise of their pastoral duties to conduct an occasional visitation of this monastery.[15]

Justinian Law

Justinian's legislation on monasticism, while chiefly important for the East, was not without influence in the West.[16] Justinian

[14] Hefele, *Conciliengeschichte*, II, 713, 714. Thomassinus writes: "Subjecerant se monachi Africani et monasteria immediatae Carthaginiensis Primatus jurisdictioni, perdiu antequam vel Gallicani, vel Occidentales reliqui monachi, Romano Pontifici immediate et ipsi subesse ambiissent."—*Vetus et Nova Ecclesiae Disciplina*, part. I, lib. III, cap. 31, n. 9. In a later Council of Carthage (534), a Bishop Felix proposed to free the monks in a more explicit manner, but whether or not this proposal was adopted is unknown. *Cf.* Hefele, *op. cit.*, II, 735. The text of Felix's proposal is in *Mansi*, VIII, 841.

[15] "Quamobrem petitionibus fraternitatis tuae libentissime annuentes, apostolica authoritate firmamus atque decernimus, ut nullus episcoporum successorum quoque tuorum in antedicto monasterio audeat sibi potestatem aliquam penitus vindicare, nisi tantum pro Dei intuitu, pastoralem sollicitudinem gerens, familiam Christi Domini ibidem positam congruis quibusque temporibus (iuxta quod condecet) sincero animo cum suis clericis studeat visitare." *Epistola Hormisdae Papae—MPL*, LXVII, 1286.

[16] *Cf.* Tabera, "De Ordinatione Status Monachalis in Fontibus Iustinianiis,"

professed a great esteem for monasticism [17] and he believed it quite fitting that the civil government should legislate on the monastic life, maintaining that, if monasticism were preserved in high estate, it would confer benefits not only on those who adopted it but also upon the state, for, when holy men prayed for the well-being of the government with pure hands and unsullied souls, the armies of the state would be victorious and the cities well-governed.[18]

Through his approval the canons of the first four ecumenical councils received the force of imperial law.[19] Thus the canons of Chalcedon on the subjection of the monks to the bishop received a new emphasis. Not content with this, Justinian explicitly repeated in his code and novels the several points mentioned by the Council of Chalcedon on the bishops' jurisdiction over the monks added several other laws to support episcopal authority over both monks and nuns.[20]

The bishop's duty of constant vigilance was strongly emphasized. The Code stated that the monasteries should be under the bishop in whose territory they were situated; each monastery should have its own superior for whose acts and installation the bishop was responsible.[21] A little further on, after provisions had been made for abolishing double monasteries and for the appointment of chaplains and *apocrisiarii* (administrators), the Code admonished the bishops that there was need for diligent supervision, lest in these matters there be transgressions. The bishop of each city was to watch carefully over the life of the monks and reprove and punish any failures to observe the provisions of the law.[22]

In chapter four of Novel 133 the bishop's duty of supervision was treated at some length. In Constantinople an official (*exarchus monasteriorum*) who was probably a delegate of the patriarch, was

CpR, XIV (1934), 199-206; Schäfer, "Iustinianus et Vita Monachica," *ACII*, I, 173-178.

[17] N. 5; N. 133.

[18] N. 133, Pr.

[19] N. 131.1.

[20] *Cf.* C. (1.3) 22, 2; 43, 5; 46, 3; N. 123.36, 42; N. 5.9; N. 79.1.

[21] C. (1.3) 39.

[22] C. (1.3) 43.8 and 43.9.

charged with the duty of watching over the monasteries.[23] This official was to send agents into the monasteries of Constantinople and its environs to examine whether anything wrong had occurred and, if so, to punish those who had offended. The bishops of other cities were also ordered to send agents to investigate and to make corrections when necessary. The patriarch of Constantinople was singled out and told to depute upright men to this task that thereby better observance and the punishment of offenses might be assured.[24]

In Justinian law the bishop's duty of visitation, personally or through delegates, is not elsewhere so clearly marked out as a part of the duty of vigilance, yet the wide powers of the bishop over the monks, his responsibility for monastic discipline and the absence of restriction upon his authority suffice to show that the bishop had the unlimited right of visiting the monasteries and affecting such reforms as were needed.

The Influence of Gregory the Great

Up to the time of the pontificate of Gregory the Great (590-604) there was no legal restraint upon episcopal authority. Episcopal interference in the monasteries often went so far as to provoke justifiable resentment on the part of the monks. Gregory valued monasticism highly and disturbed at the unsatisfactory situation devoted much of his time and administrative ability to the task of adjusting and defining the relationship between the monks and the bishops. His letters contain many sharp rebukes to various bishops for disturbing the peace and appropiating the property of the monasteries.[25] On the other hand he reproaches certain bishops for not maintaining the monasteries in good order and for making no effort to apprehend fugitive and apostate religious.[26] Hearing of abuses in various monasteries, he sends forth his agents

[23] Granic, "Die Rechtliche Stellung und Organisation der Griechischen Klöster nach Justinianischem Recht," *BZ,* XXIX (1929), 33.

[24] N. 133.4.

[25] *MGH, Ep.,* I, v, 2; I, v, 47; I, vi, 28; I, vi, 44; I, vii, 40.

[26] *MGH, Ep.,* I, iv, 9; II, viii, 8; II, x, 3; II, x, 9.

or commissions certain abbots to go in the capacity of apostolic visitors to remedy the disorders.[27]

The view once held that Gregory exempted the monasteries from episcopal control was based on the *Constitutum,* which was supposedly issued by Gregory and ratified by twenty-two bishops in a Roman council of the year 601. The *Constitutum* is no longer regarded as authentic [28] and for the most part the phrases of this famous document are taken from two letters [29] in which Gregory forbade intrusions which would disturb monastic discipline and tranquillity. In both letters, phrases which are not incorporated in the *Constitutum* indicate that Gregory was forbidding only what he conceived to be excesses and did not intend to overthrow the canonical jurisdiction and the right of visitation which previously belonged to the bishops.[30] The same policy is revealed in other letters. Gregory reproved the bishops for oppressing the monasteries, yet it is clear from various expressions that he desired only to restrict the bishops to their canonical rights.[31] In other letters, he reminds the bishops, in his forthright manner, that they are the guardians of the monasteries situated in their territories and are

[27] *MGH, Ep.,* I, v, 55; II, viii, 9; II, ix, 20; II, xiii, 48; II, xiv, 17.

[28] *Cf.* Dudden, *Gregory the Great* (London, 1905), II, 187; Mann, *History of the Popes,* I, 20; Workman, *The Evolution of the Monastic Ideal,* p. 171.

[29] *MGH Ep.,* I, v, 49; II, viii, 17.

[30] *Eg.,* "Hanc autem scriptorum nostrorum paginam omni in futuro tempore a te vel post te episcopis ordinandis firmam statuimus inlibatamque servari ut . . . monasterium illud nulli alterius alii quam generali canonicaeve iurisdictioni deserviens remotis vexationibus ac cunctis gravaminibus divinum opus cum summa animi devotione perficiat."—*MGH, Ep.,* I, v, 49. " . . . visitandi exhortandique gratia ad monasterium, quoties placuerit, ab Antistite civitatis accedatur, sed sic caritatis officium illic Episcopus impleat, ut gravamen aliquod monasterium non incurrat."—*MGH, Ep.,* II, viii, 17. Also found in Gratian: c. 1, C. XVIII, q. 2.

[31] *Cf. MGH, Ep.,* I, vi, 28; I, vii, 12; I, vii, 32. In one letter (*MGH, Ep.,* I, v, 50) the bishop was ordered not to molest a monastery *praeter diligentiam disciplinae.* This letter found its way into the Gregorian Decretals (c. 1, X, *de statu monachorum et regularium,* III, 35). The complexus of rights included under the term *diligentia disciplinae* embraced the right of visitation and is thus interpreted by Joannes Andreae (lib. III, tit. 35, cap. 1) in his commentary on this letter in the decretals.

guilty of neglect in not watching over them.[32] However, though Gregory strongly urges the duty of vigilance, the duty of visitation is more often implied than expressly mentioned. F. Homes Dudden from his thorough study of Gregory's letters is led to conclude: "He [Gregory] did not concede to the monasteries any absolute exemption or abridge in any way the canonical jurisdiction of the bishops. . . . While on the one hand the bishop was ordered to consecrate new monasteries, to constitute (*ordinare*) abbots, to provide for the celebration of masses in the chapel, to visit the monks from time to time and to superintend discipline and punish offenders, on the other hand, he was forbidden to burden the monasteries for his entertainment, to abstract anything from the revenues, properties or charter, or to make any schedule or disposition thereof." [33]

While the successors of Gregory were not always such staunch defenders of the monks, Gregory's policy of papal protection was destined to have far-reaching results. Gregory's *privilegia* went no further than to defend the rights of the monks to manage the internal affairs of the monastery, to dispose of their property, and to elect monastic officials without undue episcopal interference.[34] It was only in later years that the Papacy granted on petition privileges which deprived the bishops of all jurisdiction and the right of visitation.

Conciliar Law from the Seventh to the Eleventh Century

From the seventh to the eleventh century the councils continued to support the bishops' jurisdiction over the monasteries. In Visigothic Spain of the seventh century monasticism was in a flourishing state. St. Isidore of Seville and St. Fructuosus of Braga had written their rules for religious and fostered and organized the monastic movement. The Fourth National Council of Toledo (633) sought to restrain the bishops from oppressing the monks, but left

[32] *MGH, Ep.*, I, v, 4; I, vi, 11; I, x, 9; I, xiv, 16.

[33] *Gregory the Great*, II, 187, 188.

[34] *Cf.* Hüfner, "Das Rechtsinstitut der klösterlichen Exemption," *AKKR*, LXXXVI (1906), 316, 317; Thomassinus, *Vetus et Nova Ecclesiae Disciplina*, part. I, lib. III, cap. 30, nn. 1-3.

the bishops in possession of the rights which the canons granted them, *viz.*, the bishops' right to install abbots, to supervise discipline and to reform all practices contrary to the rule.[35] The Tenth Council of Toledo (656) referred to the bishops' authority over nuns.[36] There were few councils in Merovingian France in the seventh century amid the breakdown there of diocesan organization. However, the Council of Rouen (*circa* 650) contains a canon commanding the bishops to be diligent in visiting the monasteries of men and women.[37] This seems to be the first canon which expressly commanded the visitation of monasteries. The statutes of St. Boniface, a collection made before the year 747, stated that abbesses and abbots should lead chaste lives and, if delinquent, were subject to correction by the bishop.[38] The bishop's power of correction over all the regulars in his diocese is again referred to in the Council of Vernon (755).[39]

Under the efforts of the Carolingian rulers to reform monasticism more legislation appeared which aimed to enforce subjection to the episcopacy and to ensure frequent visitation.[40] Among the capitularies passed under Louis the Pious appear the *Capitula de Inspiciendis Monasteriis* of the year 817.[41] According to these *Capitula* the bishops were to elect abbots as visitors and these abbots should spend some days in each monastery in order to acquaint themselves with the true state of discipline. Their power of correction extended over the abbot who was being visited, and his monks. Councils later in the century urged the bishops, either alone or in company with the *missi dominici* of the emperor, to visit

[35] C. 51—Hefele, *Conciliengeschichte*, III, 84.

[36] C. 5—Hefele, *op. cit.*, III, 103.

[37] C. 10—Hefele, *op. cit.*, III, 95.

[38] C. 11—Hefele, *op. cit.*, III, 584.

[39] C. 3—*MGH, Leges*, II, i, 3.

[40] *Cf.* Council of Frankfurt (794), c. 6—*MGH, Leges*, II, I, 74; Capitularia (802), cc. 5, 17—*MGH, Leges*, II, I, 94, 111, 214; Council of Paris (829), c. 37—Hefele, *Conciliengeschichte*, IV, 62, 63.

[41] *MGH, Leges*, II, I, 321, 322. These laws were undoubtedly written in connection with the reform of St. Benedict of Aniane (*cf. supra*, p. 9). They are mentioned here as the abbot-visitors seem to be simply the delegates of the bishops.

the monasteries and with diligence to examine into the life and conduct of canons, monks and nuns,[42] to lay down regulations for the care of the poor, to make an inventory of the goods, to see that the buildings were in repair and that the monasteries were properly enclosed.[43]

The tenth century, a period of great disorder and confusion with the life of the Church at a low ebb, furnished little legislation of any kind. In the eleventh century a few councils again found it necessary to uphold episcopal authority over the monasteries.[44]

The Development of Exemptions

While the councils from the seventh to the eleventh century consistently defended the jurisdiction of the bishops, the monasteries made repeated efforts to obtain a greater measure of freedom. And not only from this quarter was episcopal authority opposed, but also by the lay founders of monasteries, kings and others, who, controlled the temporalities and the appointment of superiors. A monastery might obtain a charter from a bishop, king or pope. By charters of privileges the bishops opposed lay domination and bound themselves to refrain from intruding in certain affairs of the monastery. The Merovingian and Carolingian rulers and nobles, in their desire to provide liberty for the monasteries they had founded, granted charters themselves or asked for charters from the papacy.[45]

These fairly numerous charters did not grant what would now be called exemption; they aimed principally at removing monastic property from all danger of outside interference (except that of the founder) and assuring the monks free election of the abbot.[46] A

[42] Council of Vernon (844), c. 3—Hefele, *Conciliengeschichte,* IV, 111; Council of Savonières (859), c. 9—Thomassinus, *Vetus et Nova Ecclesiae Disciplina,* part. I, lib. III, cap. 27, n. 3; Council at St. Macra of Fimes (881), c. 4—Hefele, *op. cit.,* IV, 542.

[43] Reform Council of Mainz (813), c. 20—Hefele, *op. cit.,* III, 760.

[44] Council of Coyaco (1050) c. 2—Hefele, *op. cit.,* IV, 756; Council of Szabolcs (1092), c. 21—Hefele, *op. cit.,* V, 205.

[45] *Cf.* Leclercq, "Exemption Monastique," *DACL,* V, I, 953, 954.

[46] Thomassinus, *Vetus et Nova Ecclesiae Disciplina,* part. I, lib. III, cap.

recent careful study concludes that not even the great Irish monasteries, which St. Columban and his followers left after them, denied by their rules or charters the spiritual jurisdiction of the bishops.[47] Yet to some extent the charters did militate against the bishop's right of visitation. For when the monasteries were strong and the episcopate weak (as in the later Merovingian period) the right of visitation was largely an illusion.[48] Some of the charters guaranteed that the monastery could not be visited except at the desire of the abbot and the abbot rarely needed to call in the bishops as he had sufficient power to punish delinquents effectively.[49]

Charters from the papacy were sought more frequently in the ninth century, for such grants of immunity or liberty came to appear not only useful but necessary to the monasteries.[50] The formulas of papal protection do not always make clear their effect upon the relationship to the bishop, yet it is certain that to the end of the tenth century complete papal exemption was very exceptional.[51] A few individual monasteries, Bobbio (as early as 628),[52] Fulda,[53] Monte Cassino and two monasteries at Benevento [54] seem to have been entirely released from episcopal jurisdiction and visitation. The popes in refusing other requests stated that it was not the policy of the papacy to remove the monasteries from the bishops' supervision and that such a course would be dan-

27, nn. 6-12. For the formulas of Marculfe with their apparently broad privileges and yet the phrase, *nihil de canonica authoritate convellitur, cf.* Leclercq, *op. cit.*, V, I, 957-959.

[47] Bitterman, "The Influence of Irish Monks on Merovingian Diocesan Organization," *American Historical Review*, CL (1935), 232-246.

[48] *Cf.* Leclercq, "Exemption Monastique," *DACL*, V, I, 960.

[49] *Cf.* Thomassinus, *Vetus et Nova Ecclesiae Disciplina*, part. I, lib. III, cap. 32, n. 4; Georg Schreiber, *Kurie und Kloster in 12 Jahrhundert* (Kirchenrechtliche Abhandlungen, Heft 65-68, Stuttgart, 1910), I, 192.

[50] *Cf.* Hüfner, "Das Rechtsinstitut der Klösterlichen Exemption," *AKKR*, LXXXVI (1906), 634.

[51] Hüfner, *op. cit.*, 640; Thomassinus, *op. cit.*, part. I, lib. III, cap. 32, nn 9-11; cap. 35, n. 10.

[52] *Privilegium Bobiensi Coenobio Datum—MPL*, LXXX, 483.

[53] *Epistola XV Zachariae Papae—MPL*, LXXXIX, 954.

[54] Hüfner, *op. cit.*, 630, 632, 639.

gerous to the monasteries themselves.[55] The monasteries, however, stretched their charters of protection to the widest possible meaning and beyond. Later, when exemption was granted, it was accepted by the monasteries as a right which had long since belonged to them.[56]

The period from the middle of the eleventh century and through the twelfth witnessed the greatest change in the status of the monasteries. The Hildebrandine reform was in full swing in the latter half of the eleventh century and more and more frequently kings and others of the laity preferred to commend the lands and goods of their donation to the Roman Church or to St. Peter. The papacy received these monasteries under its special protection and conceded various immunities, *salva apostolicae sedis auctoritate.*[57] This *tradito* of goods, by which monasteries commended to the Holy See (*päpstliche Eigenklöster*) were created, was the basis of the transition from mere protection to exemption.[58] Successive popes might not always treat the monasteries whose goods were commended to them (as representatives of St. Peter or the Roman Church) in the same way; from one pope to another the status of an individual monastery might change back from exempt to non-exempt. Yet through this *tradito* of property by lay patrons exemptions were established and multiplied rapidly.[59] Other factors combined to hasten this development. Monasticism in its older form of isolated monasteries was to a large extent giving way to systems of monasteries united into centralized orders. The Cluniacs had already reached the apex of their power; the new orders—the Camaldolese, the Vallumbrosians, the Carthusians, and especially the Cistercians and the Premonstratensians—were rising to prominence. From the new monastic forces the papacy received invaluable sup-

[55] Hüfner, *op. cit.*, 638.

[56] *Cf.* Leclercq, "Exemption Monastique," *DACL,* V, I, 953, 960. Hüfner, *op. cit.*, 641, 642.

[57] *Cf.* Schreiber, *Kurie und Kloster,* I, 46-63.

[58] Schreiber, *op. cit.*, I, 9-26, 44, 45, 66.

[59] Bishops of the twelfth century sought and received papal protection for their own monasteries in a formula containing a clause that preserved episcopal jurisdiction. *Cf.* Schreiber, *op. cit.*, I, 58, 59.

port for its reforms and, as the monks and the papacy were drawn closer together, the papal privileges granted in reward upheld the liberty of the monasteries not only against secular encroachment, but also against the jurisdictional rights of the bishops.[60]

Extensive privileges were possessed by the Cluniacs in the beginning of the eleventh century. Despite the efforts of the Council of Ansa and the bishop of Macon—in whose diocese the abbey of Cluny was situated—to declare these privileges null and in contradiction to the fourth canon of Chalcedon, the privileges remained in force and were broadened by Gregory VII, Urban II and Calixtus II.[61] These concessions withdrew not only the abbey of Cluny but also many of the affiliated abbeys and priories from the judicial and penal authority of the bishops.[62] Thus a policy of great consequence was begun by which exemption was conceded not only to individual monasteries, but to a part or the whole of a system of monasteries which constituted an order. The privileges of the Camaldolese, the Vallumbrosians, and the Carthusians developed on lines analogous to those of Cluny. Finally complete exemption was accorded to them as a mark of gratitude for their aid in the papal movement for reform.[63] The Cistercians, with papal confirmation of their constitution (*Carta Caritatis*) in 1119 and with the creation of a systematized plan of visitation, had sown the seed for their later exemptions.[64] The early Cistercians, St. Bernard in particular,[65] expressly declared their intention to seek no privileges that would impair the power of the bishops. Nevertheless, from the year 1132 privileges were received which shortly accumulated into complete exemption.[66] The Military Orders of Knight Templars and Knight

[60] Schreiber, *op. cit.*, I, 109.

[61] Hüfner, "Das Rechtsinstitut der klösterlichen Exemption," *AKKR*, LXXXVI (1906), 645-647; Smith, *Cluny in the Eleventh and Twelfth Centuries*, pp. 46, 47.

[62] Hüfner, *op. cit.*, 648, 649; Schreiber, *Kurie und Kloster*, I, 75-78.

[63] *Cf.* Schreiber, *op. cit.*, I, 78-83.

[64] *Cf.* Schreiber, *op. cit.*, I, 85, 86.

[65] *Cf. De Consideratione*, lib. III, cap. 4—*MPL*, CLXXXII, 766-769.

[66] Hüfner, "Das Rechtsinstitut der klösterlichen Exemption," *AKKR*, LXXXVII (1907), 81; Schreiber, *Kurie und Kloster*, I, 89, 90.

Hospitalers of St. John were entirely freed from episcopal jurisdiction by the year 1163.[67]

There is no need to attempt to trace the status of each order. By the end of the twelfth century the monasteries could be roughly divided into exempt and non-exempt, with perhaps the majority of the monasteries of centralized orders in the former class and most of the autonomous monasteries (*i. e.*, the Benedictine and Augustinian foundations) in the latter. The popes in various formulas mention a greater or lesser number of points in which a monastery or order is freed from the authority of the diocesan bishop,[68] but the most essential point in constituting an exemption was freedom from the penal and coercive power of the bishops. Such freedom cut at the roots of episcopal jurisdiction and was the privilege most desired by the monasteries.[69] Whether or not this immunity from the bishops' power to punish was meant to overthrow the right of visitation, it did in effect render that right futile. Monasteries enjoying such an exemption may be classed with those in which freedom from visitation is expressly mentioned or is obviously contained in phrases forbidding the bishop to exercise any and all authority over the monasteries.

Churches Attached to Monasteries

Up to the eighth and ninth centuries the monks with rare exceptions possessed only the churches and chapels for their own spiritual

[67] Hüfner, *op. cit.*, 271, 274, 275; Schreiber, *op. cit.*, I, 92-100. The Cistercians and the Military Orders are exceptional in that the *traditio* of temporalities played no part in the acquiring of their exemptions. *Cf.* Schreiber, *op. cit.*, I, 90, 109.

[68] Alexander III stressed the distinction between monasteries which paid a tax to the Holy See *in indicium libertatis* and monasteries which paid the tax *in indicium protectionis*. But he did not state that in either case this was a proof of exemption. An examination would have to be made of the particular privileges granted to such monasteries in order to decide upon the extent of their freedom from episcopal control. C. 8, X, *de privilegiis et excessibus privilegiatorum*, V, 33. *Cf.* Rieger, "Die Dekretale *Recepimus litteras* bei Blumenstock und Schreiber," *Studien und Mitteilungen zur Geschichte des Benedictiner-Ordens*, XXXII (1911), 693-699.

[69] Schreiber, *op. cit.*, I, 29-31.

needs and to such churches and chapels no parochial rights belonged. These churches and chapels like the monasteries were subject to the bishop's supervision and visitation except in so far as lay patrons, who endowed monasteries with churches, retained control and hindered the exercise of episcopal authority in these *Eigenkirchen* as they did in the *Eigenklöster*.[70] In the eighth century, when there were efforts to break down the opposition of lay patrons to episcopal authority, the first German Council, under St. Boniface, stated that every priest installed in a monastic church must receive the bishop into his church on the latter's journeys of confirmation and visitation.[71] The distinction which grew up in the eleventh century between the *ecclesia* and the *altare* had the effect of restricting the claims of patrons and bringing the churches into a closer relationship with the bishops. By the *ecclesia* was understood the church buildings and by the *altare* principally the altar with its spiritual rights and offices. Over the *altare* the bishop had full authority.[72]

From the latter half of the eleventh century, when the monasteries began to receive exemptions and were coming into possession of an increasing number of parochial churches, the question of the visitation of monastic churches enters upon a new phase. Parochial and non-parochial churches of non-exempt monasteries did of course remain subject to the bishop.[73] It is with the exempt monasteries

[70] The precise status of the *Eigenkirchen* in the ecclesiastical law of that time is still the subject of debate. *Cf.* Ulrich Stutz, *Geschichte des kirchlichen Benefizialwesens* (Berlin, 1895); "Gratian und die Eigenkirchen," *Zeitschrift der Savigny-Stiftung* (Kanonistiche Abteilung I), XXXII (1911), 1-33. For a different view and a criticism of Stutz's conclusions, *cf.* Ramon Bidagor, *La "Iglesia Propria" en España,* (Analecta Gregoriana, vol. IV, Romae, 1933). In Spain the *Eigenkirchen,* to which the care of souls was attached, were uninterruptedly visited by the bishops and subjected to the duty of providing the canonical procurations. Bidagor, *op. cit.,* 171.

[71] German Council (742), c. 3—Hefele, *Conciliengeschichte,* III, 499. For legislation in the eighth and ninth centuries supporting the bishops' authority over all the clergy as against the domination of the laity or monks, *cf.* Hüfner, "Das Rechtsinstitut der klösterlichen Exemption," *AKKR,* LXXXVII (1907), 81, 82.

[72] *Cf.* Hüfner, *op. cit., AKKR,* LXXXVII (1907), 83.

[73] *Cf.* Schreiber, *Kurie und Kloster,* II, 66.

that the question arises: Did their churches with or without parochial rights share in the freedom from episcopal jurisdiction and visitation? [74] Before attempting to answer this question a few points must be noted.

In the late eleventh and early twelfth centuries it had been the practice of lay patrons to transfer property and churches already erected directly to the monasteries.[75] Against the practice of receiving churches from the hands of laymen the councils struck hard and the Third Lateran Council (1179) seems to have achieved some measure of success.[76] Thus the transfer had to be made through the bishop and it was in his power to decide in how far the church should be subject to him and whether it should possess parochial rights.[77] In most cases the vicars in monastic churches with the *ius parochiale* were secular priests, as several councils had forbidden the monks to undertake pastoral duties without the consent of the bishop.[78] But, whether the clergy of a monastic church were secular or regular, they were under the authority of the bishop as the councils of the twelfth century emphasized repeatedly.[79] Even when the monastery had built the church and had the rights of a patron, the bishop had the right to confirm the appointment

[74] Actually most of the grants of the *ius parochiale* from bishops to churches of regulars went to the Augustinian Canons and the Premonstratensians, both of whom were non-exempt at least until the thirteenth century.—*Cf.* Schreiber, *op. cit.*, II, 32; I, 103-108. Visitation in the late eleventh and twelfth centuries is emphasized in numerous documents and was conducted every fourth year in many dioceses.—*Cf.* Hüfner, *op. cit.*, *AKKR*, LXXXVII (1907), 84; Schreiber, *op. cit.*, II, 170, n. 2.

[75] *Cf.* Clarke, *History of Tithes*, pp. 146-148.

[76] Third Lateran Council, ninth decree—Hefele, *Conciliengeschichte*, VI, 713; Council of Poitiers (1078), c. 5—Hefele, *op. cit.*, V, 116.

[77] *Cf.* Council of Clermont (1095), c. 7—Hefele, *op. cit.*, V, 222; Council of Nîmes (1096), c. 1—Hefele, *op. cit.*, V, 244; First Lateran Council (1123), c. 18—Hefele, *op. cit.*, V, 381.

[78] First Lateran Council (1123), c. 18—Hefele, *op. cit.*, V, 381. For earlier particular councils, *cf.* Schreiber, *Kurie und Kloster*, II, 41, n. 1.

[79] *Cf.* First Lateran Council, c. 22—Hefele, *op. cit.*, V, 381; Council of Rheims (1157), c. 5—Hefele, *op. cit.*, V, 568. *Cf.* Urban III (in 1186)—c. 1, X, *de capellis monachorum*, III, 37.

of the vicar and to hold him responsible for his ministry in matters spiritual.

In these several points, the conciliar legislation made no distinction between churches of non-exempt and those of exempt monasteries. It is true that, if papal exemption existed for the churches of exempt monasteries, the legislation of particular councils could not destroy it, nor would the legislation of general councils touch such churches, unless it contained a clause overruling the exemption. However, papal exemptions were as a rule limited to the monasteries themselves. The dispute in the middle of the eleventh century between the exempt abbey of Fulda and the bishop of Würzburg was a case in point. The emperor, acting with papal authority, decided that the monastery of Fulda was directly under the pope, but that the vicars of the parish churches of Fulda were subject to the bishop.[80] Schreiber's study leads him to conclude that even in the twelfth century the view, which supposes that exemptions of the monasteries extended as a rule to the churches, is erroneous. He finds that there are a number of exempt monastic churches, but that this privileged position is enjoyed by a small minority in comparison to the number of exempt monasteries.[81] Only a few of these churches appear to have been parochial churches for while the papal curia sometimes gave permission to the exempt monasteries to build churches on their lands, only rarely is there a mention of parochial rights.[82] The permission to baptize, to bury, to visit the sick, and to hold public Masses depended on the bishop and, even when conceding these rights to churches of exempt monasteries, he naturally retained the right of supervision.

The Military Orders possessed the broadest exemption and could build parish churches which were to enjoy the fullest liberty. But this privilege was confined to deserted places and was intended more for the East, "in the lands of the Saracens." [83] In the churches which were united to their houses *pleno iure,* the religious supe-

[80] Hefele, *Conciliengeschichte,* IV, 737.

[81] *Kurie und Kloster,* II, 191-196.

[82] *Cf.* Schreiber, *op. cit.,* II, 33-38.

[83] Schreiber, *op. cit.,* II, 24, 197.

riors could install priests without presenting them to the bishop.[84] Yet the churches which they possessed in such a manner were oratories and had no parochial rights.[85]

In this period, then, it seems that the bishops' right to visit monastic churches remained substantially intact. In a minority of cases the exemption extended to non-parochial churches and in a few exceptional instances to parochial churches.

The Procuration

By the *canonica procuratio* was meant the food and lodging (and sometimes the traveling expenses) which the church and the monastery had to provide for the visitor and his retinue. As far back as the seventh century legislation is met with, in connection with the general diocesan visitation, which seeks to restrain the bishop from burdening the places which he visits by staying too long or by bringing too large a retinue.[86] Before the Third Lateran Council, there was no general law on the subject. The fourth canon of the aforesaid council noted that such abuses had grown up that at times the ornaments of the churches visited had to be sold to cover the expense of the procuration. It was therefore determined that archbishops visiting their territories, according to the differences of the provinces and the resources of the churches, should be accompanied by not more than forty to fifty horses, bishops by not more than twenty to thirty, cardinals by not more than twenty-five, archdeacons by not more than five to seven, while deacons delegated by the bishops were to be content with two. No hunting dogs or birds were to be taken along; the prelates should not ask for sumptuous foods, but receive with thanks what was fittingly offered; they should not demand taxes except for the sake of charity when there was some special need. And in conclusion the attendants, spoken of above, should not be maintained in the poorer localities.[87]

[84] Third Lateran Council, c. 9—c. 3, X, *de privilegiis et excessibus privilegiatorum,* V, 33.

[85] Schreiber, *op. cit.,* II, 67.

[86] Seventh Council of Toledo (646), c. 4—Hefele, *Conciliengeschichte,* III, 95. This canon restricted the bishop to a train of fifty persons and horses and forbade him to stay in any church more than one day.

[87] C. 6, X, *de censibus, exactionibus, et procurationibus,* III, 39.

Section 2

From the Fourth Lateran Council (1215) to the Council of Trent (1545)

During the period from the Fourth Lateran Council to the Council of Trent there are a few laws urging upon the bishops the duty of visiting religious, their houses and their churches.[88] However, the important features of this period are the further growth of exemptions from episcopal visitation and the special legislation on the procuration and the visitation of nuns.

The Further Development of Exemptions

In the thirteenth century exemptions from episcopal visitation multiplied and were broadened greatly in their scope. The religious of the Mendicant Orders within a very short time after their establishment were freed from the jurisdiction of the bishops; even during the lifetime of St. Francis, the Friars Minor obtained a number of privileges which placed them among the exempt orders.[89] In 1258 Alexander IV expressly stated that the Franciscans were not subject to the judicial and penal authority of the bishops and that their houses were exempted from episcopal visitation. In general the exemptions granted to the Franciscans were extended to the Dominicans, the Hermits of St. Augustine, and the Carmelites.[90] The Celestines, with the accession of their founder, Celestine V, to the papal throne, were removed from the bishops' jurisdiction (1294).[91]

Throughout this period to the time of the Fifth Lateran Council (1513-1517) an increasing number of monasteries and entire orders

[88] *E. g.*, German National Council (1287), c. 27—Hefele, *Conciliengeschichte*, VI, 249; Council of Aquileia (1339) c. 1—Hefele, *op. cit.*, VI, 647; Council of Padua (1350), c. 20—Hefele, *op. cit.*, VI, 695; Council of Rheims (1408), decree—*Mansi*, XXVI, 1068-1076; Council of Cologne (1452), c. 16—Hefele, *op. cit.*, VIII, 54. The Gregorian Decretals suppose that visitation will be undertaken annually (c. 16, X, *de officio iudicis ordinarii*, I, 21).

[89] Hüfner, "Das Rechtsinstitut der klösterlichen Exemption," *AKKR*, LXXXVII (1907), 465.

[90] Hüfner, *op. cit.*, *AKKR*, LXXXVII (1907), 467, 469.

[91] Hüfner, *op. cit.*, *AKKR*, LXXXVII (1907), 479.

received privileges which freed them from the jurisdiction and the visitation of the bishops. The development of exemptions was not steady; their history presents a confusing picture; for they were granted, revoked, confirmed, extended and restricted by the successive popes. Yet, on the whole the tendency was to remove the regulars more and more completely from episcopal authority. Under Boniface VIII and at the Council of Vienne (1312) there were attempts to reverse the process.[92] Again at the Council of Constance (1414-1418) endeavors were made in the cause of reform to abrogate at least those exemptions which had been conceded so liberally during the Great Schism (1378-1417).[93] During the half century after the Council of Constance the growth of exemptions was somewhat retarded. Sixtus IV (1471-1484) inaugurated the era which, lasting to the Fifth Lateran Council, marked the highest point in the history of exemptions.

Churches Attached to Monasteries

In these centuries not merely the great majority of religious and their houses were removed from episcopal control, but the number of monastic churches and exempt monastic churches was continually increasing. The coming of the friars had effected almost a revolution in the traditional concepts of monasticism. In the centuries before their time the monks had more or less clung to the idea of retirement from the world and had built their monasteries outside the towns; by vocation the monks were not preachers, confessors, or missionaries. With the friars the emphasis shifted to the active life; their convents were in the towns and they were to go through the streets and the countryside, preaching, confessing, and serving the poor, the sick and the unfortunate. While putting aside the spirit of the world, they were to remain very much in the world.[94] These well-known facts are recalled here because, by this newer and somewhat different concept of the religious life, the friars and other religious were brought into fields formerly reserved to the secular

[92] Hüfner, *op. cit., AKKR,* LXXXVII (1907), 476, 477.

[93] Hüfner, *op. cit., AKKR,* LXXXVII (1907), 613, 614.

[94] *Cf.* Workman, *The Evolution of the Monastic Ideal,* pp. 270-316.

clergy. Everywhere the regulars possessed a large number of churches attached to their houses by the device of incorporation or union.[95]

The distinction, noted in the previous period, between the *ecclesia* and the *altare* had passed into the *incorporatio quoad temporalia tantum* and in addition a more complete union between the church and the monastery had developed in the *incorporatio pleno iure.* The vicar stationed at a church which was united to a monastery *quoad temporalia tantum* had to be presented by the proper religious superior for installation into his office. In so far as the care of souls was concerned the vicar was responsible to the bishop.[96] The vicar stationed at a church which, in the more complete type of union, was attached to the monastery *quoad temporalia et spiritualia* was directly appointed by the proper religious superior. Yet the fact that such a union existed between a church and an exempt monastery did not deprive the bishop of his visitatorial rights over such a church though no doubt the closer union did diminish the bishop's control.[97]

The bishops of the thirteenth century complained of the number of churches united to monasteries. In the latter half of that century every effort was made to prevent patrons from granting more churches to regulars and, in the churches which regulars possessed, to prevent regular priests from acting as vicars.[98] Besides the churches the regulars possessed a number of oratories. Gregory IX in 1227 and 1237 had granted to the Dominicans and Franciscans the right to build oratories within the limits of parishes. These oratories were not parochial churches, but the fact that in them sermons could be preached, confessions heard, and public Masses offered on Sundays meant that they were allowed to hold functions which before had belonged only to churches with the *ius parochiale.*[99] Though later

[95] For a discussion of "incorporation," *cf.* Hinschius, *Kirchenrecht,* II, 436-446.

[96] *Cf.* c. 31, X, *de praebendis et dignitatibus,* III, 5.

[97] *Cf.* c. 17, X, *de privilegiis et excessibus privilegiatorum,* V, 33.

[98] Hüfner, "Das Rechtsinstitut der klösterlichen Exemption," *AKKR,* LXXXVII (1907), 469, 470.

[99] Hüfner, *op. cit.,* 468, 469.

in the century the consent of the bishop or papal legate was necessary for these activities, these oratories were eventually freed entirely from episcopal control.

With the increasing number of exempt churches in the thirteenth century the question of whether these churches were completely removed from episcopal jurisdiction and visitation was sharply debated. In 1298 Boniface VIII, in defining the status of such churches, stated that by an exemption conceded to a church it was to be understood that the church, the canons or monks, the *conversi*, and the *oblati* were exempt, but that the bishop had jurisdiction over the priest who had the care of souls, over those matters which pertained to the care of souls and over the parishioners.[100] Thus in exempt parochial churches the bishop had the right to visit the priest, secular or regular, and to visit in all matters reguarding the care of souls, while in exempt non-parochial churches the bishop had no right of visitation.

Throughout the fourteenth century the number of exempt churches continued to multiply rapidly. Innocent XI in 1356 declared that the exempt churches of the Benedictines, the Cluniacs, the Cistercians, the Premonstratensians and also the exempt churches of any other order were not subject to the visitation of the episcopal ordinaries.[101] Yet, it does not appear that he intended to overthrow the distinction of Boniface VIII and until the time of Sixtus IV, it seems that parochial churches and parochial vicars were subject to visitation in all that touched the care of the parishioners.

Sixtus IV (1471-1484), a former general of the Franciscans, revealed his antecedents rather clearly in his policy on exemptions.[102] The most extensive exemptions were given to the Franciscans, the Dominicans, the Hermits of St. Augustine, the Carmelites, and the Canons Regular of the Lateran Congregation. The successors of

[100] C. 9, *de privilegiis,* V, 7, in VI°. *Cf.* c. 10, *de privilegiis,* V, 7, in VI°; c. un., *de capellis monachorum,* III, 18, in VI°.

[101] Hüfner, "Das Rechtsinstitut der klösterlichen Exemption," *AKKR,* LXXXVII (1907), 606.

[102] "To enumerate the good things bestowed on the Mendicant Friars and more particularly on the Franciscans during this long pontificate would be an endless task."—Pastor, *History of the Popes,* IV, 390.

Sixtus IV, namely, Popes Innocent VII, Alexander VI, and Julius II, directly or by communication bestowed almost the same broad privileges on the Servites, the Cistercians, the Canons Regular of St. Salvator and the Vallumbrosians. The result was that not only were these religious with their houses and non-parochial churches exempted, but in addition their parochial churches were removed entirely from episcopal jurisdiction and visitation. The religious superior could install and remove the parochial vicar at will and indeed as long as the vicar was in office, even though he was a secular, he participated in the exemption of the religious in the same way as a professed member of the order.[103]

The bishops could hardly tolerate such restrictions upon their authority. At the Fifth Lateran Council (1513-1517) the entire question of religious exemptions broke out. It was the climax of centuries of controversy and long and bitter debates filled the council.[104] In several matters the bishops were successful. At the eleventh session, on December 19, 1516, Leo X with the approval of the council published the bull *"Dum intra mentis,"* [105] whereby certain exemptions were abolished. The bishops regained the right to visit exempt parochial churches in all that pertained to the care of souls and to the administration of the Sacraments and could punish delinquent vicars, secular or regular.

Visitation of Nuns

Before this period no special laws were issued on the visitation of nuns. What has been said on the visitation of regulars, their monasteries and their churches applies equally to the nuns. In this period two laws appeared which pertain exclusively to nuns and which were of lasting importance.

Boniface VIII, by the constitution *"Periculoso"* in 1298, commanded that a strict enclosure be observed by all nuns. They were not to leave their monasteries, unless they were in such grave sick-

[103] Hüfner, *op. cit., AKKR,* LXXXVII (1907), 626-634.

[104] *Cf.* Hefele, *Conciliengeschichte,* VIII, 621-638; Pastor, *History of the Papacy,* VIII, 393-395.

[105] *Mansi,* XXXII, 970-976; *Bullarium Romanum,* V, 685-689.

ness as to be a source of danger to others, nor was anyone permitted to enter the enclosure, unless for a reasonable and evident cause and with the permission of the proper superior. The bishops were ordered to see to the observance of this law, not only in the monasteries subject to themselves, but also, as apostolic delegates, in those monasteries which were directly subject to the Holy See.[106] Thus exempt nuns, not subject to regular superiors, were placed under the bishops' jurisdiction and visitation in regard to the enclosure.

In the year 1312, as has been mentioned, Clement V provided a special law for the visitation of nuns in his constitution *"Attendentes."*[107] The bishops were to visit annually monasteries of nuns, both the exempt, which were immediately subject to the Holy See, and the non-exempt. The visitation was to be conducted in the same manner therein prescribed for the visitation of nuns subject to regular superiors.[108]

The Procuration

During this period the greater part of the law on visitation was concerned with the procuration. The Fourth Lateran Council stated that the procuration should be furnished to prelates only when they visited personally and observed the fourth canon of the Third Lateran Council;[109] those who received the procuration contrary to this law were bound to restitution.[110] This law was followed by the constitution *"Romana Ecclesia"* (1252) of Innocent IV[111] forbidding the visiting prelates or their attendants to receive the procuration in the form of money. Only food was to be received and no one was to presume to accept any gift in whatever manner offered. If anyone violated this law he fell under a curse from which

[106] C. un., *de statu regularium,* III, 16, in VI°.

[107] C. 2, *de statu monachorum vel canonicorum regularium,* III, 10, in Clem.

[108] *Cf. supra* p. 24.

[109] *Cf. supra* p. 49.

[110] C. 23, X, *de censibus, exactionibus, et procurationibus,* III, 39. The main piece of legislation on the subject of the procuration was and remained the fourth canon of the Third Lateran Council, though the later laws introduced certain modifications. *Cf.* cc. 6, 14, 16, 17, 19, 21, 24-27, X, *de censibus, exactionibus, et procurationibus,* III, 39.

[111] C. 1, *de censibus, exactionibus, et procurationibus,* III, 20 in VI°.

he was not freed until he restored double the amount illegitimately accepted.

As this law was not sufficient to remove abuses, the Second Council of Lyons (1274) in its twenty-fourth chapter (*"Exigit"*) added penalties. Those who presumed to transgress the constitution *"Romana Ecclesia,"* were bound within a month to restore to the church or monastery twice the amount or value of the money or gift which had been accepted. Patriarchs, archbishops and bishops who failed to make such restitution within the allotted period of time incurred the interdict *ab ingressu ecclesiae;* the clergy of lower rank who were guilty of violations were suspended *ab officio et beneficio* until they made the prescribed restitution.[112]

Boniface VIII in 1298 introduced a change. Asserting that some places and churches were involved in great difficulties by the duty of providing food for the visiting prelates and their retinues, he permitted such places and churches, if they so desired, to make an equivalent payment in money. However, the visitor could receive only one procuration or its monetary equivalent for a single day, even though he visited several places.[113]

Further grave abuses led in 1336 to Benedict XII's constitution *"Vas Electionis,"* which went into great detail on the question of the procuration. The Christian world was divided into four parts; in each region a list was made according to the ranks of the visiting prelates and the classes of churches and monasteries. According to the elaborate scales that resulted, the limits of the procuration (to be supplied in food unless those visited preferred to pay in money) that might licitly be received were set down. Besides renewing the penalties of the Second Council of Lyons for accepting gifts or for exacting an excessive procuration, Benedict XII added additional penalties against attendants of the visitors who were guilty of like practices.[114]

[112] C. 2, *de censibus, exactionibus, et procurationibus,* III, 20, in VI°.

[113] C. 3, *de censibus, exactionibus, et procurationibus,* III, 20, in VI°.

[114] In the particular councils of this period efforts were repeatedly made to enforce these various general laws on the procuration. *Cf.* Council of Saumur (1253), c. 9—Hefele, *Conciliengeschichte,* VI, 47; Council of Albi (1254), cc. 57-60—*op. cit.,* VI, 53; Council of Vienna (1267), c. 2—*op. cit.,*

Section 3

From the Council of Trent (1545-1563) to the Code (1918)

In many respects the Council of Trent exalted the powers of the bishops and for the advancement of reform curtailed exemptions. Great stress was laid upon episcopal visitation as a means for maintaining the purity of the Faith and for banishing abuses from the Church.

Non-exempt Religious and Nuns Immediately Subject to the Holy See

The twenty-fourth session of the council set forth the general law for episcopal visitation. Patriarchs, primates, metropolitans and bishops were bound to visit their respective dioceses personally or, if lawfully hindered, through the vicar general or a delegate. The visitation was to be annual, unless the size of the diocese rendered this impossible; in such a case the visitation was to be made at least every two years. The aim of the visitation was to secure sound and orthodox doctrine, to banish heresies, to establish good morals and to provide for such other things as seemed profitable for the faithful. The visitor was to content himself with a limited number of servants and horses when on his rounds and was not to burden the places visited with useless expenses. With regard to the procuration money might be substituted for food, if those visited so desired. However, where it was the custom to receive neither food nor money, no change was to be introduced. Those who presumed to receive more than was permitted in the above cases were bound to restore double the value of what had been received within a month and were liable to the penalties of the constitution *"Exigit"* of the Second Council of Lyons and to such additional penalties as the provincial councils might add.[115]

In all matters relating to visitation and the correction of morals

VI, 102; Council of London (1268), c. 19—*op. cit.*, VI, 109; Council of Langeais (1278), c. 1—*op. cit.*, VI, 185; Hungarian National Council (1279), c. 14—*op. cit.*, VI, 191; Council of London (1321), c. 2—*op. cit.*, VI, 610; Council of Marsiac (1326), cc. 38, 39—*op. cit.*, VI, 626; Council of London (1342), cc. 7, 8—*op. cit.*, VI, 676; etc.

115 Council of Trent, sess. XXIV, *de ref.*, c. 3.

the bishops had the right and authority, even as delegates of the Holy See, to regulate, correct and execute, in accordance with the canons, such things as seemed necessary for the amendment of their subjects and for the benefit of their dioceses. No exemption, appeal or complaint, even to the Holy See, would hinder or suspend the execution of those things which were commanded or decreed or adjudged by the bishops in their capacity of visitors.[116]

The visitation of churches was considered in the seventh session and the council decreed that bishops were bound to visit annually all churches, no matter in what manner they might be exempt.[117] Ecclesiastical benefices with the care of souls were to be visited each year by the ordinaries of those places. The local ordinaries were enjoind to exercise due care in providing for pastoral ministrations through competent vicars.[118]

These prescriptions applied in their full force to the visitation of non-exempt religious, their houses and their churches. Nuns immediately subject to the Holy See were to be governed by the bishops as apostolic delegates.[119] By reason of this decree and the constitution *"Attendentes"* of Clement V the bishops were still obliged to visit these nuns annually. Thus the bishops had plenary powers of visitation over non-exempt religious and nuns subject immediately to the Holy See.

Exempt Regulars

The position of the exempt regulars[120] cannot be presented in such a summary fashion, as they were not entirely free from episco-

[116] Council of Trent, sess. XXIV, *de ref.*, c. 10. This was confirmed and made more explicit by Benedict XIV in his constitution, *Ad Militantis*, March 30, 1742, §§ 6, 10, 19, 21—*Fontes*, n. 326. The Roman Congregations made it clear that, if the bishop in visitation cited the party or parties and proceeded judicially, an appeal would suspend the sentence. *Cf.* S. C. Ep. et Reg., decr. 16 Oct, 1600., ad 8—*Fontes*, n. 1586; S. C. C., 24 Apr., 1597—*Fontes*, n. 2309; S. C. C., mense Dec., 1587, ad 2—*Fontes*, n. 2194; S. C. C., 28 Nov., 1602—*Fontes*, n. 2347; S. C. C., Apr., 1710, ad 1—*Fontes*, n. 3088.

[117] Council of Trent, sess. VII, *de ref.*, c. 8.

[118] Council of Trent, sess. VII, *de ref.*, c. 7.

[119] Council of Trent, sess. XXV, *de regularibus*, c. 9.

[120] Most of the regulars were exempt, but a number of individual monasteries not attached to a centralized order (*e.g.*, many of the Benedictine

pal visitation and the extent of their freedom varied somewhat during the course of this period. It may be well to take up separately each case in which the bishop during this time from the Council of Trent to the Code had the right to visit such religious, their houses, or their churches.

I. Exempt regulars, if they were guilty of transgressions while absent from or living outside their monasteries, might be canonically visited, punished, and corrected by the ordinary of the place acting in his capacity of a delegate of the Holy See.

II. Exempt autonomous monasteries which had neglected to form congregations in accordance with the decree of the Council of Trent [121] and the constitution *"In Singulis"* fell under the jurisdiction of the bishops as delegates of the Holy See.[122]

III. The Council of Trent legislated as strongly as was possible under the circumstances against the practice of appointing superiors to hold monasteries *in commendam,* yet, realizing that the practice could not be abolished immediately, the Council decreed that bishops should visit annually even exempt monasteries held *in commendam* if regular observance did not flourish therein. The bishop should see that all necessary repairs were made and that the care of souls, if such monasteries or churches annexed to them were charged with this duty, was properly fulfilled. It seems that the bishop did not have the right to visit commendatory monasteries which were subject to the heads of orders, even though such monasteries departed from regular observance and even though the higher superiors when warned by the bishop failed to make a visitation within the subsequent six months.[123]

houses) were subject to the bishops. *Cf.* Emanuel Rodericus, *Quaestiones Regulares* (Turnoni, 1609), qu. 43, art. 3; Gaudentius, *De Visitatione,* dub. X, n. 11; Joannes De Luca, *Theatrum Veritatis et Iustitiae* (Venetiis, 1734), lib. XIV, part. I, disc. 1, 2.

[121] Council of Trent, sess. XXV, *de regularibus,* c. 8.

[122] *Cf. supra* p. 27.

[123] *Cf.* Council of Trent, sess. XXI, *de ref.,* c. 8. Chapter 21 of the twenty-fifth session seems to have removed commendatory monasteries subject to the heads of orders from the provisions of chapter 8 of the twenty-first session. *Cf.* Gaudentius, *De Visitatione,* dub. X, nn. 14, 16; Ferraris, "Visitare," n. 39.

IV. The most important extension of the bishops' visitatorial powers was in regard to small monasteries. The Council of Trent had decreed that the number in any monastery should be kept within bounds so that the religious might be properly maintained on the customary revenues or alms.[124] Urban VIII through a decree of the Congregation of the Council (June 21, 1625) [125] ordered that an examination of all the religious houses in Italy be made in order that the size of each community might be fixed. At the same time he determined that both within Italy and outside Italy any monastery that would be in the future be founded in which less than twelve religious could be maintained or were actually in residence must be subject to the visitation of the local ordinary. Innocent X sanctioned another investigation of Italian monasteries.[126] Noting that the many small monasteries, without sufficient religious for the carrying out of divine office and community exercises, were an obstacle to reform, he ordered that a number be abolished.[127] Certain small convents escaped suppression and others were shortly restored.

In 1654 Innocent X by the decree *"Ut in Parvis"* defined the status of small convents as follows: (a) Regulars of restored small monasteries were subject to the visitation and correction of the bishops until such monasteries could and actually did support twelve members. Meanwhile there were to be six religious, four of whom were required to be priests in each of these convents. (b) Other small convents, which had not been suppressed, were to have in residence at least six religious, of whom four were required to be priests if the community was to retain its exemption. Otherwise they fell under the authority of the bishop, who then had the right and duty of visitation. (c) Foundations, made later than June 21, 1625, were subject to the bishop, if there were not twelve religious residing therein. Later in the seventeenth century decisions emanating from the Congregation of Bishops and Regulars departed from these provisions [128] but still later decisions swung back to the law of the

[124] Council of Trent, sess. XXV, *de regularibus*, c. 3.

[125] *Fontes*, n. 2460, § § 11-13, 14, ultimo.

[126] *Cf.* const., *Inter Caetera*, 17 Dec., 1649—Ferraris, "Conventus," art. II, n. 2; art. I, n. 5.

[127] *Cf.* const., *Instaurandae*, 15 Oct., 1652—*Fontes*, n. 233.

[128] *Cf.* S. C. Ep. et Reg., 27 Iul. 1655—*Fontes*, n. 1791; S. C. Ep. et Reg.,

decree *"Ut in Parvis."* [129] By the latter half of the nineteenth century the law had again been so changed that Leo XIII in his constitution *"Romanos Pontifices"* (1881) [130] could write: "It has been established by common law that a house which does not have at least six religious should be completely subject to the authority of the bishop." This constitution, after noting that the Congregation for the Propagation of the Faith had repeatedly declared that such small houses in missionary countries remained exempt, went on to declare that the small houses of regulars in England and Scotland were likewise exempt. The Third Plenary Council of Baltimore asked that this constitution be extended to the United States and by a decree from the Congregation for the Propagation of the Faith (September 25, 1885), approved by Leo XIII, this request was granted.[131]

V. Churches without the care of souls. The Council of Trent had commanded that the local ordinaries visit by apostolic authority all churches in whatsoever manner exempted.[132] Yet, this regulation was not interpreted by the Congregation of the Council [133] nor by canonists [134] to apply to the churches of exempt regulars to which no care of souls was attached. In such non-parochial churches the bishop could institute a canonical visitation only in order to see that those particular laws were observed which he had passed for the pur-

29 Nov., 1657—*Fontes,* n. 1793; S. C. Ep. et Reg., 11 Sept., 1670—*Fontes,* n. 1803; S. C. Ep. et Reg., 19 Nov., 1671—*Fontes,* n. 1807. *Cf.* Gaudentius, *De Visitatione,* dub. X, n. 17; Ferraris, "Conventus," art. II, n. 23.

[129] *Cf.* Gaudentius, *De Visitatione,* dub. X, n. 17; Lucidi, *De Visitatione,* II, 57, nn. 64, 65.

[130] *Fontes,* n. 582.

[131] *Acta et Decreta Concilii Plenarii Baltimorensis* III, p. cv.

[132] Council of Trent, sess. VII, *de ref.,* c. 8.

[133] Ferraris, "Regularis," art. II, n. 6, ad 1. The response was an authentic interpretation and was approved by Gregory XV and Urban VIII. Though undated, it was subsequent to Gregory XV's constitution *Inscrutabili* of Feb. 5, 1622, which had caused some doubts on the point.

[134] *E. g.,* Gaudentius, *De Visitatione,* dub. X, n. 12; Rodericus, *Quaestiones Regulares,* II, qu. 62, art. 11; Mocchegiani, *Iurisprudentia Ecclesiastica,* I, n. 812; Lucidi, *De Visitatione,* II, 78, n. 93.

pose of providing that divine services be properly carried out, that no unlawful gain be sought therefrom, and that superstitious practices on the part of the faithful be eradicated.[135]

VI. Churches with the care of souls. The Council of Trent had ordered the local ordinaries to visit all ecclesiastical benefices with the care of souls, even though they were exempt and attached to monasteries.[136] The principle of placing the local ordinaries in a position of complete authority over the *cura animarum saecularium,* which was as a rule adopted by the Council of Trent, was made more explicit by a decree of the twenty-fifth session:

> In monasteries or houses, whether of men or women, which are charged with the care of souls of other secular persons besides those who belong to the household of those monasteries or places; the individuals who exercise that care, whether they be seculars or regulars, shall be immediately subject, in whatsoever pertains to the said cure and the administration of the sacraments, to the jurisdiction, visitation, and correction of the bishop; . . . the monastery of Cluny being exempted; and excepting also monasteries and places, in which abbots general or the heads of orders have their usual and principal residence; as also the other monasteries or houses, in which abbots or other superiors of regulars exercise episcopal and temporal jurisdiction over parish priests and their parishioners; saving, however, the right of those bishops who exercise greater jurisdiction over the places or persons above named.[137]

Gregory XV in his constitution *"Inscrutabili"* of February 5, 1622,[138] insisted on the observance of this decree and Benedict XIV, to remove all controversies, dealt with the question at great length in his constitution *"Firmandis"* of November 6, 1744.[139]

[135] Council of Trent, sess. XXII, *de observandis et evitandis in celebratione Missae.*

[136] Council of Trent, sess. VII, *de ref.,* c. 7.

[137] Council of Trent, sess. XXV, *de regularibus,* c. 11.

[138] *Fontes,* n. 199, § § 2, 4.

[139] *Fontes,* n. 349. *Cf. infra,* p. 138.

Nuns Subject to Regulars

The bishops could visit nuns subject to regulars in regard to the enclosure and the administration of temporalites.

The constitution *"Periculoso"* of Boniface VIII was renewed by the Council of Trent and, in addition, was so extended that the bishops had the duty of watching over the enclosure of all nuns, even those subject to regulars.[140] In the case of nuns subject to regulars the regular superiors also were obliged to see that the law of the enclosure was observed. This cumulative jurisdiction made it necessary to define carefully the respective rights and duties of regular superiors and bishops. From decisions and declarations of the Congregation of the Council and the Congregation of Bishops and Regulars on episcopal visitation the following points were settled: (a) The bishop was not limited to an annual visitation of the enclosure, but might visit as often as he thought fit; [141] (b) it was not necessary for the regular superior to know of or be present at this visitation; [142] (c) the bishop might visit the choir, the dormitory and the cells in so far as they related to the law of the enclosure; [143] (d) the bishop must be accompanied by a few elderly and religious persons; [144] (e) the bishop might conduct a personal visitation of each nun at the

140 Council of Trent, sess. XXV, *de regularibus*, c. 5.

141 S. C. C., 17 Nov., 1629—*Fontes*, n. 2513; S. C. C., 24 Sept., 1622—*Fontes*, n. 2434; S. C. C., 26 Maii, 1640—*Fontes*, n. 2616. The constitution *"Dubiis"* (23 Dec., 1581—*Fontes*, n. 148), of Gregory XIII and the constitution *"Salutare"* (3 Ian., 1742—*Fontes*, n. 323), of Benedict XIV forbade even the bishop admission into the enclosure except *in casibus necessariis*. The congregations interpreted this phrase to mean, not that there must be in evidence a necessity for the visitation, but rather, that any canonical visitation by the bishop constituted a legitimate necessity for entering the enclosure. *Cf.* Schaaf, *The Cloister*, pp. 110, 111.

142 S. C. C., 7 Sept., 1625—*Fontes*, n. 2462; S. C. C., 12 Aug., 1628—*Fontes*, n. 2474; S. C. C., 9 Nov., 1630—*Fontes*, n. 2526; S. C. C., 23 Feb., 1641—*Fontes*, n. 2625.

143 S. C. C., 2 et 16 Dec., 1747—*Fontes*, n. 3598; S. C. C., 27 Ian., 1748—*Fontes*, n. 3600; S. C. Ep. et Reg., 7 Iul., 1724—*Fontes*, n. 1841.

144 Gregory XIII, const. *"Dubiis,"* 23 Dec., 1581—*Fontes*, n. 148. *Cf.* Ferraris, "Episcopus," art. VI, nn. 98-104.

grille on matters pertaining to observance of the enclosure;[145] (f) the vicar general with a special mandate might conduct this visitation.[146]

The administration of the temporalities in monasteries of nuns fell under the supervision of the bishops in accordance with the constitution *"Inscrutabili"*[147] of Gregory XV. In cases of maladministration the bishop was authorized to correct and punish despite exemptions and privileges. If the bishop for a reasonable cause advised the regular superior to remove the administrator and the regular superior neglected to act, the bishop might effect the removal himself. The Congregation of the Council (June 7 and August 2, 1755) settling a controversy in the diocese of Olmauc (Olmütz) then in the kingdom of Bohemia, upheld the bishop in the right to look into the accounts and to prohibit the alienation of the dowries without a papal indult and epicopal permission.[148] To avoid further dispute on these points Clement XIII by his constitution *"Inter multiplices,"* of December 11, 1758, extended this decision to the dioceses of Paderborn, Münster, Cologne, Hildesheim and Osnabrück and made it the universal norm for all cases which might come up in the future.[149]

Thus the bishops could examine into the income and expenditures and assure themselves that the law in regard to the dowry was being observed.[150]

[145] S. C. C., 7 Mart., 1608—*Fontes,* n. 2372; S. C. C., 27 Ian., 1747—*Fontes,* n. 3600; S. C. Ep. et Reg., 7 Iul., 1724—*Fontes,* n. 1841.

[146] S. C. C., 13 Ian., 1624—*Fontes,* n. 2446; S. C. C., 2 Apr., 1661—*Fontes,* n. 2767; S. C. C., 29 Iul., 1684—*Fontes,* n. 2882.

[147] 5 Feb., 1622—*Fontes,* n. 199.

[148] *Fontes,* n. 3652.

[149] § 5 ad 10—*Fontes,* n. 449.

[150] *Cf.* S. C. C., 10 Apr., 1660—*Fontes,* n. 2765; S. C. C., 2 et 16 Dec., 1747—*Fontes,* n. 3598; S. C. Ep. et Reg., 7 Iul., 1724—*Fontes,* n. 1841.

CHAPTER III

CONGREGATIONS WITH SIMPLE VOWS

THE legal history of congregations with simple vows is comparatively brief. While communities with vows that were not solemn were in existence before the Council of Trent, it is not until the constitution *"Conditae a Christo"* (December 8, 1900) of Leo XIII that they enter into the common law as accepted institutions of the Church and it is not until the Code that their members are classed among the religious.[1]

Before the Council of Trent groups of laymen and laywomen, generally tertiaries, had formed communities and followed a life very similar to the monastic life, though they took only simple vows, or none at all, and observed no very strict enclosure. There is evidence that the Holy See in the early sixteenth century was officially aware of the existence of such groups [2] and Leo X even gave a rule of common life to some tertiaries.[3] St. Pius V saw certain dangers in this mode of life and took stern measures to bring all such communities within the pale of traditional monasticism. In his constitution *"Circa Pastoralis"* of May 19, 1566, he commanded all communities of women to take solemn vows and to observe the strict enclosure. If they failed to obey, they were forbidden to receive new candidates and if they attempted to receive new candidates the profession would be invalid.[4] By the constitution *"Lubricum vitae genus"* (November 17, 1568), the same pope condemned similar institutes of men. Within twenty-four hours all members without solemn vows should declare publicly and freely whether they desired

[1] On the refusal of the Holy See, even during the nineteenth century, to term such congregations *religiones* and their members, *religiosi*—*cf.* Larraona, "Commentarium Codicis," *CpR,* I (1920), 173-177.

[2] *Cf.* Clement R. Orth, *The Approbation of Religious Institutes* (Washington, D. C., 1931), pp. 52, 53.

[3] *Inter caetera,* 20 Ian., 1521—*Bull. Rom.,* V, 764-767.

[4] *Fontes,* n. 112, § § 3, 4, 6.

to take solemn vows. Those who so desired were to convene as soon as possible, adopt an approved rule and within a month make solemn profession. The rest, stripped of the habit, were to be dismissed and thenceforth were not to be allowed to dwell in any house of the same congregation.[5] There is considerable doubt as to whether Pius V intended to abolish by this constitution all institutes of men in which solemn vows were not taken or whether he directed his legislation only against certain ones.[6] In any event, his successors gave outright approbation in the sixteenth and seventeenth centuries to several congregations of men with simple vows [7]

The situation with congregations of women was very different. It is clear that Pius V wished to abolish all of them. His successors, while not so rigorous in their opposition, permitted them no more than a precarious existence under the jurisdiction and visitation of the bishops and withheld entirely the approval of the Holy See.[8] A reply given to the archbishop of Milan illustrates the seventeenth century attitude of the Roman authorities. The archbishop had asked if he could visit certain communities of tertiaries, not in solemn vows, both as to their churches and alleged enclosure. The Congregation of the Council with the approval of Innocent XI (February 15, 1678) replied that the archbishop could visit them and moreover he was at liberty, in accord with his judgment to disband such communities.[9] In the next century Benedict XIII took a more benign stand. For example, in his bull *"Pretiosus"* (May 25, 1727), he stated that Tertiaries of the Order of Preachers, who lived

[5] *Bull. Rom.*, VII, 725, 726.

[6] *Cf.* Larraona, "Commentarium Codicis," *CpR*, I (1920), 47, 48; Orth, *The Approbation of Religious Institutes*, pp. 48-50.

[7] Larraona has listed the institutes approved during this time—*op. cit.*, 48.

[8] *Cf.* Gaudentius, *De Visitatione*, dub. XI, n. 36; Benedict XIV, *Institutiones Ecclesiasticae*, XXIX, n. 13.

[9] Gaudentius, *op. cit.*, dub. XI, n. 35. The Ursulines, founded by St. Angela Merici (1474-1540) and the Society of Mary Ward (1585-1645) were two of the earliest and most notable efforts to create for women a newer and freer form of religious life which would permit external activities. For the attitude of ecclesiastical authorities towards the Ursulines—*cf.* Sister Monica, *Angela Merici and Her Teaching Idea*, pp. 306-361; towards Mary Ward and her society—*cf.* const, *Quamvis iusto*, 30 Apr., 1749—*Fontes*, n. 309.

in community with the vow of chastity or with the three vows, were not to be compelled to make solemn profession.[10] But his successor, Clement XII, revoked several constitutions and bulls of Benedict in so far as they deviated from the previous law. The bull *"Pretiosus"* was among the laws thus revoked.[11]

The most important document of the eighteenth century relative to congregations of simple vows was the constitution *"Quamvis iusto"* of Benedict XIV.[12] This constitution had its importance not only for the case which it settled, but also as a norm in the nineteenth century for the Congregation of Bishops and Regulars in their treatment of congregations of simple vows. In this constitution Benedict XIV directed his attention to the Institute of Mary (the English Ladies) and, without granting approval to the institute, stated that its work was laudable and therefore urged the bishops, to whom the institute was entirely subject, to treat the communities with great kindness. Since the women of this institute had not bound themselves to the law of papal enclosure, it had been possible for them to convene and elect a superioress general, in whose hands the government was placed. Benedict XIV made no objection to this office, but defined its limits in order to prevent the superioress general from encroaching upon the bishop's rights. The superioress was allowed, with the consent of the ordinary of the place, to visit the houses and inform herself of the state of discipline and the educational activities of the sisters. After the visitation the superioress general was to submit a report to the bishop who might make such provisions as he judged beneficial.

During the eighteenth century the Holy See also made further concessions by approving of both the rules and the institutes of a few congregations of men. The Brothers of the Christian Schools received approval in 1725[13] and during the pontificate of Benedict XIV the Passionists and the Redemptorists were approved.[14] In

10 *Bull. Rom.*, XXII, 523-549, § 38.

11 Const., *Romanus Pontifex,* 30 Mart., 1737—*Bull. Rom.*, XXIII, 323.

12 30 Apr., 1749—*Fontes*, n. 398, § § 22, 23.

13 *Cf.* Heimbucher, *Die Orden und Kongregationen,* II, 440-442.

14 Ward, *The Passionists,* pp. 49-51. The institute of the Passionists received the final approval from Clement XIV, in 1769. For the Redemptorists

these congregations visitation of all the houses was the duty of the superior general and with the later divisions into provinces, visitation was also undertaken by the provincials. In 1771 all Passionist communities with at least twelve members, with their houses and churches, were exempted from the jurisdiction and visitation of the local ordinaries. In 1789 and 1807 the Redemptorists received the same privileges.[15] Despite the fact that these congregations of men were approved, it was only after the French Revolution that the value of religious congregations with their adaptability to the new conditions was fully appreciated.[16] From at least as early as 1821 papal approval of both the constitutions and the institute was accorded to a congregation of sisters [17] and since that time a very large number of congregations of men and women have been approved. In the early decades of the nineteenth century the Congregation of Bishops and Regulars debated the wisdom of allowing the office of superioress general to be established in congregations of women. Accepting the constitution *"Quamvis iusto"* as a norm and concluding that the danger of conflict between the bishops and the superioress general would be more than offset by the advantage of a ruler within the society, who could supervise discipline and maintain uniformity, the Congregation of Bishops and Regulars thenceforth approved of the office.[18] Lucidi gives an extract from the rules of the Daughters of Charity as a typical example of the visitatorial rights of the superioress general:

The superioress general has the power to visit all houses and the institutes (*instituta vulgo* stabilimenti), when according to her judgment and the judgment of her consultors it is necessary. If regular observance is relaxed in any house or if there is a grave disturbance,

the apostolic brief *Ad Pastoralis* of February 25, 1749, granted approval of both rule and institute.

[15] *Cf.* S. C. Ep. et Reg., 28 Iul., 1837—*Fontes,* n. 1914; S. C. Ep. et Reg., 16 Sept., 1864—*Fontes,* n. 1933; Smetana, "Die Exemption der Kongregation des allerheiligsten Erlösers," *AKKR,* XVII, 452-454.

[16] *Cf.* Lucidi, *De Visitatione,* II, p. 248, n. 268; Bouix, *De Iure Regularium,* I, 215, 216.

[17] Bizzarri mentions such an approval of the Congregation of the Sacred Heart of Mary, Sept. 14, 1821—"Annotationes," *AKKR,* XV (1866), 441.

[18] Lucidi, *De Visitatione,* II, 292-294, nn. 355-357.

she is bound to visit that house or, if legitimately impeded, to depute another sister for the task. Before beginning the visitation she should approach the bishop, pay her respects, and receive his blessing. Opening the visitation with the usual prayers and ceremonies, she should make a personal visitation of all the sisters and then of all parts of the house. It belongs to the bishop alone to visit the church. On the occasion of the visitation the superioress examines into the administration of temporalities. In such decrees as she issues there must be nothing contrary to the decrees of the bishop.[19]

Over most of the congregations of men and women the bishops retained jurisdiction and were therefore bound to make a visitation of the houses, churches and members, with the same frequency that they were bound to visit other places in the diocese. The only limitation upon their powers as visitors was the obligation to refrain from interfering with the rules and constitutions approved by the Holy See.[20]

The beginning of the twentieth century brought the first general law on congregations with simple vows. In the constitution *"Conditae a Christo"* [21] Leo XIII first distinguished between diocesan institutes and pontifically approved institutes. With regard to diocesan institutes the bishop had the right of visiting any house in his diocese in matters concerning the pursuit of virtue, the maintenance of discipline and the administration of temporalities. His power to change the constitutions was limited if the institute had spread through several dioceses; for such changes the consent of all the bishops in whose dioceses the institute had houses was necessary.

With regard to institutes approved by the Holy See the question of episcopal rights was more difficult, Leo stated. It had been the custom to approve such an institute as a pious society of simple vows under the government of a general moderator, *salva Ordinariorum jurisdictione, ad formam sacrorum canonum et Apostoli-*

[19] *Cf.* Lucidi, *De Visitatione,* II, 304-306, nn. 379-387. For the visitation by superioresses of other congregations, *cf.* Schuppe, "Die Selbstverwaltung der neueren religiösen Frauengenossenschaften," *AKKR,* XIV (1865), 175, 176.

[20] S. C. Ep. et Reg., 27 Feb., 1863—*Fontes,* n. 1987; Schuppe, *op. cit.,* 177; Lucidi, *De Visitatione,* II, 319, nn. 436, 437.

[21] 8 Dec., 1900—*Fontes,* n. 644.

carum Constitutionum. Thereby restrictions were placed upon episcopal jurisdiction and the bishops were prohibited to arrogate to themselves the power of presidents (*praesides*) of such congregations. As to visitation it was determined that (a) in the houses of any such societies the bishop had the right of visiting the church, the sacristy, the public oratory, the place of confession and of providing appropriately in these matters; (b) in societies of priests the bishop had no right to visit in matters of conscience, discipline, and the administration of temporalities; (c) in lay institutes of men and women the bishop's visitation could and should concern itself with discipline, soundness of doctrine, morals, the enclosure and the frequentation of the Sacraments but in regard to temporalities the right of visitation extended only to examining into the administration of funds and legacies acquired for divine worship or for the benefit of that locality or diocese; (d) if the bishop found anything reprehensible in the affairs which fell within the scope of his visitation, he should not then and there settle the matter, but should bring it to the attention of the moderator and if he latter neglected to act, the bishop should provide. However, in important cases which admitted of no delay the bishop should settle the affair at once and refer his decision to the Congregation of Bishops and Regulars.

No regulations were laid down in the constitution *"Conditae a Christo"* for the visitation by higher superiors within the institutes. In the *"Normae secundum quas S. Congr. Episcoporum et Regularium procedere solet in approbandis novis Institutis votorum simplicium"* (1901) it was stated that the superior general either personally or through a delegate should visit the whole institute every third year. For any one house or province that was to be visited he might designate a visitor; but, in order to designate a visitor who was not one of his consultors it was necessary to have the consent of his consultors. The visitor was to be a religious who had made perpetual profession and was to be accompanied by a companion.[22] Though these norms were not laws and were open to exceptions, they indicate what the *stylus* of the Congregation of Bishops and Regulars demanded in the constitutions before granting approval.[23]

[22] Art. 27, n. 9; art. 255-257.

[23] *Cf.* Vermeersch, *De Religiosis,* II (130).

Conclusion

From the historical outline in the foregoing pages it is evident that visitation of religious was the object of a considerable amount of legislation throughout the centuries. At the time of the promulgation of the present Code of Canon Law systems of visitations by religious superiors were long since established in all institutes of men and were regulated for the most part by the constitutions. In congregations of women systematic visitation by the superioresses was also universally maintained. The extent of the local ordinary's visitation over the communities within his territory varied widely according to the status of the religious. Thus his right of visitation over diocesan religious was practically unlimited while he had no right to conduct of visitation of communities of male regulars save in exceptional cases. With respect to parishes connected with religious in any of the several possible ways the local ordinary had in every case at least the right to visit the church, the clergy, and to inquire into temporalities in so far as all these were concerned with the *cura animarum saecularium.*

The Code takes over in substance this previously existing legislation and while determining certain points in greater detail also introduces a number of minor alterations into the laws on the visitation of religious.

Part Two

COMMENTARY ON THE LEGISLATION OF THE CODE

CHAPTER IV

VISITATION BY RELIGIOUS SUPERIORS

THE Code does not go into details on the visitation of religious institutes by religious superiors. Canon 511 states that major religious superiors, whom the constitutions designate as visitors shall, at the times determined by the constitutions, visit all the houses subject to themselves. And these visitations they shall make in person or, if they are legitimately impeded, through others.[1] At times in the past the common law of the Church, as has been seen, regulated more specifically the way in which visitations should be made by religious officials. Today, adequate visitorial systems are provided for by the constitutions of the various orders and congregations. The Code makes no effort to set up a uniform system of visiting, but allows each order or congregation to retain the distinctive features that have been incorporated into its constitutions. The advantages of this course, which is in harmony with the general spirit of the law of the Code in this section on religious, are obvious, since religious institutes varying widely in their nature and work, require visitatorial plans which will fit in with their form of government, and which will best serve their particular needs. The Code is content to reaffirm the obligations of the constitutions, and thereby makes the visitations of the major superiors a canonical right and duty.

Canon 511 is concerned only with the visitations of major superiors.[2] Minor local superiors, having charge of not only a principal house but also one or more filial houses (in the strict sense), undoubtedly have the duty of watching over and visiting the latter,

[1] Canon 511: "Majores religionum Superiores quos ad hoc munus constitutiones designant, temporibus in eisdem definitis, omnes domos sibi subjectos visitent per se, vel por alios, si fuerint legitime impediti."

[2] Canon 488, 8°: *"Superiorum maiorum* [nomine veniunt] Abbas Primas, Abbas Superior Congregationis monasticae, Abbas monasterii sui iuris, licet ad monasticam Congregationem pertinentis, supremus religionis Moderator, Superior provincialis, eorundem vicarii aliique ad instar provincialium potestatem habentes."

but this duty is derived from their office and regulated solely by the constitutions. Of such visitations the canon does not treat.[3] Since an abbot of a monastery *sui iuris* is a major local superior, any obligation which he has by the constitutions of visiting other houses, is confirmed by this canon. Larraona refers, for example, to the constitutions of the Reformed Cistercians (Trappists) which, he indicates, prescribe that daughter abbeys be visited by the abbot of the founding abbey.[4] As a rule, however, the abbot of a monastery *sui iuris,* if obliged by the constitutions to visit at all, will be bound only to visit filial houses under his jurisdiction. For example, in the English Congregation of the Federated Black Benedictines, each abbot has the duty of visiting the simple priories, which are strictly filial, under his jurisdiction; of such priories he is the sole visitor. The constitutions give the abbot president the right to visit abbeys and conventual priories, but accord him only the right to obtain a report from each abbot on the state of discipline in the filial houses, except in cases when the president believes a personal visitation is necessary.

The term "major superiors," it should be observed, includes major superioresses. For visitations in societies of religious women, the major superioresses will be almost always either provincial or general superioresses, since Canon 511, in as much as it includes institutes of women, refers chiefly to congregations of sisters, in which the absense of the papal enclosure has permitted a union of houses under a cen-

[3] In the constitutions, all houses of a province, except the provincial house may be called filial houses, though each is a self-subsistent community with its own local superior. Only in a broad sense is it proper to apply to these the term filial houses. A filial house in the strict sense is one which does not constitute an entirely distinct community (and generally does not possess its own goods) but is a dependent part of a larger house and is ruled by a delegate, removable at the will *(ad nutum)* of the superior of the larger house. The fact that a house is, in the strict sense, filial does not necessarily indicate that it is a non-formal house *(domus non formata);* the number of religious residing therein may be sufficiently large to constitute a formal house. *Cf.* S. C. de Rel, *dub.,* 1 Feb., 1924—*AAS,* XVI (1924), 95; Maroto, "Annotationes," *CpR,* V (1924), 122-134; Schäfer, *De Religiosis,* p. 40.

[4] "Commentarium Codicis," *CpR,* VIII (1927), 355, note 458. For the original Cistercian system of visitation built on the relationship of mother and daughter abbeys, *cf. supra* p. 12.

tral government, and a division into provinces. As has been seen in the earlier stage of the development of congregations, the right of the mother general to conduct visitations was carefully circumscribed when the various rules received approbation.[5] With the trend to concede to superioresses of congregations complete dominative power over the members and the internal affairs of their institutes, the restrictions upon visitatorial rights have been largely removed. Canon 511 does not lay down any specific regulations for the visitations of major superioresses. Therefore what is set forth for the visitation of major superiors applies with equal force to the visitations of major superioresses.[6] Hence unless there is a provision to the contrary in the constitutions (which is rarely the case) the major superioresses of religious congregations, whether these be of diocesan or of pontifical right, may proceed upon their visitation without seeking the consent of the local ordinaries.

Whenever nuns of any religious order, have been and are bound by solemn vows and the papal enclosure, there exist no unions among their monasteries. Furthermore, there can be no possibility of visitation by the superioresses, since they as well as the rest of the nuns are obliged to remain within the papal enclosure. However, there are cases in which monasteries of nuns with only simple vows and the episcopal enclosure have been brought together in some sort of union. In any such cases, Canon 511 embraces in its ruling abbesses of monasteries *sui iuris,* as well as the other major superioresses, provided that the constitutions invest them with the right of undertaking visitation.[7]

The canon under consideration does not oblige nor give the right of visitation to any and all major religious superiors, but only confirms the right and duty of those designated as visitors by the constitutions. The frequency of visitations or the seasons of the year in which they are to be held, also remains as determined by the constitutions. Visitations by provincials are generally prescribed annually, whereas visitations by the superior general will hardly be more fre-

[5] *Cf. supra* pp. 67, 68.

[6] Canon 490.

[7] *Cf.* Larraona, "Commentarium Codicis," *CpR,* VIII (1927), 356, note 462.

quent than every third year, and in many institutes far less often.[8]

Major superiors designated by the constitutions to conduct visitations must fulfill this obligation in person. This is a restriction of the general rule: *Potest quis per alium, quod potest facere per seipsum.*[9] It is not necessary that the constitutions explicitly mention this restriction; by virtue of Canon 511 the obligation is made personal, and the superior specified may delegate a visitor only if he himself through some legitimate cause is hindered from performing this office. However, when the constitutions give to a superior full liberty either to visit himself or to constitute an official to undertake visitation of a whole or of a part of the institute, it cannot be said that the constitutions designate the superior in question as the necessary visitor but rather designate, disjunctively, either him or his appointee. This liberty is often given to the supreme moderator, since it is foreseen that in a large religious society the obligation of carrying out the visitation in person would leave little time for other duties. Such freedom of choice may be proved not only from the text but also from doctrinal or customary interpretations of the constitutions, yet it must be clearly established in one of these ways, for it should not be easily admitted that every phrase permitting a substitute relieves the superior of this personal duty when he is able to fulfill it.

The legitimate impediment which renders the sending of a vicar or delegate lawful may be moral or physical. Unless the constitutions provide otherwise it remains for the superior in question to decide according to the circumstances of the case when the conditions are verified by which he is excused from conducting the visitation in person. In general it may be said that the excusing cause should be grave.[10]

In some of the older centralized orders (*e. g.*, the Order of Preachers) visitations are conducted not only by the major superiors who have habitual authority, such as the provincials and superiors

[8] *Cf. Normae secundum quas S. Cong. Episcoporum et Regularium procedere solet in approbandis novis Institutis votorum simplicium* (1901) nn. 255, 256, 257, 271, 9°.

[9] Reg. 68 R. J., in VI°.

[10] Larraona, "Commentarium Codicis," *CpR,* VIII (1927), 357, 358.

general but also by officials who are elected by the chapters and who have authority only during the time of visitation. A similar practice is found in some of the monastic congregations. Thus, for example, in the English Congregation of St. Benedict the abbot president is *ex officio* visitor of all the abbeys except his own. For the visitation of the president's abbey, however, the general chapter chooses two visitors. Visitors of this type, though their powers are operative only for the duration of the visitation, appear to be major superiors acting with vicarious authority.[11]

Religious visitors, unless restricted by particular law,[12] are able to inquire about, and personally investigate into, all matters. Their visitation embraces the place (local visitation), books, documents, and other things (real visitation) and persons (personal visitation). The real property—land, buildings, and their appurtenances—is subject to their inspection and within the terms of the constitutions they may order repairs and make other provisions for its conservation. They may examine into the administration of all goods, the income and expenditures, the records of investments and Masses, etc. They also may interview any member of the community and inform themselves on the state of discipline and take measures to remedy abuses and promote better observance. In a number of ways the constitutions of the different institutes vary, both in specifying the matters to which the visitor is obliged to attend and in placing limitations upon his powers.[13]

[11] *Cf.* Larraona, "Commentarium Codicis," *CpR,* IV (1923), 46. "In constitutionibus religionum generatim fere, quando sermo fit de his Visitatoribus qui alieno nomine visitant ipsi delegati appellantur. Tamen quia in iure antiquo non adeo exacte distinguebatur inter potestatem delegatam ac vicariam, verbis non est nimis insistendum ad characterem Visitatorum in singulis religionibus definiendum. Ceterum novo iure satis consonus videretur huiusmodi character vicarius in Visitatoribus."—Larraona, "An Visitatores sint ad normam iuris Superiores maiores?" *CpR,* I (1920), 31, note 7.

[12] Visitors acting in the name of another, *i. e.,* vicarious or delegated visitors, may be subject to further restrictions. Thus delegated visitors may receive faculties for all that the ordinary visitor may do *(i. e., ad universitatem negotiorum)* or for certain matters *(i. e., ad singulos casus).*

[13] These matters are discussed more fully in Chapter IX wherein the procedure in visitation is considered.

For lists of questions (classified according to the legal status of the vari-

If the visitor is endowed with ordinary power his authority begins as soon as he enters the house or province which he is to visit. If he is acting by delegated power his authority begins when he shows his letters of delegation to the superior of that portion of the institute which is to undergo visitation.[14]

Nuns Subject to Regulars

A few words must be added on religious visitors of nuns subject to regulars. It is for the constitutions of the order of male regulars to decide which of the superiors of the order of male regulars having charge over the nuns shall conduct the visitations. The frequency of visitations is also to be determined by these constitutions. The Code contains nothing which would prohibit a regular whom the constitutions designate as visitor from making an extraordinary visitation whenever circumstances arise which in his judgment render such a visitation necessary or profitable.[15] Unless the constitutions provide otherwise, the regular visitor has the authority to inquire about, and investigate into, all matters whether relating to discipline, or the administration of temporalities and has the right and duty of correcting abuses in their regard. Nuns under the jurisdiction of regulars are also subject in certain points to the local ordinary. However, in the matters over which the local ordinary and the regular superior possess cumulative jurdisdiction, each exercises his power independently of the other. Thus, though both have custody of the enclosure, the regular visitor, without consulting the local ordinary, may punish nuns or others of his subjects who have broken the law of the enclosure.[16]

Since the papal enclosure of nuns ordinarily forbids the admission of men within its confines, special norms are required for the visitation of regular superiors. Canon 600, 1°, states that the regular superior or other visitors delegated by him when canonically visit-

ous kinds of religious institutes) which the religious visitors may ask, *vide* Mothon, *Institutions Canoniques,* III, 410-429, 446-452.

[14] Piat, *Praelectiones Iuris Regularis,* I, qu. 874.

[15] For the restrictions of the pre-Code law, *cf. supra* p. 29.

[16] Canon 603, § 2.

ing the monastery of nuns may enter the enclosure but only for the purpose of inspection and on condition that they be accompanied by at least one cleric or male religious of mature age.[17] The Sacred Congregation of Religious in its instruction on the enclosure of nuns with solemn vows, February 6, 1924,[18] amplified this statement of the Code:

A. The visitor therefore may enter the cloister for local visitation only. The personal visitation must be made outside the enclosure at the grille. . . . The regular superior or the visitor may not enter the cloister except in the act of the local visitation.

B. The visitor who is about to enter the cloister for the purpose of inspection must be accompanied by at least one cleric or one male religious, who may be a lay brother, of mature age; and this companion must not leave him during the whole time he is in the monastery.

The old law went into greater detail and added several additional norms which are not in force today.[19] The following differences should be noted:

1. There is no longer a precise limit to the number of companions whom the regular superior may bring with him into the enclosure. But if others besides the single companion obligatory by law are taken within the enclosure during visitation, certainly they should be few and members either of the secular clergy or of a religious community of men.[20]

2. Neither the Code nor the instruction quoted above demands that four nuns accompany the visitor while within the enclosure. Hence, under the present law it is left to the constitutions to decide whether or not any nuns shall be in attendance.

3. If he is legitimately impeded from holding the visitation,

[17] Canon 600, 1°. "Ordinario loci aut Superiori regulari, monasterium monialium visitantibus, vel aliis Visitatoribus ab ipsis delegatis licet clausuram ingredi dumtaxat inspectionis causa, cautoque ut unus saltem clericus vel religiosus vir maturae aetatis eos comitetur."

[18] S. C. de Rel., *Instructio de clausura monialium votorum solemnium,* § III, 2°—*AAS,* XVI (1924), 98.

[19] Canon 6, 6°.

[20] Schaaf, *The Cloister,* p. 114.

the regular superior may delegate another religious to conduct both the local visitation within the enclosure and the personal visitation at the grille.

4. The regular superior is not obliged to inform the bishop of the diocese of the time of any visitation which he may undertake, whether it be the ordinary visitation which he is obliged to make at stated intervals according to the constitutions of his order or an extraordinary visitation which he believes necessary on account of special circumstances.[21]

If there are extern sisters (*sorores externae*) attached to a monastery of nuns, the regular superior is to visit them at the same time.[22] Extern sisters profess the same rule and constitute one religious family with the nuns; they are also subject to the same superioress. However, the extern sisters take only simple vows. The special purpose of these sisters is to serve the monastery and the church annexed to the monastery by undertaking such tasks as may or must be performed outside the enclosure.[23] Their residence is a separate house or a part of the monastery outside the enclosure of the nuns. As a rule they are not permitted to enter within the enclosure of the nuns. However, as their own residence has an enclosure much the same as that of congregations of women, the prescriptions of Canons 604, § 1, and 600, 1°, are to be applied.[24] Accordingly the visitor should enter this enclosure with at least one companion (a cleric or a male religious of mature age) and only

[21] For the old law, *cf. supra* p. 30. *Nuns (moniales)* with simple vows (*cf.* Canon 488, 7°) are subject as a general rule to the local ordinary (*cf.* S. C. de Rel., 23 Iun., 1923—*AAS*, XV [1923], 358). However, in the exceptional cases in which communities of nuns with simple vows are by special privilege subject to regular superiors, the rules given above for the visitation by regular superiors of communities with solemn vows and the papal enclosure are applicable.

[22] S. C. de Rel., "Statuta a sororibus externis Monasterium Monialium cuiusque ordinis servanda," 16 Iul., 1931—*CpR,* XII (1931), 410, art. 11.

[23] *Loc. cit.,* art. 3, 5, 8. These sisters are not to be confused with the lay nuns *(conversae)* who, when bound by solemn vows and the papal enclosure, must necessarily confine their service to duties within the monastery.

[24] La Puma, "Statuta a Sororibus Externis Servanda," *CpR,* XIII (1932), 348, art. 6.

for the purpose of inspection. The personal visitation of the sisters must be held some place outside its confines. As the extern sisters are subject to the regular superior in the same manner as the nuns, he may conduct an inquiry into all aspects of their religious life. Thus he may ask about the observance of the enclosure, the rule, and the special statutes that bind them. This is all part of the one canonical visitation of the monastery; from the statutes of 1931 for extern sisters, the regular superior derives no right to conduct a separate visitation of these sisters at other times.[25]

[25] La Puma, *op. cit.*, p. 352, art. 11.

CHAPTER V

THE LOCAL ORDINARY'S VISITATION OF RELIGIOUS OF DIOCESAN CONGREGATIONS

CANON 512 [1] contains provisions for the external visitation of religious by the local ordinary. External visitation means visitation by one who does not belong to the religious institute that is visited. The local ordinary may indeed be a religious but in his canonical visitations as in the other official acts of a local ordinary he is exercising powers that are his as an ecclesiastical rather than as a religious superior. Canon 512 lists the various visitations which the local ordinary must undertake in accordance with the different canonical status of the several types of religious. Before taking up the question of the extent of the local ordinary's visitatorial authority over religious of diocesan congregations it is advisable to consider which of the local ordinaries have the right and duty of conducting the visitations mentioned in Canon 512.

The Local Ordinary

The "local ordinary" is a generic term used to signify the following officials: the residential bishop, the abbot or prelate *nullius*, and their vicars general, the administrator, the vicar or prefect apostolic, and those who, failing the aforesaid, succeed to the government according to the law or approved constitutions.[2] Thus, since the term includes those who succeed to the government of a vacant see, the vicar capitular (in a diocese or in an abbacy *nullius* or prelature *nullius*)[3] and the pro-vicar or pro-prefect (in an apostolic vicariate or prefecture)[4] are local ordinaries during an interregnum.

[1] Canon 512, § 1. "Ordinarius loci per se vel per alium quinto quoque anno visitare debet: . . ."

[2] Canon 198.

[3] Within eight days after the vacancy of the see the chapter (or diocesan consultors, *cf.* Canon 427) upon whom the government immediately devolves, must elect a vicar capitular (or administrator). *Cf.* Canons 327, § 1; 431, § 1; 432. Since the chapter or diocesan consultors enjoy such brief authority, there is no need to speak of the possibility of their sending forth visitors.

[4] In an apostolic vicariate or prefecture authority passes directly to the pro-vicar or pro-prefect. *Cf.* Canon 309, § 1.

There is no doubt that the residential bishop, the abbot or prelate *nullius*, the vicar general and the vicar or prefect apostolic have the right to visit in accordance with Canon 512. Further, since the vicar delegate, appointed by the local ordinary of a mission territory, has practically the same authority as the vicar general of a diocese [5] this official has the powers granted by Canon 512.

The rights and duties of the apostolic administrator, in regard to visitation as in other matters, are determined by his letters of appointment.[6] If they contain no provisions to the contrary the following rules of Canon 315 hold:

(1) The administrator permanently constituted has the same rights and duties as the residential bishop (and hence may conduct visitations); (2) the temporary administrator has the same rights and duties as the vicar capitular but, if the see is occupied, the temporary administrator may visit the diocese according to the prescriptions of the law.[7] The inference appears to be that the vicar capitular cannot visit the diocese for after stating that the temporary administrator has the same rights and duties as the vicar capitular Canon 315, § 2, 1° immediately seems to make an exception, *sed, sede plena potest* [*Administrator*] *diocesim visitare ad tramitem iuris*. Accordingly Blat [8] and Toso [9] conclude that the vicar capitular does not

[5] ". . . Elargitus est [Benedictus XV] Ordinariis Missionum potestatem nominandi *Vicarium Delegatum*, si eo indigeant, cui practice concessa sit omnis iurisdictio in spiritualibus et temporalibus, qua ex Codice I. C. uti potest Vicarius Generalis in dioecesi.

"Ex hac concessione, omnibus Superioribus Missionum facta, nunc tu poteris Vicarium Delegatum nominare, qui gaudeat omnibus facultatibus Vicario Generali tributis, ad normam Canon 368, § 1, 2°. . . ."—S. C. de Prop. Fide, 8 Dec., 1919, II—*AAS*, XII (1920), 120.

[6] Canon 314.

[7] Canon 315, § 1. "Administrator Apostolicus permanenter constitutus iisdem iuribus et honoribus fruitur, iisdemque obligationibus tenetur, ac Episcopus residentialis.

§ 2. "Si ad tempus datus sit:

1°. "Eadem iura ac officia habet, ac vicarius Capitularis; sed, sede plena, potest diocesim visitare ad tramiten iuris; . . ."

[8] *Commentarium Textus Codicis Iuris Canonici*, II, *(De Personis)*, n. 333.

[9] *Ad Codicem Iuris Canonici Commentaria Minora* (Romae, 1923), II *(De Personis)*, 137.

possess the right of visitation. However, the Code does not indicate elsewhere that the vicar capitular is unable to conduct visitations. On the other hand Canon 435 does state clearly that the ordinary jurisdiction of the bishop in spiritual and temporal affairs passes to the vicar capitular with the exception of those things which are *expressly* prohibited to him by law.[10] There is no express prohibition in the present law which denies to the vicar capitular the right to visit like a bishop. The old law permitted the vicar capitular to visit the religious of the diocese in so far as they were subject to the bishop's ordinary jurisdiction or to the bishop's jurisdiction as perpetual delegate of the Holy See. However, the vicar capitular was obliged to wait until a year had elapsed since the last visitation.[11] In the Code there is no trace of even this restriction. Hence, it seems necessary to conclude that the vicar capitular has the same right of visitation as that which belonged to the residential bishop or abbot *nullius* or prelate *nullius* to whom he succeeds.[12] Further, since the temporary administrator has the same powers as a vicar capitular he may conduct visitations in accordance with Canon 512 whether the see be occupied or vacant.

In missionary territories when the pro-vicar or pro-prefect succeed to authority, they take over the entire government without any restriction in regard to the right of visitation.[13] Hence it appears that if five years have elapsed since the last visitation of any of the religious mentioned in Canon 512, the pro-vicar or pro-prefect is bound to visit them.

The prescription of Canon 512 that the visitation of religious should take place every five years is in harmony with the law which states that the general diocesan visitation must be completed within

[10] Canon 435, § 1. "Sicut ad Capitulum ante deputationem Vicarii Capitularis, ita deinde ad Vicarium Capitularem transit ordinaria Episcopi iurisdictio in spiritualibus et temporalibus, exceptis iis quae in iure expresse sunt eidem prohibita."

[11] S. C. C., 13 Sept., 1721—*Fontes*, n. 2332. *Cf.* D. Bouix, *Tractatus de Capitulis* (Parisiis, 1882), pp. 73-78; Cayo Castillo, *La Potestad del Cabildo en Sede Vacante o Impedida del Vicario Capitular* (The Catholic University of America, Canon Law Studies, n. 4, Habana, 1919), p. 84.

[12] Canon 6, 6°.

[13] *Cf.* Canon 309, § 2.

five years.[14] Although vicars and prefects apostolic have no obligation to make a general visitation, within any stated time, of the regions entrusted to them,[15] yet as local ordinaries they appear to be obliged to conduct a quinquennial visitation of the places mentioned in Canon 512.

The local ordinaries, who are bound to make this quinquennial visitation, cannot dispense themselves from the obligation;[16] there is no legal impediment to a more frequent exercise of this right. Indeed, when disorders arise and an extraordinary visitation appears to be the best or only remedy, the local ordinary would be obliged by natural law to use this means.

It is to be observed that, while the local ordinary must personally conduct the general visitation of his territory unless impeded through some legitimate cause,[17] he has full liberty to carry out the visitations prescribed by Canon 512 either personally or through a vicar or delegate.[18]

If the local ordinary has neglected to carry out the visitation to which he is obliged by law the right devolves upon the metropolitan in accordance with Canon 274, 5° [19] but the metropolitan must first

[14] Canon 343, § 1. Abbots and prelates *nullius* are also bound to complete the general visitation of their territories within five years (*cf.* Canon 323, § 1).

[15] Canon 301, § 2.

[16] Larraona, "Commentarium Codicis," *CpR,* VIII (1927), 441.

[17] Canons 343, § 1; 301, § 2.

[18] In many dioceses there exist officials who are termed directors of religious, supervisors of sisters, etc. Such officials are not contemplated by the Code; whether or not they have the right to conduct visitation depends entirely upon the faculties which they have received from the bishop. *Cf.* Goyeneche, "Quaenam sunt attributiones Directoris Congregationis dioecesanae?" *CpR,* XIV (1933), 357.

[19] Canon 274: "In dioecesibus vero suffraganeis Metropolita potest tantum: . . .

5 ° "Canonicum visitationem peragere, causa prius ab Apostolica Sede probata, si eam Suffraganeus neglexerit; tempore autem visitationis, potest praedicare, confessiones audire etiam absolvendo a casibus Episcopo reservatis, de vita et honestate clericorum inquirere, clericos infamia notatos Ordinariis ipsorum, ut eos puniant, denuntiare, notoria crimina, manifestas et notorias offensas tum sibi tum suis forte illatas, iustis poenis, censuris non exclusis, punire."

inform the Holy See and receive its approval. At the time of visitation the metropolitan may preach, hear confessions even absolving from cases reserved to the bishop, inquire about the life and probity of the clerics, denounce infamous clerics to the local ordinary in order that the latter may punish them, and he himself, with just penalties including censures, may punish notorious crimes and any manifest and notorious affronts and insults which may be offered to him and his attendants. It is evident that Canon 274, 5° is speaking of the general diocesan visitation, yet as the metropolitan becomes the canonical visitor of the diocese and as the visitation of religious is part of the visitation of the diocese [20] the rights of Canons 512 and 513 belong to the metropolitan during his visitation.

Diocesan Congregations

The local ordinary has complete jurisdiction over the houses of diocesan religious in his territory. A religious congregation of diocesan right comes into being through the will of the local ordinary [21] and remains diocesan until approved in some manner by the Holy See.[22] Though such a congregation has spread through several dioceses, it does not thereby attain to any measure of independence relative to the several local ordinaries in whose dioceses the houses exist.[23] Hence in treating of the visitation of such congregations Canon 512, § 1, 2° simply makes the broad statement that the local ordinary should visit their houses every five years whether the congregation be of men or women.[24]

When the local ordinary or his delegate visits houses of women religious he may enter the enclosure only for the purpose of inspec-

[20] *Cf.* Canon 344.

[21] The Holy See is consulted, but it is the local ordinary who issues the decree of erection (Canon 492, § 1).

[22] *Cf.* Canon 488, 8°.

[23] *Cf.* Canon 492, § 2. Also *Normae secundum quas S. Congregatio de Religiosis in novis religiosis Congregationibus approbandis procedere solet,* cap. 1, 3-5—*AAS,* XIII (1921), 313.

[24] Canon 512, § 1. "Ordinarius loci per se vel per alium quinto quoque anno visitare debet: . . .

2°. "Singulas domos sive virorum sive mulierum Congregationis iuris dioecesani."

tion accompanied by at least one cleric or male religious of mature age.[25] The male religious may be a lay brother. The Code does not state the maximum number of companions who may enter the enclosure with the visitor. However, if others besides the companion required by law are brought in, they should be few and either clerics or male religious of mature age. The companion (or companions) should remain with the visitor during the tour of inspection which may cover all parts of the house and garden, etc. The visitation of persons and the examination of accounts and the like must take place outside the enclosure. It need hardly be mentioned that sisters of diocesan congregations are bound only by the episcopal (or more properly the partial) enclosure which does not hinder their egress from its confines. Hence all business of the visitation apart from the tour of inspection is to be carried out with the sisters in an office or any other room of the convent outside the limits of the enclosure.

In visiting men religious the local ordinary may, of course, hold the entire visitation within the enclosure. However, in the extent of the local ordinary's visitatorial powers there is no distinction between the visitation of women and men religious. In both cases the local ordinary proceeds with unlimited powers of inquiry and inspection.[26] He may question any and all religious and investigate into all such matters of religious discipline as he deems useful for the uncovering of abuses and the advancement of good order. It is also within his power to examine into the accounts of all the temporal affairs of the house.[27] Such an examination is not imposed by

[25] Canon 604, § 1: "In domibus etiam Congregationum religiosarum sive pontificii sive dioecesani iuris clausura servetur, in quam nemo alterius sexus admittatur, nisi ii de quibus in can. 598, § 2 et can. 600, aliique quos ex iustis ac rationibus causis Superiores admitti posse censuerint."

Canon 600, 1°: "Ordinario loci aut Superiori regulari, monasterium monalium visitantibus, vel aliis Visitatoribus ab ipsis delegatis licet clausuram ingredi dumtaxat inspectionis causa, cautoque ut unus saltem clericus vel religiosus vir maturae aetatis eos comitetur."

[26] Augustine, *Commentary,* III, 136; Schäfer, *De Religiosis,* p. 181; Fanfani, *De Iure Religiosorum,* n. 70.

[27] Canon 535, § 3. "Loci Ordinario ius insuper esto cognoscendi:

1°. "De rationibus oeconomicis domus religiosae iuris dioecesani; . . ."

law upon the local ordinary as a necessary part of the visitation. If he has made arrangements according to which the superiors furnish him with accounts of the administration at frequent intervals outside the time of visitation,[28] he may find it entirely unnecessary to go into these matters while holding the canonical visitation.

When the local ordinary has completed his inquiry into whatever matters, spiritual and temporal, he deemed useful to investigate, he may remedy whatever departures from the canons and constitutions have been noted and punish those who have been at fault.[29] However, the visitor should bear in mind that, notwithstanding the plenitude of his authority over diocesan religious, he is an external superior. Particularly when he believes it advisable to leave behind him decrees regulating certain points of discipline for the future, he should act with caution. Visiting a house which belongs to a congregation existing in several dioceses, the local ordinary cannot lay down decrees which in effect abrogate provisions of the constitutions.[30] Moreover, the decrees should not be of such a nature as to impair or render difficult the exercise of the dominative power of the general, or provincial, or local superiors. For diocesan congregations the relationship between the dominative power possessed by the religious superiors and the extensive jurisdiction enjoyed by the external superiors, the local ordinaries, is defined by the Code only in part.[31] Each religious and each house are parts of a moral body whose normal life is directed, for the most part, by its own religious superiors. Membership in a diocesan congregation

[28] The general law requires an annual report from the administrators of churches, pious places canonically erected, and confraternities (Canon 1525, § 1).

[29] *Cf. infra,* Chapter IX: *Procedure in Visitation.*

[30] *Cf.* Canon 495, § 2.

[31] "Haec potestas [Ordinarii loci] nec accurate definitur nec fere valet, sub hoc respectu iuridico limitibus certis ac fixis circumscribi ac proinde ut unitas regiminis spiritus et ministeriorum conservari possi, ex parte Ordinariorum maxima prudentia ac moderatione opus est in exercenda eorum potestate; semperque etiam supposita bona voluntate, praedictae unitati pericula imminebunt et quidem eo maiora ac frequentiora quo plures erunt dioeceses ad quas extendatur Congregatio." — Larraona, "Commentarium Codicis," *CpR,* V (1924), 144, nota 94.

binds individuals much more closely together than membership in a confraternity or pious association and for a religious congregation to function effectively and retain its unity a considerable measure of autonomy is essential.[32] In certain important matters the Code demands the intervention of the local ordinary; but, he may not so multiply matters in which his permission is required as to destroy that freedom of action which is necessary for the government of internal affairs and thereby to weaken the structure of the congregation.

By way of summary the following norms may be set down: (1) The visitor may and indeed should investigate into everything, even the internal affairs of the community; (2) when by corrections made then and there the visitor is able to settle difficulties or eradicate disorders, he may do so directly or through the superior as he thinks best; (3) when it is necessary to provide for cases or situations that will recur frequently in the future and for which the canons do not require the local ordinary's intervention, it is advisable that the religious superiors, as far as possible, be left to deal with these matters, though the visitor in his decrees may outline the method.

The Mother House

In connection with the visitation of diocesan institutes it is necessary to consider in particular the visitation of the mother house. By the term "mother house" (*domus princeps seu generalitia*) is understood a religious house which is the residence not only of a local superior and his subjects but also of the superior general (or provincial) with his assistants, for these latter are under the obligation common to all religious of dwelling within a house of their own institute.[33]

I. The first point to be noted in regard to the visitation of such houses is that therein the dowry funds are administered if they belong to an institute of religious women. According to Canon 550 the dowries must be administered at the house of the habitual resi-

[32] *Cf.* Maroto, "Annotationes," *CpR,* II (1921), 323-329.

[33] *Cf.* Canon 508.

dence of the superioress general or provincial; the local ordinary should carefully watch over the preservation of the dowries and should demand an account especially on the occasion of visitation.[84] This account should include the dowries of novices which are to be invested after their first profession as well as the dowries of the professed religious which have been invested.[85] The local ordinary is to see that the dowries of all the religious who are still living have been kept intact and are being administered with proper care. As to dowries already invested, he should assure himself that they were actually placed in safe licit, and productive investments after his consent had been previously obtained.[86]

There seems to be little doubt that the local ordinary whose consent is required for the investment and who has the right to demand an account of the administration is the ordinary of the place where the mother house is situated.[87] Schäfer [88] suggests that the right of vigilance and visitation belongs to the ordinary of the place in which the religious, from whom the dowry has been received, resides. Hence, he concludes that the superioress general or provincial should send to each local ordinary an account of the dowries of those religious who are stationed in the houses in his territory. The words of neither Canon 550 nor Canon 535, § 2, are helpful in settling the question. However, the obvious purpose of receiving the account of the administration of the dowry funds is to permit the local ordinary to check up on the manner of administration and see to it that the prescriptions of the pertinent canons are being fulfilled. The local ordinary according to Canon 2412, 1°, is to

[84] Canon 550, § 1. "Dotes caute et integre administrentur apud monasterium vel domum habitualis residentiae supremae Moderatricis aut Antistitae provincialis.

§ 2. "Ordinarii locorum conservandis religiosarum dotibus sedulo invigilent; et praesertim in sacra visitatione de eisdem rationem exigant."

Canon 535, § 2. "In aliis mulierum religionibus [*i. e.*, in Congregationibus], ratio administrationis bonorum quae dotes constituunt, Ordinario loci reddatur occasione visitationis et etiam saepius, si Ordinarius id necessarium duxerit."

[85] Larraona, "Commentarium Codicis," *CpR*, XIV (1933), 350.

[86] *Cf.* Canon 549.

[87] Coronata, *Institutiones Iuris Canonici*, I, 706.

[88] *De Religiosis*, p. 288.

inflict penalties, including even deprivation of office, upon superioresses who in any way expend the dowry funds contrary to the prescriptions of Canon 549. This right and duty of supervision to insure the proper administration of the dowries extending as it does even to the infliction of penalties can be exercised only by the local ordinary who has authority over the administrators. It would be contrary to fundamental legal principles to assert that a local ordinary may correct and punish a religious residing outside his territory. Hence, it appears necessary to conclude that the right to supervise the dowry funds, to receive an account on visitations, and to punish maladministration in accordance with Canon 2412, 1°, belongs to the local ordinary of provincial or general houses wherein the dowries are administered.

II. In connection with the visitation of the mother house another question of considerable importance remains to be discussed, *viz.*, whether the general and his staff (the general curia)[39] are subject to the visitation of the local ordinary within whose territory the mother house is situated. It will rarely happen that the offices of general superior of the institute and that of local superior of the mother house will be united in one person as it would be difficult for one person to discharge competently the duties of the two superiorships. Yet, whether united or not, it is possible to distinguish clearly the general and his staff in their official capacity from the superior of the local community. No doubt exists as to the right of the local ordinary to visit the local superior and the latter's subjects in the mother house in precisely the same manner that he may visit any other house of diocesan religious within his territory. Further, there is no doubt that if the congregation is confined to one diocese he may visit the general and his staff and investigate into all the temporal affairs of the institute. The debatable question is whether the local ordinary, within whose territory the general has his habitual residence, may canonically visit the general curia and investigate into the administration of the general funds, if the diocesan congregation has spread through several dioceses.[40] This question is

[39] Or the provincial and his staff, if the congregation is divided into provinces, as is sometimes the case even in diocesan institutes.

[40] In the latter case the local ordinary of the mother house cannot bring

not clearly answered in the Code and most of the commentators do not treat of it explicitly. Bastien [41] and Larraona [42] adopt the view which denies this right to the local ordinary. D'Ambrosio [43] maintains the opposite position.[44] D'Ambrosio's view seems to be more in accord with the Code and legal principles.

Canon 512, § 1, 2°, certainly subjects the mother house to the visitation of the local ordinary within whose territory it is situated. This should be taken to mean the entire house: *ubi lex non distinguit nec nos distinguere debemus.* If a distinction is to be introduced between the general curia and the rest of the community, there must be clear and compelling reasons for so doing. There are clear reasons for making such a distinction in Canon 512, § 2, 3°,[45] which treats of the visitation of lay congregations of pontifical right. Pontifical institutes are approved by the Holy See and according to the principle expressly stated in the constitution *"Conditae a Christo"* and which now runs through the legislation on pontifical institutes, the authority of the local ordinaries is thereby restricted.[46] On the contrary, diocesan institutes are entirely under the authority of the local ordinaries according to the law.[47] In the case of a diocesan

within the purview of his visitation accounts of property of individual houses outside the local ordinary's territory, even though these accounts have been sent in to the general by the local superiors.

41 *Directoire Canonique à L'Usage des Congrégations à voeux simples,* n. 305.

42 "De Visitatorum potestate applicandi poenas in can. 2413 statutas," *CpR,* X (1929), 373-376.

43 "De Domo Generalitia Instituti Polydioecesani quoad Canonicam Visitationem can. 512, § 1, n. 2, praescriptam et quoad poenas can. 2413 sancitas," *Ap,* I (1928), 417-422.

44 In apparent agreement with D'Ambrosio, though their statements are brief and not explicit, are Augustine *(Commentary,* III, 136), Fanfani *(De Iure Religiosorum,* n. 70) and Schäfer *(De Religiosis,* p. 181).

45 A comparison between Canon 512, § 1, 1°, and Canon 512, § 1, 2°, does not help towards a solution, for there are no superioresses higher than a local superioress in monasteries of nuns.

46 *Cf. supra,* p. 70.

47 Canon 492, § 2. "Congregatio iuris dioecesani, quamvis decursu temporis in plures dioeceses diffusa, usque tamen dum pontificiae approbationis aut laudis testimonio caruerit, remanet dioecesana, Ordinariorum iurisdictioni ad norman iuris plane subiecta."

congregation which is represented in several dioceses, Canon 492, § 2, is not to be understood as calling for collective jurisdiction to be exercised by all the local ordinaries acting in unison. It is clear from the Code that the complete subjection is maintained as a rule by the exclusive, independent and complete jurisdiction of each local ordinary over the houses and the religious in his territory.[48] To this general rule there are only two exceptions. Alterations in the constitutions require the collective consent of all the local ordinaries; the foundation of a new house is dependent upon the consent of both the local ordinary of the mother house and the local ordinary of the place of proposed establishment.[49] It is therefore in agreement with the general rule to interpret Canon 512, § 1, 2°, as investing the local ordinary with the right of visiting this house in its entirety.

Further reasons may be adduced in confirmation of this view. If the local ordinary of the mother house does not possess the right of visiting the general curia, no provision is to be found in the Code for subjecting the curia to visitation. As D'Ambrosio notes,[50] the consequent exemption would establish the general curia of a diocesan congregation in a more independent status than the Code grants to the Supreme Moderator and council of a pontifical congregation, who are bound by Canon 510 to submit to the Holy See a quinquennial report on the state of the institute.[51] Since the Holy See has no direct concern with diocesan congregations, it does not demand this measure of supervision. Thus, if the general curia of these congregations were not subject to the visitation of the local ordinary, there would be a case in which the law places these congregations in a more favorable position than pontifical congregations —an anomaly which is not easily admitted.

Moreover, were the general curia of diocesan institutes exempted

[48] *Cf.*, *e. g.*, Canons 498; 506, § 4; 547, § 4; 647, § 4; 652.

[49] Canon 495.

[50] "De Domo Generalitia Instituti Polydioecesani," *Ap*, I (1928), 420.

[51] It is particularly noteworthy in this connection that for a pontifical congregation of women the report must be signed, not only by the superioress general and her council, but also by the local ordinary of the place where they reside (Canon 510).

from visitation, how could this be reconciled with the complete subjection to the local ordinaries as stated in Canon 492, § 2? It has been suggested that while no provision is made in the Code for the delegation of one visitor by all the local ordinaries, yet the way is open to such a plan.[52] But since it is the general rule that the authority of each local ordinary is limited to the houses and members within his territory, the collective action of other local ordinaries would not augment the power of the local ordinary over the mother house within his territory.[53]

The chief objection to admitting the subjection of the general curia to the visitation of the ordinary of the place is that this subjection would give that prelate predominant control over the congregation, while the tendency of the law has been rather to diminish his control and place him on a parity with the local ordinaries of the other houses. Undeniably, in the evolution of the law on diocesan institutes, the local ordinary of the mother house has lost several of his former rights,[54] but it is far from clear that in the present law he is deprived of the right in question. Canon 506, § 4,[55] is not to be taken as an argument against this right, but rather by way of analogy, as a basis in support of it. Both this canon and the declaration of the Sacred Congregation of Religious deny to the local ordinary of the mother house the right to preside over the election of the superioress general when held outside his territory; but they both affirm the exclusive right of the ordinary of the place where the election is held to preside over the election. Though the exercise of this right involves the confirmation or rejection of the one elected superioress general and thereby indirectly affects the entire congregation, the local ordinary within whose territory the electoral body sits proceeds with independent and exclusive jurisdiction. This

[52] *Cf.* Larraona, "De Visitatorum potestate applicandi poenas in can. 2413 statutas," *CpR,* X (1928), 376, note 24.

[53] If the latter has the authority to visit by himself, the procedure is superfluous; if he has not, the procedure is of doubtful legality. And apart from the legality, combined action to visit or to delegate a visitor would be cumbersome and, for congregations represented in a large number of dioceses and in several parts of the world, practically impossible.

[54] *Cf.* Larraona, *op. cit.,* 374, note 19.

[55] *Cf.* S. C. de Rel., 2 Iul., 1921—*AAS,* XIII (1921), 481.

is in harmony with the opinion that even though the right of visiting the general curia indirectly affects the entire congregation, the local ordinary within whose territory the general curia resides may proceed with independent and exclusive jurisdiction.

Finally, it is to be noted that to uphold this right is not to surrender the congregation to the control of the local ordinary of the principal house to the detriment of the interests of the other local ordinaries. Visitation is for the purpose of removing abuses and promoting good order; the corrections made and the remedies proposed must be in agreement with canon law and the constitutions of the congregation. By these fairly definite standards the visitor's discretionary powers are circumscribed.[56] Acts which would impair the limited autonomy necessary to any institute for the maintenance of unity and acts prejudicial to the rights of other local ordinaries exceed the authority of the visitor. Against such an abuse of power there remains a remedy through recourse to the Holy See.

Accordingly, therefore, it seems proper to conclude that the general (or provincial) and his staff are subject to personal visitation by the local ordinary of the mother house and that the general (or provincial) funds are subject to the latter's supervision, a right which he may exercise on the occasion of visitation.[57]

[56] It is hard to think of any matter left to the discretion of the visitor which would be of such importance to the whole congregation as the acceptance or rejection of one elected superioress general. Yet a single local ordinary is free to exercise this right *pro conscientiae officio* (Canon 506, § 4)—a phrase which may be interpreted widely. *Cf.* Larraona, "Commentarium Codicis," *CpR*, VIII (1927), 106, 107.

[57] The view that the administration of property held by the whole institute or by a province is subject to the vigilance of the local ordinary of the mother house is also put forth by Vromant *(De Bonis Ecclesiae Temporalibus*, n. 236), Vermeersch-Creusen *(Epitome*, I, n. 510) and Schäfer *(De Religiosis*, p. 250). Larraona ("Commentarium Codicis," *CpR*, XIV [1933], 416-418), is of the opposite opinion.

CHAPTER VI

THE LOCAL ORDINARY'S VISITATION OF RELIGIOUS OF PONTIFICAL CONGREGATIONS

SECTION 1

CLERICAL CONGREGATIONS OF PONTIFICAL RIGHT

RELIGIOUS congregations of pontifical right, both clerical and lay, enjoy a considerable measure of independence [1] and yet in a great number of points remain subject to the local ordinaries' jurisdiction. It is impossible to set forth the extent of their subjection in a few general statements. The matter is further complicated by the fact that clerical congregations of pontifical right are in several respects treated by the law in a different way from lay congregations of pontifical right. In general these clerical congregations—whether exempt or not—are granted a greater degree of autonomy. In matters which concern their religious life and internal government they are almost completely independent of the local ordinaries,[2] though they are subject in matters pertaining to the Christian life and priestly ministry. Since Canon 512 considers in separate sections the visitation of clerical and lay congregations the same course is followed here.

Canon 512, § 2, 2°, concedes to all clerical congregations of pontifical right a very broad freedom from the local ordinary's visitation.[3] The local ordinary's visitation is confined to the

[1] Hence, they are sometimes called, in a broad sense, exempt; but the Code reserves the term exempt to indicate a still greater freedom from the local ordinary's authority. *Cf.* Dominicus Prümmer, *Manuale Iuris Canonici,* (4 ed., Friburgi Brisgoviae: Herder, 1927), n. 339, nota 2; Pejska, *Ius Canonicum Religiosorum,* p. 41.

[2] *Cf.* Canon 618, § 2.

[3] Canon 512, § 2. "[Ordinarius loci] visitare quoque eodem tempore debet: . . .

2°. "Singulas domos Congregationis clericalis iuris pontificii etiam exemptae, in iis quae pertinent ad ecclesiam, sacrarium, oratorium, sedem ad sacramentum poenitentiae; . . ."

church, the sacristy, the public oratory and the confessionals. To this extent and only to this extent both exempt and non-exempt clerical congregations of religious are subject to the visitation.[4]

Public oratories are as usual placed on the same legal basis as churches.[5] The term "church" is used without qualification and accordingly, whether it be parochial or not, it is subject to visitation. The local ordinary should see that it is kept in proper repair as befits a temple of God, that the vestments, altar linens, sacred vessels, etc., are clean and worthy for use in divine service. The local ordinary is also to examine the confessionals to see that they conform to the requirements of law.[6] The confessionals of which the canon speaks, are those destined for hearing the confessions of the faithful, whether or not they be erected in a church or in a public oratory.[7] Semi-public oratories and confessionals erected there for the benefit, not of the faithful in general, but of the religious do not fall within the ambit of the local ordinary's visitation.[8]

The Code does not indicate the manner in which the local ordinary should make corrections, if he finds anything amiss. As Larraona suggests,[9] it seems that the procedure set forth for the episcopal visitation of all pontifical congregations in the constitution *"Conditae a Christo"* [10] should be followed. Therein it was stated that, if the bishop should find anything worthy of reproof, he should first admonish those in charge. He should deal with the matter himself only if they neglect to act. However, in an affair of greater

[4] Only a few clerical congregations are exempt, *e.g.*, the Passionists and the Redemptorists. These two congregations had by privilege received an exemption from visitation as broad as that of regulars, which they enjoyed up to the Code. (*Cf. supra,* p. 68.)

[5] *Cf.* Canon 1191, § 1.

[6] *Cf.* Canon 909.

[7] *Cf.* Canon 908.

[8] Larraona, "Commentarium Codicis," *CpR,* VIII (1927), 447; Goyeneche, "Consultationes," *CpR,* III (1922), 335, 336; Wernz-Vidal, *Ius Canonicum,* III, 123, note 91.

[9] "Commentarium Codicis," *CpR,* VIII (1927), 448.

[10] *Cf. supra,* p. 70.

moment which admits of no delay the bishop may settle the question immediately and send his decree to the Sacred Congregation of Religious.[11]

Temporalities

On the occasion of the canonical visitation the local ordinary may exercise the right of vigilance over certain temporalities. His right of vigilance in regard to temporal goods owned or administered by religious of any pontifical congregation is, roughly speaking, limited to certain goods which must be expended for purposes other than the maintenance of the congregation and its members. The basis of this restriction is Canon 618, § 2, 1°, which states that in institutes of pontifical right the local ordinary may not inquire into temporal affairs save for the dispositions of Canons 533-535. The only section in these canons pertaining to pontifical institutes which grants the local ordinary the right of inquiry into temporalities, other than the dowry-funds, is Canon 535, § 3, 2°,[12] which in turn has reference to the property mentioned in Canon 533, § 1, 3°, 4°. These brief statements of the law abound in difficulties and have given rise to many conflicting opinions when considered, as they must be, in conjunction with other more general canons, which also deal with the local ordinary's right of vigilance over temporalities. In order to state the extent of the local ordinary's right of vigilance and visitation with some semblance of order, it will be well to present the pertinent laws separately, though actually these laws overlap.

The laws which pertain to this question are the following: (I) Canon 533, § 1, 3°; (II) Canon 533, § 1, 4°; (III) the canons on trusts (particularly Canon 1516, § 3); (IV) the canons on pious foundations (particularly Canon 1550).

I. Canon 533, § 1, 3°, demands the consent of the local ordinary for the investment of funds which have been donated or bequeathed to the house of a religious congregation for expenditure locally on

[11] That this is the correct procedure may also be inferred from Canon 618, § 2, 2°.

[12] Canon 535, § 3. "Loci Ordinario ius insuper esto cognoscendi: . . .

2°. "De administratione fundorum legatorumque de quibus in can. 533, § 1, nn. 3, 4."

divine worship or on works of charity.[13] Into the administration of such funds the local ordinary may inquire by virtue of Canon 535, § 3, 2°. It is important to set forth the meaning of the somewhat vague terms and phrases of Canon 533, § 1, 3°.

(a) In the first place, the term *fundi* is equivalent to property, real or personal, in any form.[14]

(b) The phrase *tributi legative* indicates that the property may have been acquired through a gift *inter vivos* or by any testamentary disposition (*i. e.*, by will, legacy, or gift *mortis causa*).

(c) By the term *domui* is meant either a collegiate moral person (*i. e.*, the religious community) or a non-collegiate person (*e. g.*, a church) which is a subordinate part of the house.[15] Hence, if property for the ends specified in Canon 533, § 1, 3°, has been given, devised or bequeathed, not to a house of a congregation, but to a province or the institute itself, the property does not fall within the scope of this law and the local ordinary has no right of supervision over such property. It would be improper to assert that though the Code is silent, such property is by analogy (Canon 20) subject to the local ordinary's vigilance. No true analogy exists, for while a religious house of even a pontifical institute is within the diocese and subject to some extent to the local ordinary, the province (as such) or the institute of pontifical right is subject in no sense to any local ordinary. In general, laws on the relationship of the local ordinary and religious, in so far as these laws pertain to any person or part of a pontifical institute, should not be extended; for it is well recognized that by the fact of pontifical approbation the local ordinary's authority is sharply restricted. Specifically in this case Canon 618, § 2, 1° is so worded as to make an extension of

[13] Canon 533, § 1. ". . . praevium consensum Ordinarii loci obtinere tenentur:

3°. "Superior vel Antistita domus Congregationis religiosae, si qui fundi domui tributi legative sint ad Dei cultum beneficentiamve eo ipso loco impendendam; . . ."

[14] *Cf.* Larraona, "Commentarium Codicis," *CpR*, XIII (1932), 31; Wernz-Vidal, *Ius Canonicum*, III, 175; Vermeersch-Creusen, *Epitome*, I, n. 606.

[15] Larraona, *op. cit.*, 32; Wernz-Vidal, *op. cit.*, III, 174, 175, nota 9.

the local ordinary's authority, on the basis of a dubious analogy, unwarranted.[16]

(d) The phrase *ad Dei cultum beneficentiamve* indicates that the purposes for which the property is to be expended may be of a wide variety. The service of God would embrace any religious services or ecclesiastical functions, while the word "benefit" should be taken broadly as equivalent to any works of piety and charity. Thus, for example, foundations for Masses, a light before the Blessed Sacrament, scholarships in support of schools, the endowment of a bed in a hospital, etc., would all be included. The criterion which determines that the property is subject to the local ordinary's vigilance is that the purpose for which the property is given is other than for the benefit of the religious.[17]

(e) The phrase *eo ipso loco impendendam* sharply delimits the law by specifying that before the property can fall under the local ordinary's authority it must be property of which its revenue or value is to be expended in that place. It is debated whether *that place* is simply that city (town or village) or whether it should be interpreted more broadly as synonymous with that diocese. The broader interpretation appears to be correct for reasons which may be briefly stated: (1) the purpose of the law appears to be to allow the local ordinary to watch over property which is not for the benefit of the religious, but which concerns him as the guardian of the interests of the diocese; (2) the relationship of a religious house is not its relationship to a city, town or village, but to the diocese. Its subjection, if any, is to the ordinary of the diocese; (3) moreover, a city or town is not an ecclesiastical division of territory; when the term "place" is used in canon law it may be

[16] Larraona, *loc. cit.;* Wernz-Vidal, *loc. cit.;* Nebreda, "Studia Canonica," *CpR,* VII (1926), 323; Vermeersch-Creusen, *Epitome,* I, n. 606.

[17] *Cf.* Vermeersch-Creusen, *Epitome,* I, n. 606; Vromant, *De Bonis Ecclesiae Temporalibus,* nn. 67, 68, 234; Nebreda, "Studia Canonica," *CpR,* VII (1926), 324. Larraona would extend the phrase *ad Dei cultum* to include property for the upkeep of the church.—"Commentarium Codicis," *CpR,* XIII (1932), 33. But it seems clear that property for the upkeep of a religious church (even though parochial) of a pontifical congregation, exempt or non-exempt, is under the exclusive care of the religious superiors (Canon 630, § 4). *Cf. infra,* p. 140.

presumed to refer to a parish or diocese and in this case no one restricts the term to the parish; (4) the constitution "*Conditae a Christo*" (§ 2, n. XI), which is the source of this law, uses the phrase place or diocese.[18] It may be assumed that the term "diocese" is omitted from the present law simply because the word "place" is used so commonly for diocese; thus, for example, the phrase "the ordinary of the place." Hence it seems that if the value of property is to be expended in the diocese, the local ordinary has the right of supervising its administration.[19]

A further question which has been the subject of much dispute is whether Canon 533, § 1, 3°, refers to houses of exempt pontifical congregations as well as to those of non-exempt congregations. While the question cannot be definitively settled, it seems more probable that exempt congregations are not included. The following reasons are the basis for this opinion: (1) when the Code wishes to include exempt religious under a law it usually mentions them explicitly,[20] unless the law rests upon some legal principle which is so broad that no doubt may arise as to its application to exempt religious. In Canon 533, § 1, 3°, exempt religious are not mentioned and it is not at all clear that any legal principle demands their inclusion. (2) It seems that among the funds mentioned in Canon 533, § 1, 3°, pious foundations are included. Pious foundations in churches of exempt religious are under the exclusive supervision of the major superiors (by virtue of Canon 1550). The doubt as to the extent of Canon 533, § 1, 3°, should be resolved in harmony with Canon 1550 and hence exempt religious should be excluded.[21] (3) The constitution "*Conditae a Christo*" apparently stated that the administration of funds and legacies given for divine services or for the benefit of inhabitants of the diocese might be examined by the local ordinary only in the case of lay congre-

18 *Fontes*, n. 644.

19 Vermeersch-Creusen, *op. cit.*, I, n. 606; Nebreda, *op. cit.*, 323, 324; Schäfer, *De Religiosis*, p. 239. Larraona (*op. cit.*, 34, 35) is of the opposite opinion.

20 Thus, for example, in a very similar case Canon 512, § 2, 2°, employs the phrase, *etiam exemptae*.

21 Canon 18.

gations.[22] Moreover, the constitution *"Conditae a Christo"* did not overrule exemptions. Canon 533, § 1, 3°, certainly extends the provision of this constitution to all non-exempt congregations, even though clerical, but since it is at least doubtful that a change has been made in regard to exempt clerical congregations, the interpretation of the present law which in this respect is in harmony with the old law should be preferred.[23] Hence it seems that exempt congregations are not included under Canon 533, § 1, 3°.[24]

The following conclusions may be drawn from what has been presented:

I. Canon 535, § 3, 2°, in so far as it refers to Canon 533, § 1, 3°, grants the local ordinary no authority over temporalities given to a house of an exempt congregation.

2. These canons do authorize the local ordinary to supervise the investment and the administration of property given to the house of a non-exempt pontifical congregation (but not if given to the province or the congregation as such) for divine worship or for the benefit of works of piety or charity in that diocese.

II. Canon 533, § 1, 4°, speaks of money given to a parish, to a mission, or to religious—inclusive of regulars in an order—for the benefit of a parish or mission and by Canon 535, § 3, 2°, the local ordinary is empowered to inquire into the administration of such money.[25] In the first place it may be remarked that the term "money" as used here embraces all forms of property, real or per-

[22] § 2, n. XI—*Fontes,* n. 644.

[23] Canon 6, 4°.

[24] Vromant, *De Bonis Ecclesiae Temporalibus,* n. 234; Nebreda, "Studia Canonica," *CpR,* VII (1926), 320-322; Bastien, *Directoire Canonique à l'usage des Congrégations à voeux simples,* n. 316; Jansen, *Ordensrecht* (3 ed. Schöningh: Paderborn, 1921), p. 109. Of the opposite opinion, Wernz-Vidal, *Ius Canonicum,* III, 175, 176; Larraona, "Commentarium Codicis," *CpR,* XIII (1932), 25-31; Schäfer, *De Religiosis,* p. 238.

[25] No doubt the most usual case in which religious have the administration of money for a parish or mission will be the case in which the religious have charge of the parish or mission. Yet, since religious who have no care of souls and who are living in a house to which no parish or mission is attached may nevertheless have received money for a parish or mission, the question is considered here.

sonal, and the capital and/or the income therefrom. This is evident from an examination of the way in which the term "money" is used throughout Canon 533. It makes no difference in what manner the property has been conveyed; it may be by gift *inter vivos* or by any testamentary disposition.[26] It is necessary only that the property be given by the donors to or for a parish or mission.[27] The meaning of the term "parish" is clear enough; [28] the term "mission" has been interpreted by canonists as referring to a quasi-parish, to a definite vicariate or prefecture apostolic and also to a particular missionary territory not yet erected into a prefecture or vicariate.[29] Canonists have reasonably concluded that if money is given for the missions in general or for missions of a certain territory embracing several vicariates or prefectures, Canon 533, § 1, 4°, and the correlative provision of Canon 535, § 3, 2°, are not applicable.[30] However, the religious are bound to expend all such money exclusively for the missions. When this money has been allocated and sent to various missions, its administration is then subject to the vigilance and visitation of the local ordinaries of the various missions.[31] However, when money is given for a definite parish or mission, the local ordinary who has the right to supervise the administration is the local ordinary, not of the place where the money was given, but of the parish or mission for which it was given.[32] It follows, there-

[26] Larraona, "Commentarium Codicis," *CpR,* XIII (1932), 92.

[27] For the norms to be applied when it is doubtful whether property is given to the religious for their institute or for a parish (or mission) *cf.* Canon 1536, § 1; Leo XIII, const. *Romanos Pontifices,* 8 Maii, 1881, § 26—*Fontes,* n. 582; Larraona, *op. cit.,* 94-97; Nebreda, "Studia Canonica," *CpR,* VII (1926), 264-266.

[28] *Cf.* Canon 216, § 3.

[29] *Cf.* Larraona, *op. cit.,* 93, 94; Schäfer, *De Religiosis,* p. 239; Vromant, *Ius Missionariorum,* n. 106.

[30] Vermeersch-Creusen, *Epitome,* I, n. 606, II, n. 857; Fanfani, *De Iure Religiosorum,* n. 155; Nebreda, "Studia Canonica," *CpR,* VII (1926), 267.

[31] *Cf.* S. C. de Prop. Fide, instr. (Ad Vicarios Praefectosque Apostolicos, etc.), 8 Dec., 1929—*AAS,* XXII (1930) 112, 113; S. C. de Prop. Fide, responsum (De Usu et Administratione Eleemosynarum per Unionem Missionariam Franciscanam Collectarum), 28 Iul., 1932—*Perodica* XXII (1933), 162.

[32] Vermeersch-Creusen, *loc. cit.;* Vromant, *De Bonis Ecclesiae Temporalibus,* n. 66; Schäfer, *De Religiosis,* p. 239.

fore, that the local ordinary visiting a religious house of an exempt or non-exempt congregation may inquire (by virtue of Canon 535, § 3, 2°, and Canon 533, § 1, 4°) only about property held or administered by the religious of that house for a parish or mission under his jurisdiction. However, property donated to or for a parish or mission does not include property given to or for the church fabric of a religious parochial church of pontifical institute.[33]

III. The local ordinary also has the right of vigilance over certain trusts of which religious of pontifical institutes are trustees. In this matter, it is to be noted, the law recognizes some distinction between exempt and non-exempt religious trustees.

Canon 1516, § 1,[34] prescribes that a cleric or a religious who has become the trustee of goods for a pious cause,[35] either through a gift *inter vivos* or through any testamentary disposition, must render to the ordinary a complete account of the goods so received and of the obligations attached thereto. The second paragraph of the same canon states that the ordinary should demand that goods held in trust be safely invested and he has the right and duty of watching over the fulfillment of the trust (even by visitation). The

[33] *Cf. infra*, p. 140.

[34] Canon 1516, § 1. "Clericus vel religiosus qui bona ad pias causas sive per actum inter vivos, sive ex testamento fiduciarie accepit, debet de sua fiducia Ordinarium certiorem reddere, eique omnia istiusmodi bona seu mobilia seu immobilia cum oneribus adiunctis indicare; quod si donator id expresse et omnino prohibuerit, fiduciam ne acceptet.

§ 2. "Ordinarius debet exigere ut bona fiducaria in tuto collocentur et vigilare pro executione piae voluntatis ad normam can. 1515. [Canon 1515, § 2. '. . . Ordinarii vigilare possunt, ac debent, etiam per visitationem, ut piae voluntates impleantur, et alii exsecutores delegati debent, perfuncti munere, illis reddere rationem.']

§ 3. "Bonis fiduciariis alicui religioso commissis, si quidem bona sint attributa loci seu dioecesis ecclesiis, incolis aut piis causis iuvandis, Ordinarius de quo in § § 1, 2, est loci Ordinarius; secus, est Ordinarius eiusdem religiosi proprius."

[35] "*Pia causa* vel *res pia* dicitur: *Quidquid* praecipue fit Dei finisque supernaturalis intuitu, ad gratiam vel gloriam coram Deo promerendam, vel in satisfactionem pro propriis vel alienis peccatis."—Vromant, *De Bonis Ecclesiae Temporalibus*, n. 146. *Cf.* Vermeersch-Creusen, *Epitome*, II, n. 834; Hannan, *The Canon Law of Wills*, nn. 97, 98.

third paragraph determines the ordinary who has the aforesaid rights and duties: (a) Whether the trustee be an exempt or non-exempt religious, the ordinary is the *local* ordinary, if the beneficiaries of the trust are churches, inhabitants or pious causes of the place or diocese. Canonists agree that if the beneficiaries are specified the local ordinary to which reference is here made is the local ordinary of the beneficiaries of the trust and not the local ordinary within whose territory the religious trustee resides.[36] (b) If the trustee is not a member of an exempt clerical institute, the ordinary is his *local* ordinary *(Ordinarius eiusdem religiosi proprius)* for trust funds other than those mentioned in (a). (c) If the trustee is a member of an exempt clerical institute the ordinary is his major superior *(Ordinarius eiusdem religiosi proprius)* for trust funds other than those mentioned in (a).

It is to be noted that authors do not consider that the local ordinary has any rights in regard to trusts of which a religious of a pontifical institute is the trustee if at the same time his institute or a part thereof is the beneficiary. The reason for this is that in such cases the trustee and the beneficiary are considered identical and hence they are not trusts in the strict sense.[37] Excluding, therefore, such property from the category of trusts, the trust funds referred to above in (b) and (c) must be goods held in trust for pious causes in a more or less general way, *i. e.,* trust funds for the benefit of pious causes of no determinate place, diocese, vicariate, or prefecture.[38]

With these points in mind the extent of the local ordinary's right of vigilance and visitation may be deduced from Canon 1516 and summed up in the following conclusions:

1. Whether the trustee is an exempt or non-exempt religious, the local ordinary has the right of supervision and visitation of

[36] Nebreda, "Studia Canonica," *CpR,* VII (1926), 328; Vromant, *op. cit.,* n. 163; Vermeersch-Creusen, *Epitome,* II, n. 836.

[37] Goyeneche, "Consultationes," *CpR,* III (1932), 226; Nebreda, "Studia Canonica," *CpR,* VII (1926), 327; Vromant, *De Bonis Ecclesiae Temporalibus,* nn. 152, 164; Fanfani, *De Iuris Religiosorum,* n. 176.

[38] Nebreda, *op. cit.,* 326; Vromant, *loc. cit.*

trusts which are for the benefit of secular churches, inhabitants, or pious causes within his territory.[39]

2. If the trustee is not an exempt clerical religious the local ordinary may also exercise his right of supervision and visitation in regard to trusts which are not for the benefit of any *determinate* place (diocese, vicariate, or prefecture).

IV. Pious foundations are temporalities conveyed in any form to a moral ecclesiastical person with a perpetual or long-term obligation of applying the annual revenues therefrom to the celebrating of Masses or the carrying out of other determinate ecclesiastical functions or works of piety and charity.[40] A pious foundation is of a fiduciary nature, but its distinctive elements are that the property is given to a moral person and that the capital is to be preserved intact for a number of years.[41] The canons prescribe: (a) that for the acceptance of a pious foundation the consent of the local ordinary is necessary; [42] (b) that for the investing of the same the decision rests with the prudent judgment of the local ordinary; [43] (c) that an annual account is to be given by the administrators to the local ordinary; [44] and (d) that to assure the faithful fulfillment of the obligation attached thereto the local ordinary has the duty of vigilance and visitation.[45] It is unnecessary to discuss these points in detail; for the purposes at hand the only relevant question is to determine into what pious foundations established in a religious house or in a church over which the religious have charge the local ordinary may inquire for the purpose of seeing that the laws and duties relative to pious foundations have been and are being properly observed and executed.

[39] If the trustee resides in another diocese, the local ordinary of course cannot visit him, but he may see to the fulfillment of the trust by demanding that an account be sent to him from the trustee and by visiting the beneficiaries (persons or places) within his territory.

[40] Canon 1544.

[41] The number of years is disputed among canonists. Ten years would appear to be the minimum. *Cf.* Vromant, *De Bonis Ecclesiae Temporalibus*, n. 346; Hannan, *The Canon Law of Wills*, n. 753.

[42] Canon 1546.

[43] Canon 1547.

[44] Canons 1549, § 1; 1525, § 1.

[45] Canons 1549, § 1; 1515, § 2.

Canon 1550 [46] states that in the case of pious foundations established in churches—even in parochial churches—of exempt religious the rights and duties referred to above as being proper to the local ordinary belong exclusively to the major superior. It seems beyond reasonable doubt that the churches referred to are religious, and not secular, churches.[47] The phrase "foundations in churches" appears to mean foundations of which the revenues are by the intention of the donor to be spent in the church and hence for ecclesiastical functions (particularly for Masses) and not for works of charity or piety that are to be performed outside the church for the benefit of a parish or mission.[48] Maroto, on the contrary, affirms that foundations for the benefit of a parish are included in the category of "foundations in churches." [49] An examination of the sources and text of Canon 1549, § 1,[50] which prescribes that in any church the rector shall keep an inventory of the obligations attached to pious foundations, shows that the canon is speaking of foundations of which the obligations are to be fulfilled in the churches. It seems probable that Canon 1550 means the same. Moreover, as has been seen Canon 533, § 1, 4°, and Canon 1516, § 3, state that money and trusts held or administered by exempt religious (even regulars) for the benefit of a parish, mission, or secular churches, inhabitants or pious causes of a diocese are under the vigilance of the local ordinary. Therefore, such an interpretation of Canon 1550 must be adopted which is in harmony with these parallel canons—*viz.*, that the phrase "foundations in churches" of exempt religious does not include foundations for charitable or pious works outside the churches and hence does not withdraw such foundations from the local ordinary's authority.[51]

[46] Canon 1550: "Si agatur de piis fundationibus in ecclesiis, etiam paroecialibus, religiosorum exemptorum, iura et officia Ordinarii loci, de quibus in can. 1545-1549, exclusive competunt Superiori maiori."

[47] Vromant, *De Bonis Ecclesiae Temporalibus*, n. 354; Vermeersch-Creusen, *Epitome*, II, n. 869; Nebreda, "Studia Canonica," *CpR*, VII (1926), 331, 332. For the definition of a religious church, *cf. infra*, p. 131, n. 10.

[48] Vromant, *op. cit.*, n. 355; Vermeersch-Creusen, *op. cit.*, I, n. 606.

[49] "Annotationes," *CpR*, VII (1926), 441.

[50] *Cf.* Vromant, *op. cit.*, 353.

[51] Vromant *(op. cit.*, n. 355) believes that the response of the Code Commission on July 25, 1926 (*cf. infra*, p. 142) confirms this view.

It is to be noted, however, that pious foundations which are given to any moral person which is part of an exempt or non-exempt pontifical institute for the maintenance of that institute or for a pious cause not distinct from it (*e. g.*, the education of its members) does not fall under the local ordinary's supervision.[52]

With these points in mind the following conclusions may be drawn. The local ordinary has the right of supervision, etc., over:

1. All foundations in secular churches which are in any way under the charge of exempt or non-exempt religious.

2. Foundations in religious churches of non-exempt religious whether the revenues are to be devoted (a) to ecclesiastical functions in the church or (b) to works of charity or piety outside the church for the benefit of a determinate parish, mission, or pious cause within the local ordinary's territory.

3. Foundations in a religious church of exempt religious when their revenues are to be devoted to the purposes mentioned in 2 (b).

The canons on pious foundations contain no special legislation on foundations given to the religious community. Since Canon 535, § 3, 2° and Canon 1516, § 3, seem to include pious foundations under the more generic terms of "funds," "legacies," and "trusts," the conclusions drawn from these canons may be applied to foundations given to religious communities of pontifical right.

V. Before concluding this section a word must be said on the right of the local ordinary to inquire into the fulfillment of the obligations assumed by religious priests in accepting the manual stipends for Masses. Canon 842 states that the right and duty of watching that Mass obligations be fulfilled in secular churches belongs to the local ordinary; in churches of religious to their superiors.[53] Canon 843 prescribes that rectors of churches and other pious places,[54] both secular and religious, in which stipends are

[52] Vromant, *op. cit.*, 356; Hannan, *The Canon Law of Wills*, n. 771; Goyeneche, "Consultationes," *CpR*, III (1922), 269.

[53] Clearly this canon refers to both founded and manual Masses, but it is necessary to consider only the latter here, as the local ordinary's right of supervision over founded Masses falls under the general rules for pious foundations which have been set forth above.

[54] The term rector is not to be understood in the narrow sense of Canon 479, § 1, but must be taken more broadly as applying to pastors (Canon 216,

usually received, must have a special book in which they should accurately mark down the number, the intention, the amount of the stipend received and the celebration of the Masses.[55] The ordinaries are obliged to inspect these books at least once a year, either personally or through another. Since the term ordinaries is used without qualification it may refer to either the local ordinaries or the major superiors of exempt clerical institutes.[56] If the church is a religious church of an exempt clerical institute, the major superior certainly has the right to examine the book for the manual Masses and if the church is a religious or secular church and served by religious other than members of an exempt clerical institute, this right certainly belongs to the local ordinary. As to churches which are secular and yet in the care of exempt clerical religious who therein exercise the ministry, it is not clear from the wording of the canons which ordinary possesses the right of inspecting the books. However, as the term ordinaries apparently means the ordinaries of the rectors mentioned in Canon 843, § 1,[57] it seems that in a secular church under the charge of a religious rector of an exempt clerical institute the Mass book is to be examined by the religious ordinary. The view that the right does not belong to the local ordinary is confirmed by a declaration of the Congregation of Bishops and Regulars on May 11, 1904. The Congregation declared that the bishop in visitation could not examine the books for the manual Masses in a parish of the Friars Minor.[58] While the declaration was only for a particular church of the Friars Minor it is based on the principle that the exemption of exempt clerical

§ 1), chaplains and every priest having charge of a church or chapel. Charles F. Keller, *Mass Stipends* (Washington, D. C., 1925), p. 152.

[55] For founded Masses a different book is to be used (*Cf.* Canon 1549, § 2).

[56] Felix M. Cappello, *De Sacramentis* (Romae: Marietti, 1928), I, n. 712; Keller, *op. cit.*, p. 155; Ayrinhac, *Legislation on the Sacraments*, p. 152.

[57] *Cf.* Innocentius XIII, const., *"Nuper,"* 23 Dec., 1697, § § 19, 23—*Fontes*, n. 260.

[58] S. C. Ep. et Reg.: "Mens est, quod exemptio a iurisdictione episcopali fratribus Minoribus S. Francisci competens extenditur etiam ad Missas manuales: ideoque Episcopus in visitatione canonica nullam sibi vindicare potest inspectionem librorum Missarum manualium in paroecia fratrum Minorum in casu." *Fontes*, n. 2047.

institutes extends to manual Masses. Hence it is proper to conclude that in a church whether secular or religious, which is served by religious of an exempt clerical institute the local ordinary cannot examine the book for the manual Masses.

SECTION 2

Lay Congregations of Pontificial Right

Lay congregations are institutes either of women religious in which only simple vows are taken or of men religious in which only simple vows are taken and in which the majority of the members are not priests.[59] Canon 512, § 2, 3° is concerned with the visitation of lay congregations of pontifical right; evidently this section does not include lay orders.[60]

In visiting houses of lay congregations, the local ordinary is first of all to subject to his inspection the places to be visited in clerical congregations of pontifical right. As far as these places are concerned, there is no distinction between clerical and lay congregations and it is unnecessary to repeat what has been said on this matter.[61]

However, in lay congregations the local ordinary is also to inquire into several matters of internal discipline according to the prescriptions of Canon 618, § 2, 2°.[62] The rights granted and the du-

[59] Canon 488, 4°. Yet this is not to be insisted upon too rigorously. If a large minority are priests, the institute may be clerical. Sometimes it is possible to determine whether an institute is lay or clerical by its special end (*e.g.*, if the special work of the institute requires sacerdotal powers). *Cf.* Schäfer, *De Religiosis*, pp. 51, 52.

[60] Canon 512, § 2: "[Ordinarius loci] visitare eodem tempore debet: . . .

3°. "Singulas domos Congregationis laicalis iuris pontificii non solum in iis, de quibus in superiore numero, sed etiam in aliis, quae ad internam disciplinam spectant, ad normam tamen can. 618, § 2, n. 2."

[61] *Cf. supra*, p. 99.

[62] Canon 618, § 2: "In religionibus tamen iuris pontificii Ordinario loci non licet: . . .

2°. "Sese ingerere in regimen internum ac disciplinam, exceptis casibus in iure expressis; nihilominus in religionibus laicalibus ipse potest ac debet inquirere num disciplina ad constitutionum normam vigeat, num quid sana doctrina morumve probitas detrimenti ceperit, num contra clausuram peccatum sit, num Sacramenta aequa stataque frequentia suscipiantur; et, si Superiores

ties imposed by this section are very broad. The inquiry of the local ordinary is to discover: (a) whether discipline is maintained conformably to the constitutions; (b) whether sound doctrine and good morals have suffered in any way; (c) whether there have been offenses against the law of the enclosure; (d) whether the reception of the Sacraments is regular and frequent.[63] It is impossible and unnecessary to attempt an enumeration of the particular points which fall under the extensive terms of "discipline," "sound doctrine" and "good morals." In canonical practice the local ordinary's right of inquiry into matters of regular observance is almost unlimited. He may conduct a personal visitation (according to the norms of Canon 513, § 1) of the religious of the community and he may inspect the house, in so far as it appears necessary or useful for the acquiring of knowledge on the observance of the enclosure and other points of discipline. When visiting sisters he must conduct the personal visitation outside the enclosure. He may enter the enclosure only for the purpose of inspection, accompanied by at least one cleric or male religious of a mature age.[64]

The procedure for correcting abuses is clearly outlined in Canon 618, § 2, 2° and offers no difficulties. If the local ordinary discovers any grave abuses, he is to advise the superiors of the fact. The canon does not specify which superiors. It is reasonable to suppose that in most cases it will suffice to place the facts before the local superior, as the latter in ordinary circumstances will have enough power and good will to effect a remedy. In cases, however, in which the local superior is incapable of restoring good order or is himself the cause of discord and abuses, it will be necessary to acquaint the provincial or general superior with the state of affairs. When the religious superiors do not effect the requisite improvements within a reasonable time, the local ordinary shall take such action as the case demands. For affairs of greater importance which admit of no delay

de gravibus forte abusibus admoniti opportune non providerint, ipse per se consulat; si qua tamen maioris momenti occurrant, quae moram non patiantur, decernat statim; decretum vero ad Sanctum Sedem deferat."

[63] *Cf.* Canon 595, § 1, 3°; 595, § 2.

[64] Canons 604, § 1; 600, 1°. In regard to this point what has been said in treating of the visitation of diocesan sisters is applicable. *Cf. supra,* p. 89.

a different procedure is prescribed. At such times the local ordinary is to settle the matter immediately. It it within the power of the visitor to decide when a situation necessitates immediate action on his part. The visitor's decree, containing the facts of the case and the course pursued, is to be forwarded to the Holy See. The visitor seems to be obliged to send his decree to the Holy See, not only when he has immediately acted in grave matters, but also when he intervenes upon the failure of the superiors to remedy the abuses he has pointed out.

Temporalities

There is no necessity of treating at length of the local ordinary's right of inquiry into the administration of temporalities as lay congregations of pontifical right are subject to the local ordinary in this matter to the same extent as clerical congregations of pontifical right.[65] It may be observed that, though there is nothing which absolutely prohibits a lay congregation of pontifical right from receiving by special concession the privilege of exemption,[66] yet as a matter of fact such lay congregations seem, as far as may be ascertained, to be invariably non-exempt. Hence, what has been set forth above on the local ordinary's right of supervision over temporalities of non-exempt clerical congregations of pontifical right is applicable here.[67]

The Mother House

The visitation of the mother house (the residence of the provincial or general superior) of a lay congregation of pontifical right presents two special points which must be briefly considered.

I. In institutes of women, the dowries, if any are demanded by the constitutions, will be administered in the provincial or general house. When conducting a visitation of such a house the local ordinary should inquire into the administration of the dowries. The laws cited and the conclusion drawn from them in the discussion above on dowries in diocesan institutes are applicable here.[68]

[65] Canon 618, § 2, 1°.

[66] *Cf.* Canon 618, § 1.

[67] *Cf. supra*, pp. 100-112.

[68] *Cf. supra*, p. 91.

II. The second question is whether the local ordinary in visiting a mother house may conduct a visitation of the provincial (or general) curia. The answer, it seems, should be in the negative. The local ordinary in accordance with Canon 512, § 2, 3°, may visit the local superior and the latter's subjects and also the major superior and his staff in their unofficial capacity as members of the community. But the local superior should not extend his visitation to an inquiry into the official actions and affairs of the major superior and his staff.

Leo XIII stated in the constitution *"Conditae a Christo"* that the fact that a religious congregation has received pontifical approbation restricts to some extent the jurisdiction of the local ordinaries and, as has been noted, the Code frequently recognizes that fact. A province of a pontifical congregation is not properly within a diocese. It is an administrative division which transcends diocesan limits and is generally composed of houses established in a number of dioceses. Hence the province as such is not subject to any local ordinary. Canonists generally agree that property held by the province (except the dowry-funds) does not come under the supervision of the local ordinary. Thus in interpreting Canon 533, § 1, 3°, which in conjunction with Canon 535, § 3, 2°, gives the local ordinary supervisory authority over certain property of individual houses, canonists do not consider it legitimate to extend the law so as to include property given to a province of a pontifical institute.[69] Similarly Canon 512, § 2, 3°, which gives the local ordinary authority to visit individual houses should be interpreted strictly as granting the local ordinary the right to conduct a visitation only in such matters as are properly the affair of the individual house (or houses) within his territory.[70] Hence the acts and the affairs of the provincial curia, and much more the general curia, should not fall within the scope of the local ordinary's visitation.

[69] *Cf. supra*, p. 101.

[70] *Cf.* Canon 618, § 2, 2°.

CHAPTER VII

THE LOCAL ORDINARY'S VISITATION OF REGULARS[1]

SECTION 1

NUNS SUBJECT TO THE LOCAL ORDINARY OR IMMEDIATELY SUBJECT TO THE HOLY SEE

CANON 512, § 1, 1°, imposes upon the local ordinary the duty of making a quinquennial visitation of monasteries of nuns who are under his jurisdiction or under the immediate jurisdiction of the Holy See.[2] The term "nuns" (*moniales*) is used throughout the Code for women religious with solemn vows, or, unless it appears otherwise from the nature of the case or from the context, for women religious whose vows are normally solemn, but which, by a disposition of the Holy See, are simple in certain regions.[3] There is no need to enter into a discussion about the differences of the legal status of nuns with solemn vows and nuns with simple vows.[4] Both

[1] From their relationship to the local ordinary as visitor, regulars must be divided into three classes: (1) Nuns subject to the local ordinary or immediately subject to the Holy See; (2) nuns subject to male regulars; (3) male regulars. The extent of the local ordinary's visitatorial powers in respect to these three classes varies widely. In conducting a visitation of nuns subject to himself or immediately to the Holy See the local ordinary proceeds with plenary authority while in visiting nuns subject to regulars, he is normally restricted to an investigation into the observance of the enclosure. As a rule the local ordinary has no right of visitation over male regulars.

[2] Canon 512, § 1: "Ordinarius loci per se vel per alium quinto quoque anno visitare debet:

1°. "Singula monalium monasteria quae sibi vel Sedi Apostolicae immediate subiecta sunt."

[3] Canon 488, 7°.

[4] Reference may be made to Maroto, "Annotationes," *CpR*, I (1920), 257-265; IV (1923), 323-330. It is no longer necessary for the nuns of France and Belgium (and the United States) to remain in simple vows, for since June 23, 1923 (*cf. AAS*, XV [1923], 357) they are able, upon application to the Holy See, to obtain permission for solemn vows and the papal enclosure.

types of nuns, so long as they are subject to the local ordinary or directly the Holy See, are included under this section of the canon. For both types the extent of the local ordinary's visitation is the same. It is also to be noted that between nuns subject to the local ordinary and nuns subject immediately to the Holy See no juridical distinction exists in regard to visitation, except that in visiting the former the local ordinary acts by his own ordinary jurisdiction while in visiting the latter the local ordinary proceeds by vicarious apostolic authority, *i. e.*, as a vicar of the Holy See.[5] In both cases the scope of the visitation is identical.

The Enclosure

The enclosure which, as a rule, prevents the local ordinary as well as any other man from entering within its confines renders it necessary to lay down special rules for the visitation. Nuns with solemn vows have the papal enclosure, while nuns with simple vows have the episcopal (or partial) enclosure.[6] There are a number

The S. Congr. of Religious began its instruction of Feb. 6, 1924, on the enclosure of nuns with solemn vows (*cf. AAS,* XVI [1924], 96) by stating that very many nuns of France and Belgium had already taken action to secure this permission. In the United States, during the nineteenth century there were only five convents of nuns in which solemn vows were taken. *Cf.* S. C. Ep. et Reg., *Causa Americana Votorum,* 30 Sept., 1864—Lucidi, *De Visitatione,* III, 463-477. Since the turn of the century several other convents have received permission to take solemn vows.

[5] By the Fifth Council of the Lateran and by the Council of Trent the bishops were delegated by law to visit nuns directly subject to the Holy See (*cf. supra,* pp. 54, 58). In the present law, in the exercise of this right, the local ordinary uses ordinary jurisdiction. Vermeersch-Creusen, *Epitome,* I, n. 277; Larraona, "Commentarium Codicis," *CpR,* VIII (1927), 442. Yet, as Maroto states, the authority is vicarious, for the canon expressly states that these nuns are immediately subject to the Holy See (*i. e.,* exempt *de iure* from the local ordinary). The exemption remains the general principle and the cases in which these nuns are brought within the powers of the bishops are special concessions made to the bishops by the Holy See. *Cf.* Maroto, *Institutiones Iuris Canonici* (Romae: 1919), n. 699 (8a), nota 1.

[6] "Principium generale post Codicem prout etiam olim erat, est: Non habentur vota solemnia absque clausura papali, nec datur clausura papalis absque solemnitate votorum. Exceptiones dari possent."—Schäfer, *De Religiosis,* p. 421.

of differences in the laws on these two kinds of enclosures, yet they are both the same in the manner in which they permit the admittance of a male visitor.[7]

Accordingly the following rules may be set forth for the visitation of both types of nuns.

1. The local ordinary visiting the monastery of nuns, or other visitors delegated by him, may enter the enclosure, but only for the purpose of inspection and on condition that they be accompanied by at least one cleric or male religious of mature age.[8]

2. The visitor therefore may enter the enclosure for the local visitation only. The personal visitation must be made outside at the grille (or in any room outside the enclosure in the case of a community with simple vows and the episcopal enclosure).

3. The visitor who enters the enclosure for the purpose of inspection must be accompanied by at least one cleric or male religious who may be a lay brother of mature age; and this companion must not leave the canonical visitor during the whole time that the latter is in the monastery.[9]

4. Besides the one companion required by law, the local ordinary or his delegated visitor may bring other attendants within the enclosure during the tour of inspection. The Code does not limit the number, but they should be few and ought to be members either of the secular clergy or of a religious community of men.[10]

5. The local ordinary or his delegated visitor may enter the enclosure for local visitation not only at the time stated by law (*i. e.*,

[7] *Cf.* Canon 600, 1° and Canon 604, § 1. In Canon 600 the word *moniales* means nuns with solemn vows (*cf.* Commissio Pontif., 1 Mart. 1921 ad 2—*AAS*, XII [1921], 178). Canon 604, § 1, on the episcopal enclosure which binds sisters and nuns with simple vows, refers back to Canon 600 and thereby makes the prescription of the latter canon obligatory upon all female religious with simple vows and the episcopal enclosure.

[8] Canon 600, 1°.

[9] S. C. de Rel. *Instructio de Clausura Monialium Votorum Solemnium*, 6 Feb., 1924—*AAS*, XVI (1924), 98.

Rules 2 and 3 are no more than restatements of Canon 600, 1°. Hence, though given as norms for nuns with solemn vows, they apply to the visitation of female religious with simple vows.

[10] *Cf.* Schaaf, *The Cloister*, pp. 113, 114.

every five years), but whenever in the prudent judgment of the local ordinary a canonical visitation is required.[11]

While these rules for the holding of canonical visitation obtain both for nuns with episcopal as well as the papal enclosure, the local ordinary will, of course, recall, when inquiring into observance of the cloister that the papal enclosure is governed by laws which differ in several notable respects from the laws of episcopal enclosure.[12]

Visitation of Other Matters

The visitatorial powers of the local ordinary extend to all matters. The entire house, including the cells, the garden, the chapel or church, etc., are subject to his inspection. In the personal visitation of the nuns at the grille, the visitor may question them on any and all topics pertaining to religious discipline, their health, their work, etc., and he may correct all faults and abuses. Both the questioning and correction should be according to the norms set forth in the chapter dealing with the procedure of visitation.[13]

The local ordinary may use the visitation as an occasion for examining the accounts of the administration. Canon 535, § 1, 1°, states that in every monastery of nuns, even if it be exempt, the superioress must furnish to the local ordinary an account of her administration once a year or even more often if the constitutions so prescribe.[14] This account of administration should include everything, all income and expenses, ordinary and extraordinary, movable and immovable goods, dowries, trust funds, etc. The accounts, prepared by the procuratrix (*oeconoma*) of the community, should be submitted according to the norms of the constitutions to the

[11] This was the rule in the old law (*cf. supra,* p. 63). Moreover, Canon 600, 1°, simply gives the visitor permission to enter the enclosure without making any distinction between ordinary and extraordinary visitations.

[12] For the papal enclosure, *cf.* Canons 597-603, 605, 606, § 1, 2342. For the episcopal enclosure, *cf.* Canons 604-607.

[13] *Cfr infra,* pp. 149-162.

[14] Canon 535, § 1: "In quolibet monialium monasterio etiam exempto:

1°. "Administrationis ratio, gratis exigenda, reddatur semel in anno, aut etiam saepius si id in constitutionibus praescribatur, ab Antistita Ordinario loci . . . " *Cf.* Canon 512, § 3.

superioress or also to her consultors, to be approved, or verified and should then be given to the local ordinary.[15] The account may also be given to the visitor delegate of the local ordinary for inspection and review.[16] If the constitutions do not prescribe that the accounts be submitted more frequently than every year, the local ordinary has no right to demand more than an annual report. Hence, if the annual report has already been submitted before the time of visitation, the local ordinary has no right to demand a second report during the time of the visitation.[17] The administration of the funds from the dowries should be investigated by the local ordinary during the visitation, even though the annual report on the general finances (including the dowries) had before been sent to him.[18]

If the local ordinary does not approve of the account of the administration, he can apply fitting remedies, including removal from office of the procuratrix and the other administrators, if the circumstances demand it.[19] There may be a number of reasons which would lead the local ordinary to disapprove of the administration of the temporalities. The administrators may have failed against canon law, for example, by making investments without his consent,[20] by illicitly alienating property [21] or by spending the dowry funds.[22] It is not only transgressions of the canons, but also other actions, which to his prudent judgment seem to be proof of maladministration, that may reasonably cause the local ordinary to withhold his approval. Thus, for example, careless or fraudulent bookkeeping, useless expenses or, on the other hand, failure to

[15] Larraona, "Commentarium Codicis," *CpR,* XIV (1933), 347.

[16] *Cf.* Canon 199, § 1.

[17] *Cf.* Larraona, *op. cit.,* 346.

[18] Canon 550, § 2: "Ordinarii locorum conservandis religiosarum dotibus sedulo invigilent; et praesertim in sacra visitatione de eisdem rationem exigant." This refers to all women religious (*cf.* Schäfer, *De Religiosis,* p. 289) and hence is broader than the similar provision of Canon 535, § 2, as the latter applies only to sisters.

[19] Canon 535, § 1, 2°: "Si ratio administrationis Ordinario non probetur, ipse potest opportuna remedia adhibere, etiam removendo, si res postulet, oeconomam aliosque administratores; . . . "

[20] *Cf.* Canon 533, § 1, 1°.

[21] *Cf.* Canon 534.

[22] *Cf.* Canon 549.

make reasonable expenditures for the needs of the community, etc., may properly lead the local ordinary to disapprove and to intervene. The remedies which the local ordinary uses will depend upon the circumstances of each case. They may be recommendations or commands, specifying a different course of action, or they may be penalties directed against the administrators.[23] It is within the power of the local ordinary to remove any of the administrators from office. This removal may or may not be of a penal character. Thus, removal for not preserving the dowry funds intact is a penalty prescribed by law,[24] while removal of an administrator who, despite excellent intentions and a careful observance of the canons, is incapable of handling business affairs, is in no sense of a penal nature. When an administrator has been removed it is not within the power of the local ordinary to select her successor; whoever, by the constitutions, has that right and competence under ordinary circumstances, also has the power to fill the vacancy in this case.[25]

Extern Sisters

Extern sisters, who belong to the community of nuns are to be visited at the same time. This is part of the local ordinary's visitation of the monastery. It is to be conducted according to the same rules which govern the religious ordinary's visitation of extern sisters who belong to a community of nuns that is subject to a regular superior.[26]

SECTION 2

NUNS SUBJECT TO REGULARS

Canon 512, § 2, 1°, states that every five years the local ordinary should visit the monasteries of nuns, which are subject to regulars,

[23] *Cf., e. g.,* Canons 2347; 2348.

[24] Canon 2412, 1°.

[25] "Non tamen negamus Ordinarium in novorum administratorum electionem diversimode intervenire posse. Ex. gr., aliquos excludendo qui in iisdem aut similibus conditionibus versantur ac illi qui fuerunt, requisita imponendo." —Larraona, "Commentarium Codicis," *CpR,* XIV (1933), 348.

[26] *Cf. supra,* pp. 82, 83.

in those matters which relate to the law of the enclosure.[27] This is a restatement of the pre-Code law, except that the visitation is no longer obligatory every year, but only every fifth year, and the local ordinary no longer proceeds as a delegate, but as a vicar of the Holy See. Substantially therefore the present law is the same as that before the Code and is to be interpreted in the light of the declarations of the Holy See and the statements of approved authors under the old law. Unnecessary repetition may be avoided by stating succinctly the norms for this visitation and by giving references in the footnotes to the pages where the various points have already been treated more fully.

1. The local ordinary is not limited to the quinquennial visitation; he may in his prudent judgment undertake at other times extraordinary visitations and these are to be governed by the same rules as ordinary visitations.[28]

2. It is not necessary that the regular superiors know of, or be present at, the local ordinary's visitation.[29]

3. The local ordinary may enter within the enclosure only for the purpose of inspection in conformity with Canon 600, 1°; he may visit the choir, the dormitory and the cells, etc., in so far as they relate to the law of the enclosure.[30] Thus, for example, he may see that the windows are constructed in such a manner as to prevent as far as possible those within from being seen by, or seeing persons outside.[31]

4. While within the enclosure the visitor must be accompanied by at least one cleric or male religious of mature age.[32]

[27] Canon 512, § 2. "[Ordinarius loci] visitare quoque eodem tempore debet: 1. Monasteria monialium, quae regularibus subduntur, circa ea quae ad clausurae legem spectant; imo etiam circa alia omnia, si Superior regularis ea a quinque annis non visitaverit; . . ."

[28] *Cf. supra*, p. 63.

[29] *Cf. supra*, p. 63.

[30] *Cf. supra*, p. 63.

[31] *Cf.* Canon 602; S. C. de Rel., instr., 6 February, 1924, § 2—*AAS*, XVI (1924), 96.

[32] *Cf. supra*, p. 118.

5. The visitor may conduct a personal visitation of the nuns at the grille (*i. e.*, the visitor may question the nuns in accordance with Canon 513, § 1), on matters pertaining to the enclosure.[33]

6. The local ordinary has full liberty, as in the other visitations enumerated in Canon 512, to empower a delegate to conduct the visitation in the same manner as he himself would do.

7. On the occasion of the visitation the local ordinary may take the opportunity to receive an account of the administration of all temporalities.[34] He should especially inquire into the administration of the dowry-funds. With regard to the inquiry into the administration of temporalities, what has been said above in treating of nuns not subject to regulars [35] has equal force here, except that when the removal of an administrator in a monastery of nuns subject to regulars seems advisable, the local ordinary should request the regular superior to effect the removal. Only if the latter fails to act may he deal with the case himself.[36]

8. If the regular superior has not visited the nuns within the past five years, then the local ordinary should visit them in all matters.[37]

[33] For the old law, *cf. supra*, p. 63. Commissio Pontif., 24 Nov., 1920: "Utrum ad normam can. 512, § 2, 1° et can 513, § 1 officum Ordinarii loci sit visitare quinto quoque anno monasteria monialium, quae Regularibus (etiam exemptis) subduntur, circa ea quae clausurae legem spectant eo, qui in can. 513, exponitur modo. Resp: *Affirmative*."—*AAS*, XII (1920), 575.

[34] Even though a report must be submitted to the regular superior, the local ordinary also has the right to receive a report at least annually and more frequently if the constitutions so state. Commissio Pontif., 24 Nov., 1920: "Utrum vi canonis 535, § 1, 1°, si monasterium monalium subiectum sit Superiori regulari (etiam exempto), administrationis ratio reddenda sit Superiori regulari et etiam Ordinario loci. Resp.: *Affirmative*."—*AAS*, XII (1920), 575.

[35] *Cf. supra*, p. 119.

[36] Canon 535, § 1, 2°.

[37] *I. e.*, in the same manner as he should visit the nuns mentioned in Canon 512, § 1, 1°. In no place does the Code oblige the regular superior to visit nuns every five years, but undoubtedly all constitutions of regulars to which nuns are subject demand visitation at even more frequent intervals.

Section 3

Male Regulars

The local ordinary has no right to visit in any way the houses or members of religious orders of men. Canon 615 states that regulars, both men and women, including novices, except those nuns who are not subject to regular superiors, are exempt together with their houses and churches from the jurisdiction of the local ordinary, except in the cases provided by law. Moreover Canon 344, § 2, determines that the bishop may visit exempt religious only in the cases expressed in law. Neither in Canon 512, which is the principal canon dealing with the visitation of religious, nor elsewhere in the Code is the local ordinary given the right to visit the houses of orders of men or the members (professed or novices) residing therein.[38] Before the Code the bishop had the right of visiting small houses of male regulars, except in missionary territories;[39] but from the latter half of the nineteenth century the Holy See frequently urged bishops not to use this right, unless special circumstances demanded its exercise.[40] Now the Code has definitely abrogated even this right of visitation. The only law which deals specifically with non-formal (small) houses and their relationship to the local ordinary is Canon 617, § 2, which mentions that every non-formal house remains under the special vigilance of the local ordinary, who, if abuses arise and become a source of scandal to the faithful, can himself provisionally deal with them. This special vigilance need not be discussed here. It suffices to note that the right of vigilance does not include the right of visitation and non-formal houses of regulars are not by Canon 617, § 2, made subject to the local ordinary's visitation.[41]

[38] This view is held by all canonists. *Cf., e.g.,* Fanfani, *De Iure Religiosorum,* n. 70; Wernz-Vidal, *Ius Canonicum,* III, 123; Creusen, *Religieux et Religieuses,* n. 75.

[39] *Cf. supra,* p. 60.

[40] *Cf.* Lucidi, *De Visitatione,* II, cap. IV, n. 67; Piat-Appeltern, *Compendium Iuris Regularis,* qu. 549.

[41] Coronata, *Institutiones Iuris Canonici,* I, 807; Vermeersch-Creusen, *Epitome,* I, n. 720. The right of vigilance and visitation, as the terms are used in the Code, are, while not the same, very similar and the precise dis-

All non-parochial churches of regulars (or more precisely, all their churches without the care of souls) are also exempt from the local ordinary's visitation. As has been seen, they enjoyed this privilege before the Code. In the present law Canon 615, § 1, simply states that churches of regulars are exempt, except in such cases in which the law expresses the contrary. Canonists interpret this exemption to include freedom both from jurisdiction and from visitation wherever no contrary provisions are set forth in the law.[42]

The single contrary provision whereby the local ordinary in special circumstances may visit such churches is expressed in Canon 1261.[43] Canon 1261 provides that if the local ordinary passes laws for his territory concerning the matters referred to in the first paragraph, *viz.*, abuses in divine worship, superstitious practices, anything alien to the faith or out of harmony with ecclesiastical traditions, or anything which has the appearance of shameful gain, —then according to the second paragraph of this canon all religious,

tinction between them is difficult to define in general terms. Both rights imply a certain amount of jurisdiction; a person or place may be subject to vigilance or visitation, though in a general sense exempt (*cf.*, *e.g.*, Canons 1491, § 1; 344, § 1). Visitation, however, is the broader term and the right of visiting signifies that one may go to a place (or person) and subject the place (or person) to an investigation. The right of vigilance does not extend so far; when the Code wishes to include visitation under vigilance the former is expressly mentioned (*e.g.*, Canon 1515, § 2). However, when one has the right of visiting a place in reference to a certain matter, it is certainly legitimate for him while there to exercise a right of vigilance possessed in regard to other points. In such cases it is at times all but impossible to show wherein visitation and vigilance differ.

[42] *Cf.*, *e.g.*, Vermeersch-Creusen, *Epitome,* I, nn. 581, 717; Fanfani, *De Iure Religiosorum,* n. 51; Coronata, *Institutiones Iuris Canonici,* I, 807; Jansen, *Ordensrecht,* p. 86; Goyeneche, "Consultationes," *CpR,* VI (1925), 357-360.

[43] Canon 1261, § 1: "Locorum Ordinarii advigilent ut sacrorum canonum praescripta de divino cultu sedulo observentur, et praesertim ne in cultum divinum sive publicum sive privatum aut in quotidianam fidelium vitam superstitiosa ulla praxis inducatur, aut quidquam admittatur a fide alienum vel ab ecclesiastica traditione absonum vel turpis quaestus speciem praeseferens.

§ 2. Si loci Ordinarius leges pro suo territorio hac in re tulerit, etiam religiosi omnes, exempti quoque, obligatione tenentur easdem servandi; et Ordinarius potest eorundem ecclesias vel publica oratoria in hunc finem visitare."

even though exempt, are bound to observe these laws; and the local ordinary for this purpose may visit their churches and public oratories.[44] Clearly, the non-parochial churches of regulars fall within the scope of this canon. Cardinal Gasparri in his capacity of President of the Pontifical Commission for the Interpretation of the Code declared in reply to several doubts: (a) that the laws referred to in Canon 1261 were not diocesan laws which merely reaffirmed the general laws of the Church, but diocesan laws with a different content; (b) that the visitation mentioned in Canon 1261, § 2, was not the ordinary quinquennial visitation; (c) that the visitation therein referred to could be undertaken only when the local ordinary had positive knowledge that particular laws passed by him were not being observed in the churches of exempt regulars.[45]

[44] For the old law, *cf. supra,* p. 61.

[45] "In Urbe N., tempore quo ecclesiae urbis quinquennali visitationi subdebantur, misit Ordinarius loci suum delegatum ad visitandum templum Societatis Iesu in illa urbe exsistens. Superiore praedictae Societatis non reluctante, delegatus Ordinarii visitavit templum et sacrarium eodem modo, quo ecclesiae non exemptae visitari solent.—Re audita, Praepositus Provincialis praedictae Societatis protestationem Ordinario porrexit, in qua cum debita reverentia ei inculcare conabatur, templum Societatis Iesu vi exemptionis visitationi loci Ordinarii obnoxium non esse. Quod si vero de visitatione iuxta can. 1261, § 2, agatur, illam supponere leges particulares in materia in praedicto canone expressa latas, hancque visitationem totam quantam differre ab illa quinquennali. Ordinarius affirmat, se allatas rationes non agnoscere seque ius habere etiam exemptorum regularium templa visitandi.—Ad rem dirimendam quaeritur.

I. "Utrum Ordinarius loci templa Societatis Iesu in sua dioecesi existentia modo praedicto quinto quoque anno visitare possit—Et quatenus negative:

II. "Utrum in casu, quo leges dioecesanae (*e. g.,* synodales) non quidem novam materiam iuxta can. 1261 afferunt, sed solum leges ecclesiasticas urgent, Ordinarius ad visitationem manum apponere possit—Et quatenus negative:

III. "Utrum visitatio, de qua in can. 1261, § 2 eodem modo instituenda sit, ac solita quinquennalis visitatio ecclesiarum non exemptarum.—Et quatenus negative:

IV. "Utrum ad visitationem iuxta can. 1261, § 2 extendi possunt responsa S. C. EE. et RR. ante novum Codicem data, ut nempe Ordinarius visitationis iure in tantum solum generatim utatur, in quantum positivam habeat notitiam leges particulares a se latas *in ecclesiis regularium exemptorum* non observari.

"Responsum datum 8 Apr., 1924—Ad I, II, III, *negative;* ad IV *affirmative.*"—Wernz-Vidal, *Ius Canonicum,* III, 429, nota 32.

This response was never promulgated by publication in the *Acta Apostolicae Sedis* and hence the question has been raised as to whether it has the force of an authentic interpretation.[46] Yet there should be no reasonable doubt that this is an authentic interpretation. According to Canon 17, § 2, an authentic interpretation which is declaratory of words which are in themselves certain needs no promulgation and certainly the President of the Commission acting alone can give authentic interpretations to doubts which are of lesser importance or which offer no great difficulty.[47]

[46] *Cf.* Marcellus, "De Exemptione Ecclesiarum Regularium a Canonica Episcopi Visitatione," *CpR,* IX (1928), 244, nota 2 (by Hippolytus).

[47] *Cf.* "Pontificia Commissio Ad Codicis Canones Authentice Interpretandos,"—*AAS,* XI (1919), 480, nota 1. *Cf. Disquisitio Circa Ius Ordinarii Dioecesani Visitandi Ecclesias Regularium* (Ad Claras Aquas, 1936), p. 15.

CHAPTER VIII

THE LOCAL ORDINARY'S VISITATION OF PARISHES IN CHARGE OF RELIGIOUS

THE law on the local ordinary's visitation of parishes, quasi-parishes and mission stations which are in any of the several possible ways connected with religious, is not contained in Canon 512, but is found in several canons scattered through the Code. Therefore it seems best to treat this subject in a separate chapter.

It is well known that every parish or quasi-parish is under the jurisdiction of a local ordinary. The present law does not contemplate the situation which, as has been seen, often existed in the later Middle Ages, wherein a parish under the care of religious was exempted in regard to the church, the clergy in charge and in the parishioners.[1] It is a fundamental principle, upheld in the Code even more vigorously than in the Council of Trent, that the *cura animarum saecularium* is entirely under the jurisdiction of the local ordinary. Most parishes are secular parishes in which the church, the parochial benefice and the parochial clergy are secular. A number of parishes, however, are in some way connected with religious and in respect to such parishes the question arises as to whether and, if so, in how far, the Code because of this relationship between the religious and the parish has provided special laws for the visitation of the local ordinary. The endeavor of this chapter is to set forth the special rules which govern the visitation of such parishes and to take up only incidentally the law which governs the visitation of parishes in general. Yet this incidental question may well be disposed of first.

[1] This was termed a union *plenissimo iure*. At present the term is sometimes employed in reference to a parish which is outside a diocese and which constitutes a part of an abbey or prelature *nullius* [*dioecesis*].—*Cf.* Sebastianelli, *De Personis*, p. 416; Wernz-Vidal, *Ius Canonicum*, II, 182. The relationship between such a parish and the abbot or prelate *nullius* is in practically every respect the same as the relationship between a parish in a diocese and the residential bishop.

Visitation of parishes is part of the general visitation of the diocesan or quasi-diocesan territory and hence is regulated by the laws on general visitation. The residential bishop of a diocese and the abbot or prelate *nullius* have the duty of visiting the parishes within their respective territories every five years.[2] In the United States it is still obligatory for bishops to visit each parish every third year.[3] Vicars and prefects apostolic, on the other hand, are bound to visit the quasi-parishes and mission stations at no definite interval, but whenever there is need.[4] However, none of the aforesaid local ordinaries may fulfill this duty through another unless legitimately impeded from personally performing the office themselves. Even in regard to the vicar general, Canon 343, § 1, explicitly states that the bishop may send him only when he himself is legitimately hindered. It is clear that the ordinaries of quasi-diocesan territories are similarly restricted in assigning the duty of visitation to their vicars general or (in missionary territories) to their vicars delegate.[5] Be-

[2] Canon 343, § 1: "Ad sanam et orthodoxam doctrinam conservandam, bonus mores tuendos, pravos corrigendos, pacem, innocentiam, pietatem et disciplinam in populo et clero promovendam ceteraque pro ratione adiunctorum ad bonum religionis constituenda, tenentur Episcopi obligatione visitandae quotannis diocesis vel ex toto vel ex parte, ita ut saltem singulis quinquenniis universam vel ipsi per se vel, si fuerint legitime impediti, per Vicarium Generalem aliumve lustrent." Canon 323, § 1: "Abbas vel Praelatus *nullius* easdem potestates ordinarias easdemque obligationes cum iisdem sanctionibus habet, quae competunt Episcopis residentialibus in propria dioecesi."

[3] "Unus quisque igitur Episcopus saltem unoquoque triennio totam diocesim perlustrare teneatur. . . ."—*Acta et Decreta Concilii Plenarii Baltimorensis* III, tit. ii. n. 14. . . . "as regards the period of time within which the visitation must be completed, the three year limit of the Council is still our rule since the *saltem singulis quinquenniis* of the Code leaves the way open to the stricter particular law."—Barrett, *A Comparative Study of the Councils of Baltimore and the Code of Canon Law* (Washington, D. C., 1932), p. 67.

[4] Canon 301, § 2: "Regionem sibi concreditam, quandocumque sit opus, debent ipsi per se vel, si legitime impediti fuerint, per alium visitare eaque omnia in visitatione expendere, quae ad fidem, bonos mores, Sacramentorum administrationem, praedicationem verbi Dei, festorum observantiam, cultum divinum, iuventutis institutionem, disciplinam ecclesiasticam referuntur."

[5] *Cf.* Canons 323, § 1: 301, § 2. For the meaning of the phrase "legitime impediti," *cf. supra,* p. 78.

sides being subject to the local ordinary's visitation, parishes are also subject to the visitation of the vicar forane (rural dean) of the district. Canon 447, § 1, enumerates the several matters over which the vicar forane has the right and duty of vigilance. The following paragraph of the same canon states that, in order that he may report on these matters, the vicar forane should, at such times as have been determined by the bishop, visit the parishes of his district.

Such in brief are the general laws which set forth by whom and when parishes are to be visited. Over parishes which are in no way connected with religious the local ordinary has plenary visitatorial powers. When a parish is connected with religious in some manner, the local ordinary's right of visitation is often by that very fact limited in certain respects. But in order to determine what limitations upon the local ordinary's visitatorial authority exist in cases of parishes connected with religious it is necessary to consider first the several possible relationships between a parish and religious.

The Several Possible Relationships Between a Parish and Religious

Parishes [6] connected in some way to religious may first of all be classified as religious or secular parishes. The religious parish is one incorporated (united) *pleno iure* with a religious house, *i. e.,* united in regard to matters spiritual and temporal. The secular parish is either incorporated (united) *quoad temporalia tantum* or is in spiritual affairs under at least the temporary charge of religious clergy.

In the religious parish the parochial benefice is united, by an indult of the Holy See, as an accessory benefice to the religious house.[7] The religious community is the habitual pastor but the re-

[6] A parish is made up of (a) a certain territory with definite boundaries; (b) the parishioners; (c) the church which serves their needs; (d) the parochial benefice, *i. e.,* the pastoral office and the right to receive the revenues from the dowry attached to the office; (e) the pastor, *i. e.,* either a priest or a moral person (*e. g.,* a religious community) which must appoint a vicar for the actual care of souls. *Cf.* Canons 216, § 3; 451, § 1.

[7] *I. e., unio minus principalis. Cf.* Vermeersch-Creusen, *Epitome,* II n. 753; Nebreda, "Studia Canonica," *CpR,* VII (1926), 117.

ligious superior must name and designate a priest from the religious institute to assume the actual care of souls. The confirmation of this parochial vicar rests with the local ordinary.[8] It appears that if assistant vicars are required on account of the number of parishioners or for other reasons, they should also be drawn from the institute to which the parish is united.[9] The Code does not state that the church of a religious parish is necessarily a religious church.[10] This indeed is the more usual situation, but it may happen that the church is a secular church though the parish is religious.[11]

In a parish united *quoad temporalia tantum* to a religious house the parochial benefice remains secular in regard to the rights and duties over spiritual matters attached to it. The religious house participates only in the revenues of the parish. The religious superior presents for the local ordinary's confirmation a secular priest

[8] Canons 452, § 1; 471, § § 1, 2; 1425, § 2. For relationship between the community and the parochial vicar, *cf.* Canons 609, § 1; 415.

[9] The Code has no specific legislation on this point, but it seems that, since the one parochial vicar is so selected, by analogy (Canon 20) the assistant vicars are to be chosen in the same way. For a thorough discussion of the matter, *cf.* Bastnagel *The Appointment of Parochial Adjutants and Assistants,* pp. 163-174.

[10] Maroto offers a definition of a religious church: "Et quidem ecclesia proprie religiosa est illa quae alicui Religioni legitime est plene addicta ex iure dominii seu proprietatis vel saltem ex usu stabili per perpetuo aut quasi perpetuo, non autem si communitati religiosae fuerit concessa ad usum precarium sive indefinite sive ad certum tempus sive modo transitorio, eoque minus si ecclesia saecularis curis alicuius privati religiosi, tamquam rectoris, committatur."—"Annotationes," *CpR,* VII (1926), 438. As Maroto notes, this is a modification of the definition of a religious church which he had previously given.—*Cf.* "Annotationes," *CpR,* II (1921), 101. Mayer appears to accept Maroto's earlier definition. *Cf.* "Die nicht inkorporierte Klosterpfarrei," *AKKR,* CXII (1932), 478, 479. However, the later definition of Maroto is in substantial agreement with definitions given by other canonists who have touched the matter.—*Cf.* Vermeersch-Creusen, II, nn. 476, 869; Nebreda, "Studia Canonica," *CpR,* VII (1926), 116, 263; for citations of other authors in agreement with the latter definition of Maroto, *cf.* Nebreda., *op. cit.,* 331, 332.

[11] Nebreda, *op. cit.,* 330; Maroto, "Annotationes," *CpR,* VII (1926), 438. Benedict XIV also refers to secular churches in parishes united *pleno iure* to religious houses. *Cf. De Synodo Dioecesana,* lib. V, cap. 7, n. 3.

to exercise the care of souls. A papal rescript is necessary to effect such a union.[12]

The third type of parish connected with religious is had when the parish is not incorporated with the religious house in any manner, but is entrusted to religious priests in order that they may assume the care of souls. This has sometimes been termed a union *quoad spiritualia tantum.* Apostolic nuncios, internuncios, and delegates may grant in particular cases or temporarily to bishops the faculty of placing religious priests in charge of parishes when there is a dearth of secular priests.[13] A similar faculty has been given to missionary bishops.[14] It has been thought that the exercise of this faculty does not have the effect of incorporating the parishes with the religious house, but rather places the parish under a religious priest in whom vests the title of pastor.[15] The view has also been advanced that the Code itself contemplates such a relationship. The phrase *"paroecia religiosis concredita,"* [16] it has been said, refers not to a religious parish, but to an unincorporated secular parish, in which the title of pastor vests not in the religious house, but in the religious priest who has charge of the parish.[17] Whether or not the Code in using the phrase *paroecia religiosis concredita* implies such an arrangement is a question to which no definitive answer need be attempted here, since it is not essential to the determining of

[12] Canons 1425, § 1; 1423, § 2. Such unions seem to be rather rare. *Cf.* Nebreda, "Studia Canonica," *CpR,* VII (1926), 330, n. 90.

[13] "Concedendi in casibus particularibus, vel ad tempus, Ordinariis dioecesanis facultatem praeficiendi paroeciis religiosos in defectu sacerdotum saecularium, de consensu tamen suorum Superiorum, et cum clausula ut saltem duo alii religiosi cum parocho cohabitent, servatisque in reliquis sacrorum canonum dispositionibus."—*Index Facultatum Quas, Pro Locis Missionis Suae, Nuntiis, Internuntiis et Delegatis Apostolicis Penes Civitates Seu Nationes, Post Codicis Iuris Canonici Publicationem Tribuere SSmus Dominus Noster Decrevit, Ceteris Abrogatis,* n. 48 (in Vermeersch-Creusen, *Epitome,* I, 527).

[14] S. C. Prop. Fide, 9 Dec. 1920,—*AAS,* XIII (1921), 18.

[15] *Cf.* Bastnagel, *The Appointment of Adjutants and Assistants,* p. 158; Vromant, *De Bonis Ecclesiae Temporalibus,* n. 354.

[16] Canons 456, 472, 2°, 475, § 1.

[17] Mayer, "Die nicht inkorporierte Klosterpfarrei," *AKKR,* CXII (1932), 468, 473. Admittedly such a status may arise only through an indult or faculty from the Holy See.—*Op. cit.,* 472. *Cf.* Canon 1442.

the visitatorial rights of the local ordinary.[18] Actually the Holy See does approve of an arrangement in which the parish is placed under the charge of religious clergy and yet remains a secular parish. In this arrangement according to Mayer,[19] the parish church may be either a religious or a secular church. The charge of the parish may be assumed temporarily or permanently.[20]

18 A few reasons may be given which make one hesitate to accept the view that the Code speaks specifically of such a relationship: (1) The notes to the sources which Gasparri gives for Canon 456 (which speaks of the *paroecia religiosis concredita*) and for Canon 1425, § 2 (which is concerned with the parish *pleno iure unita*) are the same, and these sources have reference to parishes *pleno iure unitae.* Gasparri's notes to the sources, though printed with the Code, are not part of the Code; yet their value in determining the meaning of doubtful phrases is universally recognized. In this case they indicate that the *paroecia religiosis concredita* means the *paroecia pleno iure domui religiosae unita.* (2) If the two phrases refer to entirely different statuses, Canon 472, 2° and 475, § 1, make no provision for a parish united *pleno iure,* when such a parish is vacant or the pastor incapacitated. (3) Historically the terms *parochus religiosus* and *vicarius religiosus* have been used indiscriminately to signify the religious parochial vicar of a parish united *pleno iure* to a religious house. (*Cf.* Notes to sources of Canons 454, § 5; 456.) Hence, it is doubtful if one can insist that when the Code uses the term *parochus religiosus* it is referring to a situation in which the title of pastor strictly belongs to the religious priest who has the care of souls and not to the religious house (*cf.* also Canon 415, § 2, 2°). Only in Canon 630, § 1, is it clear that *parochus religiosus* means only the religious priest who has the care of souls.

It seems a more acceptable hypothesis that the phrase *paroecia religiosis concredita* refers to any parish under the spiritual care of religious, whether united *pleno iure* or not. It is clear from a comparison of Canon 456 with Canon 1425, § 1, that the phrase cannot refer to a parish united to a religious house *quoad temporalia tantum.*

19 "Die nicht inkorporierte Klosterpfarrei,"*AKKR,* CXII (1932), 478, 479.

20 "Die Konzilskongregation gibt die Erlaubnis zur Übertragung einer Pfarrei an Religiosen nur unter der Bedingung, dass der Bischof die Pfarrei den Religiosen ohne Erlaubnis des Heiligen Stuhles nicht wieder abnimmt, m.a.W. auch die Übertragung einer Säkularpfarrei an Religiosen kann ähnlich einer Union (can. 1423, § 3) vom Bischof nur für dauernd, nicht auf Zeit vorgenommem werden."—Mayer, *op cit.,* 472. Yet certainly there are cases in the United States in which parishes are only temporarily entrusted to religious. This involves no injustice to either the local ordinary or the religious, if it is clearly understood in the initial agreement that the charge is only for a time. However the permission of the Holy See is required.

The only distinctive marks of such an arrangement are that the parish remains secular, is in no way incorporated with the religious house, and if entrusted permanently to religious the title of pastor belongs strictly to the religious priest who exercises the care of souls. In other details each case may have its peculiar features according to the contract entered into by the local ordinary and the religious.

With this summary statement relative to the status engendered by the various ways in which parishes may be connected with religious it is possible to take up the question of the local ordinary's visitation. This may be treated under three headings: (a) the clergy; (b) the church; (c) the temporalities of the parish.

The Clergy

All religious pastors or religious parochial vicars are in every respect save in regular observance subject to the jurisdiction, visitation and correction of the local ordinary, just as secular pastors. This is the comprehensive rule of Canon 631, § 1.[21] It is substantially the same as the law set forth by the Council of Trent and the legislation which appeared in the period subsequent to that council and prior to the present Code. In only one point does the present law introduce a change. The Tridentine decree exempted from visitation churches and their religious pastors or vicars, if the churches were attached to houses in which an abbot general or the head of an order had his usual and principal residence. The constitution *"Firmandis"* (November 6, 1744) of Benedict XIV sustained this exemption and determined with more precision the cases to which it was applicable.[22] In Canon 631, § 1, this exemption is overruled by an explicit statement to the effect that the religious pastor or vicar exercising his ministry in a house or place where major superiors have their ordinary residence is, like any other religious pastor or vicar, subject entirely to the local ordinary,

[21] Canon 631, § 1: "Idem parochus vel vicarius religiosus, licet ministerium exerceat in domo seu loco ubi maiores Superiores religiosi ordinariam sedem habent, subest immediate omnimodae iurisdictioni, visitationi, et correctioni Ordinarii loci, non secus ac parochi saeculares, regulari observantia unice excepta."

[22] *Cf. supra,* p. 62.

except in matters touching his regular observance. It is evident that Canon 631, § 1, admits of no exception. Whether the religious is a member of an exempt or non-exempt institute makes no difference.[23] Even if the parish is a religious parish (*i. e.*, united *pleno iure*), the priest having the care of souls is subject to the local ordinary's jurisdiction, visitation, and correction in accordance with Canon 631 and Canon 1425, § 2.[24]

Benedict XIV in the constitution *"Firmandis,"*[25] did not content himself with reasserting the subjection of religious pastors and vicars to the bishop, but listed a number of points which he apparently considered worthy of the visitor's special attention. As the constitution is in this regard simply a more explicit statement of the present law [26] it is advisable to recall the points therein enumerated. The local ordinary has the right and duty to examine: (a) whether the pastor exercises the care of souls by a legitimate title; (b) whether he has been and is observing the law of residence; (c) whether he attends the conferences on cases of conscience; (d) whether he applies Mass for the people on the days determined by law; (e) whether he carries out all things prescribed by law as to preaching and instructing children in Christian doctrine; (f) whether he sets aside certain days for hearing the confessions of the faithful; (g) whether he is zealous in assisting the sick and dying and administers the Sacraments in good time; (h) whether he gives to boys and girls the proper instruction before Confirmation and First Communion; (i) whether before permitting the faithful to marry in *facie ecclesiae* he makes the requisite investigations to ascertain that no impediment exists, that they consent freely to marriage and, finally, that they are instructed in Christian doctrine, particularly

[23] However, the religious pastor or vicar, if he is a diocesan religious or a member of a lay congregation, is as a religious subject to the local ordinary's visitation in regard to regular observance, by virtue of Canon 512.

[24] Canon 1425, § 2: "Sin autem *pleno iure*, paroecia fit religiosa et Superior potest sacerdotem e sua religione ad curam animarum excercendam nominare, sed Ordinarii loci est eundem probare et instituere, eiusque iurisdictioni, correctioni, et visitationi ipse subesse debet in iis rebus quae ad curam animarum pertinent, ad normam can. 631."

[25] *Fontes*, n. 349, § 9.

[26] *Cf.* Canon 6, 3°.

in the principal mysteries of the Faith; (j) whether he keeps in good order the book in which are recorded the baptisms, confirmations, marriages, and the spiritual status of his parishioners *(status animarum)*.

In a similar way assistant vicars, since they share in the care of souls, are to be visited by the local ordinary.

The local ordinary's right of correction is considered in Canon 631, § § 2, 3.[27] When the local ordinary finds that the pastor or parochial vicar has failed to fulfill his duty properly, he may pass suitable decrees and inflict penalties. In this the local ordinary has a cumulative right with the religious superior, but in case of conflict the decree of the local ordinary prevails. The local ordinary may even proceed to remove the pastor or vicar, since they hold office at his will *(ad nutum)*. It is necessary only to advise the religious superior of his intention. The local ordinary does not need the consent of the religious superior nor need he give to the religious superior the reasons for the removal. Yet there should be good grounds for the removal as the Code indicates by permitting recourse *in devolutivo* to the Holy See.

What has been said of religious pastors and vicars in charge of parishes is applicable to all missionaries engaged in the care of souls in quasi-parishes and mission stations.[28] The Sacred Congre-

[27] Canon 631, § 2: "Ordinarius loci, ubi eum suo muneri defecisse compererit, opportuna decreta condere ac meritas in eum poenas statuere potest; in quo nihilominus Ordinarii facultates minime privativae sunt, sed Superior ius cumulativum cum ipso habet, ita tamen ut, si aliter a Superiore, aliter ab Ordinario decerni contingat, decretum Ordinarii praevalere debeat.

§ 3: "Quod attinet ad parochi vel vicarii religiosi remotionem e paroecia, servetur praescriptum can. 454, § 5; . . ."

[28] Canon 296, § 1. "Etiam missionarii regulares subiiciuntur Vicarii et Praefecti Apostolici iurisdictioni, visitationi, et correctioni in iis quae pertinent ad missionum regimen, curam animarum, Sacramentorum administrationem, scholarum directionem, oblationes intuitu missionis factas, implementum piarum voluntatum in favorem eiusdem missionis.

§ 2. "Quamvis Vicariis et Praefectis Apostolicis nullo modo liceat, praeter casus in iure praevisos, se in disciplinam religiosam ingerere quae a Superiore dependet, si tamen circa ea, de quibus in superiore paragrapho, conflictus oriatur inter mandatum Vicarii aut Praefecti Apostolici et mandatum Superioris, prius praevalere debet, salvo iure recursus in devolutivo ad Sanctam Sedem et salvis peculiaribus statutis a Sede Apostolica probatis."

gation for the Propagation of the Faith, in its instruction of December 8, 1929, to promote concord and union in missionary territories, touched upon the question of the removal of missionaries. It urged the ecclesiastical superior of the mission territory to effect removals in the ordinary circumstances with the counsel of the religious superior. However, for very grave reasons the superior of the mission territory may proceed to remove a missionary without awaiting the consent of, or furnishing reasons to, the religious superior in accordance with the norm of Canon 454, § 5.[29]

The Church

In considering the local ordinary's right of visiting parochial churches of parishes connected in any way with religious, it is necessary to treat specifically only of the churches of regulars. Secular churches are completely subject to the local ordinary's visitation even though the parish is under the charge of religious or is incorporated with a religious house. Similarly, by virtue of Canon 512 religious churches of diocesan congregations or of pontifical congregations, even though the latter be exempt, are subject in their entirety to the local ordinary's visitatorial powers. Hence, apart from churches of regulars there is no question about the right of the local ordinary to conduct a local visitation of parochial churches.[30]

Churches of regulars are exempt according to Canon 615. Yet, when such a church becomes at the same time a parochial church, it becomes subject to the jurisdiction and visitation of the local ordinary *in so far as it serves the parish.* This was the law before the Code[31] and undoubtedly remains the law today. No canon of the Code mentions expressly the local ordinary's right to visit such

[29] *AAS,* XXII (1930), 114, 115.

[30] In considering the visitation of churches of parishes connected in some way with regulars, it is of prime importance to know whether the *church* is secular or religious. As has been seen (*cf. supra,* p. 131), this does not depend upon the type of relationship between the *parish* and the religious. The church may be secular, though the parish is in the strict sense religious, and vice versa.

[31] *Cf. supra,* p. 62.

churches of regulars; yet, that the local ordinary possesses this right is a corollary from the fundamental principle that he has complete jurisdictional and visitatorial rights over all that concerns the *cura animarum saecularium.* Apparently since the Code explicitly affirms the right to visit and correct any and every religious pastor and vicar, it was not thought necessary to state that the right of visitation extended to any and every religious parochial church.[32] The one change from the pre-code law is the following: Parochial churches attached to houses wherein the major superiors of regulars reside are no longer exempt, but are placed in the same category as other parochial churches of regulars.[33] It is, therefore, the common teaching of canonists that all the churches of regulars which are also parochial churches are subject to the visitation of the local ordinary in all things that concern the care of souls.[34] Canonists also agree that the constitution *"Firmandis"* [35] of Benedict XIV, which presents a complete list *(taxative)* of such matters as fall within the ambit of the local ordinary's visitation, is still applicable as norm for interpreting the present law. The constitution states that regulars must receive into their parochial churches missionaries which the bishop sends ahead of him on his visitation. These missionaries may administer the Sacraments of Penance and the Eucharist, preach and perform such other actions as they have been commissioned to undertake as a preparation for the visitation. As to the local visitation, the bishop may visit: (a) not all the altars, but only that altar in which the Blessed Sacrament is preserved and

[32] Though Canon 512 speaks only of the local visitation of houses and monasteries, it is evident that the religious residing therein are also subject to visitation. Similarly when Canon 631, § 1, states that all the parochial clergy, though religious, are to be visited, it is clear that the local visitation of the parochial church in which they exercise their ministry is also enjoined.

[33] *Cf.* Canon 631, § 1.

[34] *Cf., e.g.,* Fanfani, *De Iure Religiosorum,* n. 449; Coronata, *Institutiones Iuris Canonici,* I, p. 808; Melo, *De Exemptione Regularium,* p. 154; Haring, "Nochmals die Aufsicht des Dechants über Regularseelsorger," *ThPrQS,* LXXXII (1929), 563, 564. Vromant had expressed the view that such churches are exempt, *Ius Missionariorum,* II, 87; but he subsequently indicated his adherence to the common opinion, "De Regimine Paroeciarum et Quasi-Paroeciarum Religiosis Sodalibus Concreditarum," *JP,* XIII (1933), 280.

[35] *Fontes,* n. 349, § § 5, 7.

consequently the tabernacle; (b) the baptismal font; (c) the confessionals; (d) the pulpit; (e) the sacristy in regard to the vestments used in administering the Sacraments; (f) the sepulchres and the cemetery for receiving the bodies of parishioners; (g) the campanile, if the bells serve the parish; (h) all sacred vessels used for preserving consecrated particles, holy oils, baptismal water or holy water for the parishioners.

It may be added that the same norms are also applicable to churches of regulars which are quasi-parochial or are used as mission stations where quasi-parishes have not yet been erected.[36]

Temporalities

In order to set forth as clearly as possible the extent of the local ordinary's right of inquiry on the occasion of visitation into the administration of the temporalities connected with a parish,[37] it seems advisable first to attempt a classification of the property which constitutes these temporalities and to add a few words of commentary where necessary.

I. Property acquired by the religious clergy or by the religious house for the institute. The income received by religious pastors or vicars as a means of support and in recompense for their services in the parish passes to the institute according to the norms of Canon 580, § 2, and Canon 582. The sources and the amount of the salary and legitimate perquisites of the religious pastor (and assistant religious vicars) may vary widely.[38] Thus, their support

[36] Vromant, "De Regimine Paroeciarum et Quasi-Paroeciarum Religiosis Sodalibus Concreditarum," *JP,* XIII (1933) 280.

[37] The Third Council of Baltimore stressed the importance of this inquiry: "Quum vero, inter cetera, in temporalem Ecclesiarum administrationem accurate inquirere maximi intersit, si fieri potest [Episcopus] secum ducat duos convisitatores, vel saltem unum, hosque eligat ex praestantioribus inter presbyteros, et praesertim ex iis qui in bonis temporalibus Ecclesiae administrandis scientia et experientia excellere noscuntur."—*Acta et Decreta Concilii Plenarii Baltimorensis III,* tit. II, n. 14. While the bishop no longer has the obligation to bring co-visitors with him (*cf.* Canon 343, § 2), it seems that he is still required in the United States to examine into the temporalities which are under his jurisdiction. *Cf.* Barrett, *A Comparative Study of the Council of Baltimore and the Code of Canon Law,* p. 67.

[38] *Cf.* Canon 463, § 1.

may be derived from the local ordinary, from the government, from stole fees, from the income accruing by reason of the dowry of the benefice, from a portion of certain collections, etc. But whatever the source may be, all property which is not given for the benefit of the parish[39] and which by law, custom or special agreement with the local ordinary passes to the parochial clergy as a remuneration for their ministerial activities may be placed under this heading.

When a parish is united in temporalities (whether the union be *pleno iure* or *quoad temporalia tantum)* to a religious house, the house receives a part or all of the income from the dowry of the benefice.[40] In each case particular arrangements presumably will have been made between the local ordinary and the religious house (or will have been imposed by the Holy See), which arrangements will determine the dowry of the benefice and what portion of it the house shall enjoy for its support. Such income may for the purposes at hand may be placed under the same heading with the income received by the religious clergy for their parochial activities.[41]

II. Property for the church fabric. By virtue of Canon 630, § 4, if a parochial church is religious church, it belongs to the religious superiors to receive, retain, collect and administer offerings for its erection, upkeep, and decoration, whereas these rights belong to the local ordinary if the church is secular.[42] As to the property for the fabric of a religious church it may simply be noted here that the canon gives the exclusive right of administration to religious superiors without drawing any distinction between exempt and non-exempt religious. In regard to the property for the fabric

[39] Canon 630, § 3. "Bona quae ipsi [parocho vel vicario religioso] obveniunt intuitu paroeciae cui praeficitur, ipsi paroeciae acquirit; cetera acquirit ad instar aliorum religiosorum." For the norms to be applied when the intention of the donor is doubtful—*Cf.* Canon 1536, § 1; Leo XIII, const. *"Romanos Pontifices,"* 8 Mai, 1881—*Fontes,* n. 582, § 26.

[40] Canons 1425, 1472, 1473.

[41] *Cf.* Goyeneche, "Consultationes," *CpR,* X (1929), 41.

[42] Canon 630, § 4. ". . . sed eleemosynas pro ecclesia paroeciali aedificanda, conservanda, instauranda, exornanda accipere, apud se retinere, colligere aut administrare pertinet ad Superiores, si ecclesia sit communitatis religiosae; secus ad loci Ordinarium." *Cf.* Canons 1182; 609, § 1 (415, § 3, 3°). For the meaning of the term "religious church" *vide supra,* p. 131, n. 10.

of secular churches which are under the care of religious, it is debated whether this canon gives the local ordinary: (a) the exclusive and direct right of administration; or (b) a cumulative right of administration with the religious pastor (or parochial vicar); or (c) merely the right of vigilance and visitation of the religious pastor's administration.[43] The dispute is of no practical importance here. The normal procedure would appear to be to allow the pastor (or vicar) to administer the property and whether he performs this task as a delegate of the local ordinary or in his own right, in either case the local ordinary has the right of subjecting the manner of administration to scrutiny on the occasion of his visitation.

Canon 630, § 4, is not concerned with the source whence the property for the church fabric is derived. There may be a fund invested, the revenues of which are sufficient for the building and upkeep of the church, or it may be the practice to deduct a certain sum from the general collections, or both the revenues from an investment and a part of the collections may be allocated to the maintenance of the church. The arrangements will differ according to the conditions, expressed or implied, under which the religious undertook the charge of the parish. The only point pertinent to the question of whether the local ordinary has the right of supervising the administration of the property for the church fabric is whether the church is religious or secular.

III. Offerings for the benefit of the parishioners. Canon 630, § 4, permits the religious pastor (or vicar) under the vigilance of his superiors, to accept, collect, administer, and dispense, with due regard for the will of the donors, offerings given in any way for the benefit of parishioners or Catholic schools or pious places connected with the parish.[44] Such offerings become the property of the parish.[45]

[43] Nebreda has presented the three opinions in more detail.—"Studia Canonica," *CpR*, VII (1926), 196-198.

[44] Canon 630, § 4. "Non obstante voto paupertatis, eidem [parocho sive vicario] licet eleemosynas in bonum paroecianorum, vel pro scholis catholicis aut locis piis paroeciae coniunctis, quovis modo oblatas accipere aut colligere, et acceptas sive collectas administrare, itemque, servata offerentium voluntate, pro prudenti suo arbitrio, erogare, salva semper vigilantia sui Superioris; . . ."

[45] Canon 630, § 3. "Ex hoc canone liquet [etiam] paroeciam incorporatam

IV. Funds and legacies referred to in Canon 535, § 3, 2°, and Canon 533, § 1, 4°. Canon 631, § 3, provides that in a parish under the charge of a religious pastor (or vicar) the prescriptions of Canon 533, § 1, 4°, and of Canon 535, § 3, 2°, should be followed.[46] The meaning of these canons has already been considered in Chapter VI.[47]

V. Pious foundations established in the parish church. The rule of Canon 1550, which has been discussed (in Chapter VI) [48] applies in the same way to parochial churches as to non-parochial churches.

VI. Manual Mass stipends. Manual Mass stipends are acquired by the religious in charge of a parish if they celebrate the Masses in conformity to the obligations assumed upon accepting the stipends. Such stipends then pass to the institute according to the norms of Canons 580, § 2, and 582 and hence could be brought under the first heading (I). However, as Canons 842 and 843, § 2, set forth special rules on the local ordinary's right to supervise the fulfillment of the obligations attached to manual stipends, such stipends are here placed under a special heading. Canons 842 and 843, § 2, have already been discussed and it is unnecessary to repeat what has previously been set forth on this point.[49]

In connection with the subject of the temporalities of a parish and the local ordinary's right of supervision the following question was put to the Commission for the Interpretation of the Code:

> Whether in virtue of Canons 631, § 3; 535, § 3, 2°; 533, § 1, 3° and 4°, the Ordinary of the place has the right to demand an account of the administration of funds and legacies of a religious parish, to which Canon 1425, § 2, refers. *Response:* In the affirmative without prejudice to the prescriptions of Canon 630, § 4, and Canon 1550.[50]

Religioni esse subiectum dominii potestateque frui pergere nedum bona habendi sed et alia acquirendi."—Goyeneche, "Consultationes," *CpR,* X (1929), 40.

[46] Canon 631, § 3: "(Quod attinet ad parochi vel vicarii religiosi remotionem e paroecia, servetur praescriptum can. 454, § 5) et quod [attinet] ad bona temporalia [servetur] praescriptum can. 533, § 1, n. 4, et can. 535, § 3, n. 2."

[47] *Cf. supra,* pp. 100-106.

[48] *Cf. supra,* p. 108.

[49] *Cf. supra,* p. 110.

[50] 25 Iul., 1926—*AAS,* XVIII (1926), 393.

There is no need to comment at length on this response. The meaning of Canons 631, § 3; 535, § 3, 2°; 533, § 1, 3° and 4°, has already been set forth. It should, however, be recalled that the church of a religious parish is not necessarily a religious church. In the event that it is a religious church, the freedom from the local ordinary's authority conceded by Canon 630, § 4, and Canon 1550 is not impaired by the other canons above enumerated. Specifically, Canon 630, § 4, places the property for the fabric of any religious church of a pontifical institute, exempt or non-exempt, under the exclusive care of the religious superiors and withdraws such property entirely from the local ordinary's jurisdiction.[51] And Canon 1550 determines that with regard to foundations established in religious churches, parochial or non-parochial, of exempt religious the major superiors have complete jurisdiction to the exclusion of the local ordinary. Yet these foundations, most probably, must be for religious services or ecclesiastical functions, for it seems that foundations, even though established in religious churches of an exempt institute, but which are for the benefit of works of charity in the parish or mission, fall under the authority of the local ordinary.[52] These two provisions (of Canon 630, § 4, and Canon 1550), the response states, are not affected by Canons 631, § 3; 535, § 3, 2°; 533, § 1, 3° and 4°.

With these preliminary considerations disposed of, it is possible to state summarily the extent of the local ordinary's right of supervision over property connected with a parish, following the classification of property given above.

Parishes connected in some way with diocesan religious, whether the parochial church is secular or religious, offer no difficulty. Visiting such parishes the local ordinary has plenary powers of inquiry with regard to the temporalities.

[51] The conclusion that the property for the fabric of religious churches of even non-exempt pontifical institutes is withdrawn entirely from the local ordinary's authority is evident from the text of Canon 630, § 4, and from Canon 618, § 2, 1°. *Cf.* Goyeneche, "Consultationes," *CpR,* III (1922), 271; Nebreda, "Studia Canonica," *CpR,* VII (1926), 195; Maroto, "Annotationes," *CpR,* VII (1926), 440; Mayer, "Die nicht inkorporierte Klosterpfarrei," *AKKR,* CXII (1932), 479.

[52] *Cf. supra,* p. 109.

In parishes connected in some way with religious of a pontifical institute, his right is in various points restricted, depending chiefly on (a) whether the church is religious or secular; and (b) whether the religious are or are not exempt clerical religious.

For parishes under the spiritual care of religious of an exempt clerical institute, whether the parish be incorporated *pleno iure* or simply entrusted to religious priests, the following rules, in reference to the types of property enumerated above, obtain:

I. Property acquired by the religious or religious house for the institute. The local ordinary may not concern himself in any way with such property.

II. Property for the church fabric (*cf.* Canon 630, § 4). If the church is secular the local ordinary has at least the right to supervise the administration of such property, if not directly to administer it. If the church is a religious church, the local ordinary has no right of inquiry, since such property is under the exclusive jurisdiction of the religious superiors.

III. Offerings for the benefit of the parishioners (*cf.* Canon 630, § 4). The local ordinary has the right to supervise the administration and to demand an account of all such property.[53]

IV. The funds and legacies referred to in Canon 535, § 3, 2°, and Canon 533, § 1, 4°. Whether these are given to the religious for the parish or directly to the parish and are simply administered by the religious, the local ordinary has the right to inquire and to demand an account of the administration.

V. Pious foundations established in the parish church (*cf.* Canon 1550). If the church is a secular church the local ordinary has all the rights and duties listed in Canons 1545-1549 for all foundations. If the church is religious and the pious foundations are for ecclesiastical functions in the church, the aforesaid rights and duties belong exclusively to the major superiors. If the church is religious and the foundations are for the benefit of some work of charity outside the church, in the parish or within the local ordinary's territory,

[53] As such offerings clearly fall under Canon 533, § 1, 4°, and Canon 535, § 3, 2°, they could be placed under the subsequent heading (IV); however, as the Code mentions them separately (in Canon 630, § 4), the same has been done here.

it seems more probable that the local ordinary, rather than the major superior, has the authority over these foundations.

VI. Manual Mass stipends (*cf.* Canons 842, 843, § 2). Whether the church is a secular or a religious church, the local ordinary has no right of vigilance in regard to obligations arising from manual stipends, nor may he examine the book in which the manual Masses are recorded.

For parishes under the spiritual care (whether incorporated *pleno iure* or simply entrusted to the ministry) of religious of a pontifical institute which is not an exempt clerical institute, the following rules may be succinctly set forth:

In regard to the property mentioned in I, II, III and IV, the same rules obtain as are given above for parishes under the care of religious of exempt clerical institutes.

V. Pious foundations in the parish church. If the religious are priests of an exempt lay institute, the same rules obtain as for the religious of exempt clerical institutes. If the religious are not exempt, all pious foundations are under the authority of the local ordinary.

VI. Manual Stipends for Masses. Whether the church be secular or religious, the local ordinary may examine the book in which manual Masses are recorded.

CHAPTER IX

THE PROCEDURE IN VISITATION

IN Canon 513 [1] is contained the only legislation of the Code directly and explicitly treating of the procedure in the visitation of religious. This canon indeed considers only the most important points, but other questions, of which there is no mention and yet which relate to the manner of conducting the visitation, may be conveniently discussed in this chapter. Two such questions, the announcement and the ceremonies, can be first of all summarily disposed of.

The Announcement and the Ceremonies

Although the Code does not state that the visitation must be announced, ordinarily an announcement should be sent some days before the visitation is to begin so that the religious may prepare themselves for it.[2] But there is no canonical obligation [3] and the visitor upon occasion may find it advisable to visit a community unexpectedly.[4] Notice of the local ordinary's visitation of a parish must be sent sometime in advance to the pastor if the latter is to have the opportunity to make the necessary preparations and to announce to the people beforehand the time of the local ordinary's arrival.

[1] Canon 513, § 1. "Visitator ius et officium habet interrogandi religiosos quos oportere iudicaverit et cognoscendi de iis quae ad visitationem spectant; omnes autem religiosi obligatione tenentur respondendi secundum veritatem, nec Superioribus fas est quoquo modo eos ab hac obligatione avertere aut visitationis scopum aliter impedire.

§ 2. "A decretis Visitatoris recursus datur in devolutivo tantum, nisi Visitator ordine iudiciario processerit."

[2] Piat-Appeltern, *Compendium Iuris Regularis,* qu. 520. Can. 2413 contains the phrase, *post indictam visitationem,* suggesting that an announcement is the general rule.

[3] The constitutions may oblige a religious visitor to communicate the day and hour of his intended arrival.

[4] Gaudentius, *De Visitatione,* dub. I, n. 3.

The Code provides no rules for the attendant ceremonies of visitation. The *Pontificale Romanum* (tit., *Ordo ad visitandas parochias)* makes provisions for the ceremonies of parochial visitation by the local ordinary.[5] For visitation of communities by religious superiors, it remains for the constitutions to determine in what way the visitor shall present his credentials, how the religious shall pay their respects to the visitor, whether the visitation is to be opened and closed with an exhortation and prayers and in general to arrange for such kindred matters. The local ordinary is at liberty to follow his own discretion on these points when he visits religious houses. It is, however, the general custom to open the visitation with an address by the visitor in which are explained the purposes of visitation, the liberty of all the religious to speak freely with the visitor, the extent and the limit of their obligation to answer questions or to volunteer information, etc.[6] At the end of the visitation, it is usual for the visitor to give a short conference on the religious life and to conclude it with a general absolution (if the visitor is a priest) and prayers for the dead.

The Nature of Visitation

To hold a visitation is to exercise an act of government. Canon 513 expressly states that those who are visitors possess the right of questioning the religious and the right of personally investigating into places and things (*e. g.*, documents and books) which come under their authority—and implicitly states that visitors also possess the right of issuing decrees to remedy abuses and to promote good order. Obviously these three rights will vary in nature and extent as the authority of one visitor varies in nature and extent from that of another.[7] It is first of all evident that Canon 513 is treating of

[5] *Cf.* Pius Martinucci, *Manuale Sacrarum Caeremoniarium* (Romae: Pustet, 1915), IV, 357-385; Adrian Fortescue, *The Ceremonies of the Roman Rite Described* (London: Burns, Oates & Washburne, 1930), 394-408.

[6] *Cf.* Bastien, *Directoire Canonique*, pp. 282, 283.

[7] They differ in nature for in exercising these rights an ordinary of person or place is using voluntary jurisdiction or judicial power while a religious visitor of a lay or non-exempt institute is using merely dominative power. Likewise the extent of these rights varies as the scope of the visitation is restricted or unrestricted.

any and all visitors who possess true authority—complete or partial, jurisdictional or dominative—over the religious to be visited. Thus it includes visitors apostolic, episcopal, and religious, whether acting in their own name or by vicarious or delegated authority, so long as they are empowered to hold a visitation in the true sense. Frequently a superior (*e. g.*, a provincial) enjoying habitual authority is endowed by particular law with faculties which permit him during the visitation to dispose of matters ordinarily beyond his powers. And often the power of the local superior is suspended or greatly curtailed.[8] When a competent superior sends a delegate into a religious community with no other power but to observe the state of discipline and to submit a report on his return, then such a one may often be called a visitor, though actually he is rather an inspector whose authority falls far short of the visitors considered in Canon 513.[9]
discipline and by fatherly admonitions and corrections to promote good order and the religious spirit of the community. It is evident that the Code has not changed the nature of visitation. The bishop undertaking the general diocesan visitation is ordinarily obliged to proceed in a paternal way.[11] The legislator has not thought it necessary to repeat this injunction for the visitors of religious but intimately, to inquire in a paternal way into the observance of superiors an opportunity to know their spiritual children more

Traditionally visitation has been considered primarily a paternal rather than a judicial procedure.[10] Its predominant aim was to give

recursus in devolutivo tantum; in aliis vero causis, etiam tempore visitationis,

[11] Canon 345. "Visitator, in iis quae obiectum et finem visitationis respiciunt, debet paterna forma procedere, et ab eius praeceptis ac decretis datur

[10] ". . . monentur omnes et singuli [partriarchae, primates, metropolitani, et episcopi] ad quos visitatio spectat, ut paterna charitate Christianoque zelo omnes amplectantur . . ."—Council of Trent, sess. XXIV, *de ref.*, c. 3. The older canonists were agreed that the visitor of religious should ordinarily proceed as a father, *e. g.*, Reiffenstuel, lib. V, tit. I, n. 153; Gaudentius, *De Visitatione*, dub. XIV, n. 30; De Peyrinis, *Religiosus subditus et Praelatus*, tom. I, qu. I, cap. 16.

[8] Coronata, *Institutiones Iuris Canonici*, I, 648.

[9] Larraona, "Commentarium Codicis," *CpR*, IX (1928), 23-25.

Episcopus ad normam iuris procedat necesse est."

clearly they must act as fathers rather than judges,[12] though it is not forbidden that a visitor endowed with the requisite jurisdiction proceed according to a strictly judicial process if the need arises. In what follows on the visitor's right of inquiry and correction, the predominantly paternal character of visitation should be borne in mind.[13]

The Right of Questioning in General

The visitor has the right to interrogate all the religious and this includes not only the professed subjects, but also the superiors who fall under the visitor's authority, and further novices and postulants.[14] Even though he has full visitatorial rights in all matters, yet by common law the visitor is not obliged to interrogate each and every member of the community. He fulfills his duty when he questions those from whom he can elicit the information necessary or useful for the purposes of the visitation. In selecting those whom he will question, the visitor, in the absence of particular laws, is to be guided by his own prudent judgment. Not infrequently the constitutions will prescribe that all the members of the community must be questioned by the religious visitor. In any case it is advisable that the visitor should give all an opportunity to speak to him in private if they so desire. During the personal interviews the visitor's secretary or *socius* should not as a rule be present since the visitor is proceeding as a father to whom the religious of their own accord or in answer to his questions may, and at times must, communicate confidential information.[15]

Since the object of visitation is to secure the welfare of the

[12] Canon 513, § 2, indicates that to act judicially is the exception.

[13] While visitation is paternal it seeks to promote the common welfare and as a rule deals with the misconduct of an individual only in so far as his action is detrimental to the order and the good name of the community. *Cf.* Augustine, *Commentary,* III, 139; Gaudentius, *De Visitatione,* dub. proem. II, n. 4; Pejska, *Ius Canonicum Religiosorum,* p. 240.

[14] Novices and postulants are included because as members of the community they are subjects of the visitor. Larraona, "Commentarium Codicis" *CpR,* IX (1928), 25, note 516.

[15] Reiffenstuel, lib. V. tit. I, n. 293; Gaudentius, *De Visitatione,* dub. XIV, n. 42; Piat-Appeltern, *Compendium Iuris Regularis,* qu. 526; Coronata, *Institutiones Iuris Canonici,* I, 648.

community in all affairs or in regard to some point (*e.g.*, the observance of the enclosure), the visitor's questions should usually be of a type which will elicit information on matters as they touch the community as a whole. Therefore, if he has full visitatorial rights he will chiefly ask about (a) regular discipline, the observance of the vows, life in common, the care of the sick, the spirit of fraternal charity, attendance at choir and meditation, the holding of domestic meetings, conferences and the like; (b) the manner in which the superiors and officials fulfill their duties, the relations between the lectors and the students, the standard of studies; (c) temporal affairs, property, debts, method of bookkeeping, and especially Mass obligations, founded and manual.[16] The visitor may have reason to ask in detail about the faults and crimes of a particular individual, since at times it is only by directly correcting the misconduct of a certain member or members of the community that the good reputation of the religious house and a high standard of observance may be maintained.[17] Before asking others about the possible misdeeds of a particular member of the community, the visitor should have some reasonable basis for suspecting that member to be delinquent. The reason for this is sufficiently evident, for while a prudent visitor may easily inquire, for example, about the manner in which the officials of the community are discharging their duties or about the character of one who is being discussed as the possible appointee for some office, without exciting suspicions derogatory to the religious in question, he can hardly make the direct inquiries necessary to establish the guilt or innocence of a person suspected of crime without communicating the fact that the person is under suspicion.[18] Hence, when there are grounds for

[16] Augustine, *Commentary,* III, 138.

[17] Accordingly, even in paternal proceedings, the canonists distinguish between the *inquisitio generalis* (a general investigation in the life and observance of the community, not necessarily made with any suspicion of wrongdoing), the *inquisitio specialis* (an inquiry into the specific misdeeds of a particular individual, undertaken because the visitor has cause for suspecting the individual in question), and the *inquisitio mixta* (an inquiry about a specific crime but not in regard to a particular individual or vice versa). *Cf.* Wernz-Vidal, *Ius Canonicum,* VI, n. 718; Reiffenstuel, lib. V, tit. I, nn. 150-152.

[18] The authors who treat of special paternal inquisition are somewhat at

suspicion and it seems necessary for the welfare of the community or a third person to ascertain whether or not a certain religious is guilty, an inquiry should be conducted, but with secrecy and great caution, for the good name of the religious must not be unnecessarily jeopardized. Those who are asked about such matters are bound to preserve strict secrecy, though it is not necessary that they be put under oath in a paternal inquiry.[19]

The Obligation of Those Visited to Cooperate

Corresponding to the visitor's right of questioning the religious and of knowing about the affairs which relate to the visitation is the duty of the religious to answer truthfully. The visitor's questions must be legitimate, that is to say, they must be on matters over which the visitor has canonical authority *(de iis quae ad visitationem spectant)* [20] and secondly, they must not deal with affairs which a religious by natural or positive law is obliged or entitled to keep from the knowledge of the superiors. To legitimate questions a religious may not return an evasive, ambiguous, or false answer, nor may he remain silent. The constitution or the visitor (provided he has the requisite authority) may confirm this duty by a formal precept, by the vow of obedience, or by the threat of penalties upon those who refuse to reply or who reply untruthfully.

The canon imposes the duty of merely replying to questions. It is not unreasonable for the constitutions to go beyond the canon to demand that a religious even without questioning reveal certain abuses or matters connected with the government of the community, which, it is thought, will be useful or necessary for the visitor to know. The Code, of course, leaves intact the obligation of the natural law whereby a religious, upon his own initiative, may be bound to inform the visitor of disorders or crimes in order to avoid

variance. *Cf.* Reiffenstuel, lib. V, tit. I, nn. 288-290; Gaudentius, *De Visitatione,* dub. proem. II, nn. 12-14, dub. XIV, nn. 48-50; De Peyrinis, *Religiosus subditus et Praelatus,* tom. I, qu. I, cap. 16.

[19] For the special inquisition made in a paternal manner, Canons 1939, § 1; 1942, 1943 may be applied not strictly but as norms *mutatis mutandis.*

[20] Canon 513, § 1.

scandal or to eliminate danger to the community or its particular members.[21] On the other hand, the law of fraternal charity is not suspended during the time of visitation and must be taken into consideration both in answering questions and in volunteering information.

Even in the absence of positive legislation, it is clear that it would be illicit for subjects or superiors to hinder the visitor in the performance of his duties. However, the Code in Canon 513, § 1, has emphasized the unlawfulness of interference on the part of superiors by stating that it is not right for superiors to deter the religious from answering questions truthfully or to hinder in other ways the scope of visitation. The language of the canon is comprehensive. Both major and minor superiors are included in this prohibition. Commands, threats, counsels from the superior personally or through the agency of others, and all the many possible ways by which a religious might be induced to transgress his obligation of answering the visitor according to the truth, are wrongful acts. Further, it is unlawful for superiors to put obstacles in the way of attaining other purposes of the visitation. Thus, to send a religious away, to destroy documents, to hide things, to falsify accounts and the like constitute infringements upon visitatorial rights and are in violation of the canon. It is evident that what is prohibited to superiors is *a fortiori* illicit for subjects.[22] It may be noted that it is within the power of the visitor to punish interference with his rights, although the interference is not of the type for which the Code in Canon 2413 demands the infliction of penalties.[23]

The Right of Questioning in Particular

Since the personal interviews are perhaps the most important part of visitation and since the statements given above are not sufficiently detailed to determine precisely the legitimacy of certain types of questions and the extent of a subject's right or duty to

[21] Larraona, "Commentarium Codicis," *CpR,* IX (1928), 27.

[22] Canon 2413 explicitly mentions interference by subjects as well as by superiors. *Cf.* Larraona, "Commentarium Codicis," *CpR,* IX (1928), 30.

[23] Larraona, *loc. cit.*

furnish voluntary information, it may be profitable to take up particular points.

I. First of all a few words must be said on cases which pertain to the Holy Office. Canon 501, § 2, strictly forbids all religious superiors to interfere with such cases.[24] A decree of the Holy Office on May 15, 1901, was more explicit. By this decree regular superiors were forbidden, in cases which come under the competency of the Holy Office, to conduct an inquiry, to receive denunciations, to examine witnesses or the accused, to institute a trial, to pass a sentence, and in any way or under any pretext to handle such cases. But if they know of any members of their institute who were guilty or suspected [25] of such crimes (particularly those which concern the abuse of the Sacrament of Penance) they should without delay, or without communicating with anyone, or without administering a fraternal correction, denounce them to the Holy Office or the local ordinary.[26] The more summary of statement of Canon 501, § 2 (which includes all religious superiors) is to be understood in the light of the above decree. Hence no religious visitor may question or punish any religious, nor in any way interfere when there is a case which comes under the jurisdiction of the Holy Office. If the religious visitor has information which proves or creates a reasonable suspicion that a religious has been guilty of some such crime, his sole duty is to make a denunciation to the local ordinary or the Holy Office.

[24] Canon 501, § 2. "Superioribus quibuslibet districte prohibetur quominus in causis ad S. Officium spectantibus se intromittant." In general, cases which come under the Holy Office are those which are directly or indirectly concerned with faith (*cf.* Canon 247, § 1). Such are the following: (a) the crime of heresy (*cf.* Canon 2314, § 2) and other crimes which render one suspected of heresy (*cf.* Canons 2306, 2319, § 2; 2320, 2332, 2340, § 1; 2371); (b) the crime of solicitation (*cf.* Canons 904, 2368), certain violations of the seal of confession (*cf.* Coronata, *Institutiones Iuris Canonici,* I, 628), refusal of absolution unless the name of the accomplice be revealed (*cf.* Coronata, *loc. cit.*, Augustine, *Commentary,* III, 110); (c) the crime of becoming a member, if a cleric or a religious, of a Masonic sect or a similar society (*cf.* Canon 2336, § 2).

[25] Coronata (*Institutiones Iuris Canonici,* I, 628) and Augustine (*Commentary,* III, 111) indicate that there must be good grounds for the suspicion; mere gossip or rumor would not justify a denunciation.

[26] *Fontes,* n. 1254.

II. Questions concerning the religious himself which require answers that involve a partial or complete manifestation of conscience must not be asked. By Canon 530, § 1, all religious superiors are strictly forbidden to induce their subjects in any way whatever to make a manifestation of conscience to them. Therefore religious visitors must not inquire about the internal sins, virtues, temptations, and other spiritual difficulties of those over whom they have authority; such questions if asked need not be answered.[27] Episcopal and apostolic visitors, though superiors of religious, are not religious superiors and hence are not directly bound by Canon 530. Nevertheless, to assert that such visitors may inquire into matters of conscience would be to affirm a right of which there is no mention in the Code and which would be opposed to the whole spirit of ecclesiastical law, for the Church wishes to give religious full liberty in the choice of their spiritual directors and to separate clearly the external from the internal forum. It can hardly be admitted in the absence of positive statement in the common law that external visitors enjoy rights so broad as to be able to force religious to manifest the intimate workings of their souls. All visitors may indeed receive voluntary confidences made by a subject in regard to his own spiritual state, but they should confine their questions to the externals of religious discipline.[28]

III. With regard to questions concerning the faults and crimes of others, several observations are in order. First of all, it is to be noted that a visitor possessing judicial power may put such inquiries either for the sake of paternally correcting abuses or with the intent of instituting a criminal process. If the latter purpose is sought and the inquiries are made in order to obtain a judicial denunciation [29] or are part of the special inquisition preliminary to the criminal trial,[30] the prescriptions of the Code must be carefully com-

[27] Constitutions commanding a manifestation of conscience have no juridical force. *Cf.* Canon 489; Schäfer, *De Religiosis,* p. 227.

[28] Jombart, "Visite des monastères et ouverture de conscience," *NRT,* LI (1924), 624, 625.

[29] *Cf.* Canons 1935, 1936.

[30] *Cf.* Canons 1939-1946.

plied with.[31] However, such cases are exceptional. Unless the contrary is stated, the visitor's questions on the misdeeds of other religious or his command to denounce them are to be understood as coming from the visitor in his character of a father.[32] To reveal the faults or crimes of another to a superior in his quality of father constitutes a paternal denunciation. When such questions are asked, it is recognized by canonists that the obligation to manifest the truth does not extend to all cases of misconduct.[33] The visitor should explain to those unacquainted with canon law or moral theology the limits within which his command must be understood,

[31] In the actual trial, a religious who is to be questioned as a witness must first be cited (Canon 1765) and all the pertinent canons observed.

[32] Piat-Appeltern, *Compendium Iuris Regularis,* qu. 525; Gaudentius, *De Visitatione,* dub. XIV, n. 37.

[33] While this is acknowledged by all canonists, there is considerable difference of opinion on the extent and limitations of the duty of paternal denunciation. The differences, it appears, are due chiefly to the equivocal use of the word *paternal.* One source of confusion is the fact that denunciations are divided by most authors into judicial and paternal, while some add a third species, *viz.,* canonical (*e. g.,* Vermeersch-Creusen, *Epitome,* III, n. 259; Noval, *De Processibus,* n. 763). According to these latter, paternal denunciation is made to the superior as a father for the spiritual benefit of the delinquent alone and canonical is made to the superior as the moderator of the community that he may provide for its welfare. Yet, it has been noted that the visitor, though proceeding as a father (*paterna forma*—Canon 345), is concerned primarily with the common good. Hence his command to reveal the faults of others is for that end. The denunciation may properly be termed paternal but it is made to the visitor, not as a private individual, but in his official capacity. The confusion immanent in the word *paternal* also appears in discussions of dominative power. It is agreed that superiors with merely dominative power have authority only in what Vermeersch-Creusen (*loc. cit.*) term the "paternal forum," yet their authority is for the purpose of governing. The canonists who distinguish three types of denunciations consistently state that these superiors may receive canonical as well as paternal denunciations (*cf.* Vermeersch-Creusen, *Epitome,* I, n. 574), whereupon they may act only *paternally,* yet in the one case for the common good, in the other for the sole good of the delinquent. There is no need to pursue the matter further. It suffices here simply to state that commands or questions which necessitate an extra-judicial denunciation are sought by the visitor principally for the common good and hence should not include the cases to be subsequently enumerated.

lest he lead the religious to reveal things which, by the natural law, should be kept secret.[34] It may be well to set down here the limitations to be observed:

A. Ordinarily a denunciation must not be made unless a fraternal correction has first been given in private to the delinquent confrère.[35] The fraternal correction may be omitted when it is clear that no benefit may be hoped from it or that the welfare of the community or a third party cannot be safeguarded without the intervention of the visitor. These exceptions are not easily presumed, since the right of a religious to his good name with the superiors should not be esteemed lightly.[36]

B. The precept does not oblige a religious to manifest the occult faults or crimes of another unless such action is necessary to avert grave harm from the community or a third person.[37] If an occult crime that should not have been revealed actually is revealed to the visitor he may use this knowledge to correct the delinquent secretly.[38]

C. If a religious has already made amends or if he committed the offense a long time ago, there is no obligation to inform the

[34] Gaudentius, *De Visitatione,* dub. XIV, n. 38; Piat-Appeltern, *Compendium Iuris Regularis,* qu. 525; De Peyrinis, *Religiosus subditus et Praelatus,* Formularium P, cap. 9, n. 8.

[35] Matt. XVIII, 15.

[36] Piat-Appeltern, *Compendium Iuris Regularis,* qu. 525; Gaudentius, *De Visitatione,* dub. XIV, n. 62, 66; De Peyrinis, *Religiosus subditus et Praelatus,* tom. I, qu. I, cap. 16; St. Alphonsus Liguori, *Theologia Moralis,* lib. IV, cap. I, n. 57—who however adds: "longe communior et longe probilior sententia docet, bene posse denuntiare crimen occultum praelato prudenti tamquam patri, nulla praemissa correctione, si speretur sic melius emendatio fratris obtineri."—*Ibid.,* n. 243. In certain institutes (*e. g.,* the Society of Jesus), the members have renounced their right to a fraternal correction previous to being denounced and moreover the constitutions often add the obligation of revealing certain faults without awaiting questions from the visitor. Leurenius, lib. V, tit. I, qu. 23, n. 3; Larraona, "Commentarium Codicis," *CpR,* IX (1928), 27, n. 523.

[37] Piat-Appeltern, *op. cit.,* qu. 525; Augustine, *Commentary,* III, 139; De Peyrinis, *op. cit.,* Formularium P, cap. 9, n. 16; St. Alphonsus, *op. cit.,* lib. IV, cap. I, n. 57; Gaudentius, *op. cit.,* dub. XIV, nn. 49-56. Of the opposite opinion, Reiffenstuel, lib. V, tit. I, n. 296; Leurenius, lib. V, tit. I, qu. 24.

[38] Gaudentius, *op. cit.,* dub. XIV, n. 56.

visitor.[39] An exception to this rule should be made if a religious be in danger of relapsing into the same fault and if his previous fall was never known to a superior.[40]

D. Likewise the visitor should not be told of a fault committed once through weakness or because of some unusual occasion of sin, for the delinquent may be presumed to have already corrected himself.[41]

E. When it is known that others have already denounced the crime, it is not necessary to mention the matter to the visitor, unless it is clear that the latter seeks a confirmation of the knowledge he has received.[42]

F. If no remedy lies within the power of the visitor, a denunciation need not be made since no one is bound to a useless act. However, a subject should not readily assume that the visitor can provide no remedy, for, though the latter may be unable to take effective measures against the delinquent or in regard to the crime itself, he may yet be able to safeguard the welfare of the community.[43]

G. When a religious has knowledge of a crime derived from the fact that the delinquent had sought counsel from the aforesaid religious in his capacity of theologian, canonist, or spiritual director, the knowledge must not be revealed as it is a professional secret.[44]

H. When the fault or crime has already been denounced to the local superior (or provincial) the affair may not be reported to the visitor, unless the superior already informed is incapable of taking

[39] Piat-Appeltern, *op. cit.*, qu. 525; Gaudentius, *op. cit.*, dub. XIV, n. 63; St. Alphonsus Liguori, *op. cit.*, lib. IV, cap. I, n. 57; Leurenius, *op. cit.*, lib. V, tit. I, qu. 32, n. 2; Rodriquez, *Quaestiones Regulares*, tom. II, qu. 6, art. 2.

[40] Piat-Appeltern, *op. cit.*, qu. 525; St. Alphonsus, *op. cit.*, lib. IV, n. 244.

[41] *Cf.* Piat-Appeltern, *op. cit.*, qu. 525.

[42] *Cf.* Piat-Appeltern, *op. cit.*, qu. 525; St. Alphonsus Liguori, *op. cit.*, lib. IV, cap. I, n. 57.

[43] Piat-Appeltern, *op. cit.*, qu. 525; St. Alphonsus Liguori, *op. cit.*, lib. IV, cap. I, n. 57; Larraona, "Commentarium Codicis," *CpR*, IX (1928), 29, n. 527.

[44] *Cf.* Piat-Appeltern, *op. cit.*, qu. 525; Leurenius, lib. V, tit. I, qu. 38, n. 8.

effective action.[45] Even in the latter circumstance it seems that a subject may remain silent and leave it to the local superior to refer the matter to a higher authority capable of coping with the case.

I. The religious must know with certainty or have solid reasons for believing in the guilt of his confrère from the statements of usually reliable persons. Rumor or gossip is not a sufficient basis for a denunciation.[46]

With the exception of these cases all other faults and crimes must be denounced in response to the questions or commands of the visitor even though they cannot be proved.

The Use of the Information Received

In connection with this matter, a few words should be added upon the action of the visitor subsequent to receiving information of misconduct through paternal denunciations. It is impossible to set down rigid rules, since paternal procedure is touched only incidentally and obscurely in the Code and since of its nature it is a manner of acting dependent to a great extent upon equity, charity, and the discretion of the visitor. Yet an attempt may be made to sketch in broad outline the way the visitor should proceed.[47]

In the first place, the visitor should form his judgment prudently upon the matters reported, weighing well both the disposition of the ones who revealed the misdeeds and also what he may know from other sources of the character of the accused. The ac-

[45] Piat, *Praelectionis Iuris Regularis,* I, qu. 877, n. 7; Gaudentius, *op. cit.,* dub. XIV, n. 75.

[46] Leurenius, lib. V, tit. I, qu. 32, n. 2; Rodriquez, *op. cit.,* tom. II, qu. 6, art. 7; Gaudentius, *op. cit.,* dub. XIV, n. 75. Piat maintains that what is known only by hearsay is not to be revealed, unless on account of the gravity of the affair the visitor expressly includes such knowledge, *op. cit.,* qu. I, 877, n. 5; *cf.* Augustine, *op. cit.,* III, 140.

[47] The procedure is based upon the following general considerations. The visitor has received the denunciations principally for the general welfare. In harmony with the clemency and charity of paternal procedure, he should seek that end by effecting the amendment of the delinquent through mild and secret measures. When these would obviously be inadequate to attain the purpose or when they have been tried without success, the visitor may avail himself of other measures more severe, even to the full extent of his power. *Cf.* Noval, "De Ratione Corrigendi," *JP,* II (1921), 148, 149; III (1922), 36, 37, 206-210.

cused is, of course, entitled by natural law to be heard in his own defense. When the visitor, having granted a fair and patient hearing, finds that it is necessary to take action against an individual he should, recalling the paternal character of his office, act with all possible mildness. Yet he may correct not only those who are guilty of canonical crimes (Canon 2195, § 1) but also those who are culpable of infractions of the rule, particularly if those infractions are so frequent or of such a serious nature that they endanger the internal order of the house or the good reputation of the community with seculars. Unless the visitor learns that the misconduct is public (in the sense of Canon 2197, 1°), he should keep secret the information received and, in so far as it is compatible with the common good, take no action which will betray the identity of the accusers or impair the reputation of the accused. It is not a violation of secrecy for the visitor to consult with one or two others who, in the circumstances of the case, may be better qualified to decide upon the proper course to be pursued. When possible the visitor should reveal neither the name of the accuser nor of the culprit to those consulted; in any case the latter are bound to secrecy.[48] Certain religious visitors are forbidden by the constitutions to correct individual members of the community, but are to see that the corrections are made by the local superior. Whenever the visitor's power is thus restricted it appears that even information derived from paternal denunciations may be communicated to the local superior in order that the latter while preserving secrecy may take the proper measures.

If the denunciations merely establish the fact that a religious has been conducting himself in a gravely suspicious manner or that he is in proximate occasion of committing an offense, the visitor should confine himself to private admonitions.[49] Circumstances may also render it advisable, even when it is not certain that any fault or crime has been committed, to prohibit a religious from frequenting certain places or associating with certain persons of a dubious character. When a fault or crime is morally certain the

[48] Piat, *Praelectiones Iuris Regularis,* I, qu. 878; Reiffenstuel, lib. V, tit. I, n. 301.

[49] *Cf.* Canon 2307.

visitor may impose penances and administer a rebuke (*correptio*) adapted to the gravity of the misdemeanor and the condition of the person.[50] These methods of correction should first be of a private nature, if there is hope that these will be sufficient.[51] Yet a memorandum of the fact that admonitions and rebukes were administered should be made and preserved in some secret place.[52] When further action seems expedient, the visitor may in the presence of two witnesses (or a notary or by registered letter) admonish and rebuke a religious whose delinquency has been confessed or proved (even extra-judicially) by the statement of two trustworthy persons. The witnesses to such an admonition and rebuke should keep the matter secret unless later called on to testify that such measures were used.[53] When it appears that such remedies will be insufficient to achieve the desired effect, or when they have been tried (*e. g.*, by the local superior) without success, then a precept should be given telling the individual precisely what he must do or what he must avoid under the threat of punishment for transgression of the precept.[54] In grave cases, particularly when the delinquent is in danger of relapsing into the same offense, the visitor may charge a prudent religious, under secrecy, to watch over the actions of the delinquent.[55] The visitor frequently will have other methods at his disposal which are not in themselves of a penal character, but

[50] *Cf.* Canons 2308; 2313, § 2.

[51] Public penances presuppose a public crime or transgression (Canon 2312, § 2).

[52] *Cf.* Canon 2309, § 5.

[53] An admonition or rebuke administered in this way is termed public (Canon 2309, § 2). The word *public* evidently is not used in the sense of Canon 2197, 1°, but rather in the sense of Canon 1037, *viz.*, that which can be proved in the external forum. A public admonition or rebuke may be given for an occult crime as the only prerequisite is that the guilt be (at least extra-judicially) confessed or proved by the testimony of two witnesses. *Cf.* Canon 2309, § 3; Noval, "De Ratione Corrigendi," *JP*, III (1922), 207.

[54] *Cf.* Canon 2310. Visitors with only dominative powers cannot impose a precept with the threat of canonical penalties; the vicar general and delegated visitors of ordinaries may do so only if they have received the power in a special mandate or by delegated faculties. *Cf.* Canon 2220, § 2; Augustine, *Commentary*, VIII, 269.

[55] *Cf.* Canon 2311.

which may serve effectually to correct the delinquent and preserve the common good. Thus, for example, the visitor may be able to remove the religious from the occasion of sin by transferring him to some other house or by depriving him of an office which he holds *ad nutum,* though in these and similar actions plausible reasons should be advanced in order not to injure the delinquent's good name.[56]

No action in the procedure outlined above exceeds the limits of paternal correction and all the steps are within the authority of any visitor whose corrective powers are not restricted by particular law.[57] Visitors who are ordinaries must in the use of penal remedies and penances follow the letter of the Code strictly.[58] Visitors with only dominative power may impose penal remedies and penances *ad instar legis:* [59] they should take the pertinent canons as norms and not proceed in a harsher manner on the plea that their actions have effect only in the "paternal forum."

There is considerable diversity of opinion on the question whether a visitor may proceed to inflict more severe punishments when all

[56] Similarly visitors, including even those with only dominative power, may avail themselves of the powers of Canon 595, § 3 and Canon 2222, § 2, when the circumstances are verified. Noval, "De Ratione Corrigendi," *JP,* III (1922), 210.

[57] Reiffenstuel (lib. V, tit. I, n. 303), after setting forth a procedure very similar, adds: " . . . quod omnia non excedant limites correctionis paternae et potestatem superioris tanquam in filios; cum haec omnia non vindictam publicam, sed meram emendationem deliquentis, consequenter munus paternum sapiant . . . " *Cf.* De Peyrinis, *Religiosus subditus et Praelatus,* tom. I, qu. I, cap. 16; Leurenius, lib. V, tit. I, nn. 24-27; Piat, *Praelectiones Iuris Regularis,* II, qu. 508.

[58] Canons 2306-2313. The different uses of the word *paternal* may also be a source of confusion in this matter. *Paternal* and *canonical* are not necessarily mutually exclusive terms. *Cf.* Canons 2158, 2193; S. C. Ep. et Reg., instr. 11 Iun. 1880, n. 6—*Fontes* n. 2005. It is evident that *paternal* is used broadly in Canon 345 and thus it appears proper to speak of *paternal* correction as embracing any use of penal remedies or penances, even though when inflicted by ordinaries they are canonical acts.

[59] *Cf.* Schäfer, *De Religiosis.* p. 129; Pejska, *Ius Canonicum Religiosorum,* p. 242

methods of paternal correction, tried by himself or other superiors, have failed.[60] It does not seem incompatible with the character of visitation to turn to more rigorous measures when milder action has been tried without success. However, in cases of light offenses which cause little or no disturbance or scandal a repeated application of the forms of paternal correction will generally be the best or only course. But when the common good is jeopardized by the continued misconduct of a religious, the visitor is bound to exercise the fullness of his authority.[61] Accordingly religious visitors with only dominative power who have exhausted their means of correction and still find a religious incorrigible and a cause of disturbance or scandal should refer the case to a higher superior whose more ample powers may effect either the amendment or the dismissal of the delinquent. Visitors with the power of inflicting penalties[62] may safeguard the general welfare or avert harm from a third person by using their coercive power extra-judicially according to the prescriptions of the Code.[63] When a crime (in the sense of Canon 2195) is public a judicial process may be instituted by visitors who have the requisite authority.[64] A paternal denunciation cannot be adduced as a judicial denunciation. Consequently it cannot be made the basis for a special judicial inquiry, but the visitor may command the religious who revealed the crime in the paternal inquiry to make a judicial denunciation.[65] In the course of the trial which may result the one who has made the judicial denunciation may be summoned and compelled to testify.[66]

[60] *Cf.* Piat, *Praelectiones Iuris Regularis,* I, qu. 879.

[61] *Cf.* Gaudentius, *De Visitatione,* dub. XV. nn. 58-60, 76; De Peyrinis, *Religiosus subditus et Praelatus,* tom. I, qu. I, cap. 16.

[62] *Cf.* Canon 2220.

[63] *Cf.* Canon 1933, § 4.

[64] *Cf.* Canon 1933, § 1.

[65] Canon 1935, § 2. "Imo obligatio denuntiationis urget quotiescumque ad id adigitur . . . peculiari legitimo praecepto . . . " *Cf.* Vermeersch-Creusen, *Epitome,* III, n. 261, 3°; Schäfer, *De Religiosis,* p. 466; Fanfani, *De Iure Religiosorum,* p. 92.

[66] Piat, *Praelectiones Iuris Regularis,* I, qu. 880; Gaudentius, *De Visitatione,* dub. XV, nn. 75-78.

The Decrees of the Visitor

Canon 513, § 2, implies that visitors are as a rule empowered to draw up decrees after they have completed their investigation and gathered whatever information might prove of value. Under the term "decrees" must be included not only the statutes and regulations which bind the entire house (or province), but also the precepts and corrections and decisions of the visitor which relate even to a single individual.[67]

Enough has been said on the visitor's corrections of individual members of the community. On the power of issuing decrees which bind the entire house (or province) very little need be stated in general, since this power varies widely with the authority of different visitors. Visitors acting as delegates and even certain religious visitors acting in their own name may be able of themselves to decide then and there only such matters as require immediate action and for the rest submit recommendations, which do not take effect until ratified by the competent authorities. Again, certain religious visitors are obliged to confine themselves to advising the superior of the abuses discovered and may act only when the latter has proved himself culpably negligent.[68]

By common law the visitor is not bound to put his decrees in writing. However, it is advisable that a record be kept so that the visitor, if he has authority outside of the time of the visitation, may see that his commands are executed or, if he has authority only during the time of the visitation, that the higher superiors and the next visitor may assure themselves on this point.[69] For this purpose

[67] *Cf.* Canon 345.

[68] The same restriction is placed on the local ordinary in his visitation of congregations of pontifical right (*cf. supra*, pp. 99, 113).

[69] In reference to the importance of seeing that the decrees are carried out the words of Benedict XIV on the general diocesan visitation are pertinent: "Sed neque etiam satis est lustrari a vobis dioeceses, et opportunis praeceptionibus vestris curationi earum esse prospectum: restat et illud enixe perficiendum a vobis, ut quae in visitationibus constituta fuerunt, vere in effectum perducantur; nam legum etsi optimarum utilitas nulla erit, nisi quod sancitum verbis est, reipsa ab eis, ad quos pertinet, studiose praestetur."—Encycl. *Ubi Primum,* 3 Dec. 1740, § 5—*Fontes,* n. 304. The vicar forane has the right and duty of seeing that in the parishes within his territory the visitatorial decrees of the bishop are put into execution (Canon 447, § 1, 2°).

it is advisable and, in some religious institutes, obligatory that a book of visitations be preserved containing whatever the visitor thinks should be noted on the spiritual and economic status of the community and the decrees which he has issued. The misdeeds of individuals and the corrections or penalties which the visitor has applied should not be entered. If the visitor believes it necessary he should keep a secret record of these.[70] If judicial proceedings have been held the *acta* are to be preserved as prescribed in Canon 1645, § 2.

Since the purpose of visitation is to remove abuses and effect a better observance of ecclesiastical law and of the religious constitutions, the decrees should be chiefly for the purpose of determining ways and means to attain these goals or simply for the purpose of emphasizing obligations already existing. The visitor should be careful not to exceed his powers by issuing decrees contrary to canon law and the constitutions or by adding obligations *praeter legem.* The local ordinary is to be guided by his own prudent judgment in determining the manner in which the visitatorial decrees shall be promulgated and the length of time during which they shall remain in force. In the absence of specific provisions in the constitutions religious visitors, taking into account the limits of their authority,[71] are also at liberty to decide these matters as they think best.

The second paragraph of Canon 513 permits only recourse *in devolutivo* from the visitor's paternal or administrative decrees, Therefore the general principle of recourse *in devolutivo* holds: *Pareant et deinde recurrant.*[72] The decree is binding and must be obeyed until upon recourse it is modified or abrogated by the proper authority. Canon 513, § 2, in stating this principle excludes explicitly only cases in which the visitor has proceeded judicially. Yet in whatever cases the Code permits recourse *in suspensivo* against a decree or penalty, such recourse suspends the decree or penalty

[70] *Cf.* Gaudentius, *De Visitatione,* dub. VIII, n. 8. When the ordinary has given a secret admonition or rebuke a memorandum is to be made and kept in the secret archives (Canon 2309, § 5). It is a sound norm for other visitors.

[71] A provincial or even a general visitor, for example, may be able to pass regulations which will remain in force at the longest only until the convocation of the next chapter, by which they will be either ratified or repealed.

[72] Piat, *Praelectiones Iuris Regularis,* II, qu. 617.

even though the decree was issued or the penalty inflicted during visitation. Thus even if the visitor proceeding extra-judicially inflicts a vindictive penalty, recourse, taken within the proper time, will suspend the penalty in accordance with Canon 2287.[73] Likewise recourse against the decree of dismissal issued by a visitor (with the requisite authority) against a religious with temporary vows in any institute [74] or against a religious with perpetual vows in a diocesan institute [75] suspends the execution of the decree, except in a case where a serious scandal has caused the visitor to dismiss the religious in the extraordinary manner provided for in Canon 653.

When the visitor has proceeded judicially, appeals suspending the decrees are also admitted. Canon 513, § 2, does not mean to imply that such appeals are necessarily suspensive. All the judicial acts of the visitor are governed by the general laws on judicial processes. From a judicial sentence of the visitor the appeal will generally be suspensive [76] but there are important exceptions.[77]

The Procuration

By the term "procuration," as has been seen, is understood the food and lodging and sometimes also the traveling expenses which are given to the visitor and his party during the time of visitation.[78] In connection with the visitation of religious the Code makes no mention of the obligation of providing the procuration, but in the section on the general diocesan visitation Canon 346 deals with this matter and several related points.[79] This canon speaks only of

[73] Coronata, *Institutiones Iuris Canonici,* I, 468.

[74] Canon 647, § 2, 4°.

[75] *Cf.* Canon 650, § 1; Larraona, "De dimissione Religiosorum," *CpR,* XIV (1932), 55.

[76] Canon 1889, § 2.

[77] *Cf.* Canons 1917, § 2, 2243.

[78] *Cf.* Gaudentius, *De Visitatione,* dub. proem. VI, n. 1; Ferraris, "Procuratio," n. 1.

[79] Canon 346: "Studeant Episcopi debita cum diligentia, sine inutilibus tamen moris, pastoralem visitationem absolvere: caveant, ne superfluis sumptibus cuiquam graves onerosive sint, neve ratione visitationis ipsi aut quisquam suorum pro se suisve dona quodvis genus petant aut accipiant, reprobata quavis contraria consuetudine; circa vero victualia sibi suisque ministranda vel procurationes et expensas itineris, servetur legitima locorum consuetudo."

bishops, yet, since there is no law covering these questions for other local ordinaries, Canon 346 should be taken as a norm by the latter.[80] After stating that the bishops should carry out their pastoral visitation with proper diligence and yet without useless delays, the canon warns the visiting bishops not to make themselves burdensome to anyone by superfluous expenses. This might be done by bringing along a large number of companions or by demanding luxuries in food or drink. The Council of Trent, from which this canon is largely drawn, urged the visiting prelate to seek no more than a frugal fare and to be content with a modest train of servants and horses.[81] Since the time of the Council of Trent the Holy See has repeatedly refused to define the exact number that may accompany the bishop.[82] The Code, while granting the bishop the right to select as assistants any two clerics he desires,[83] does not forbid him to bring others along in the party. Accordingly it seems impossible to say anything more definite than that the bishop may take with him on visitation that limited number of assistants and servants which in his judgment appear to be necessary or useful.

The present law renews the old prohibition against accepting gifts, which was intended to prevent the visitation from being used as an occasion for exactions or as a source of revenue. The text of the canon is broad: neither the bishops nor any of their attendants may seek or, even if offered voluntarily, accept gifts of any kind whatever by reason of the visitation. All contrary customs are reprobated. Today this is a simple prohibition and the obligation to restore the value or double the value of the gifts received and the other canonical penalties of the old law[84] are no longer in force. However, the phrase *by reason of visitation* (*ratione visitationis*) should not be so restricted as to permit the seeking or acceptance of gifts on some other pretext.[85]

80 Canon 20.

81 Sess. XXIV, *de ref.*, c. 3.

82 *Cf.* Pallottini, "Episcopus," § 19, nn. 39, 40, 41, 50.

83 Canon 343, § 2.

84 *Cf. supra*, pp. 55, 57.

85 The canon, in this part, appears to be merely a restatement of the Council of Trent: " . . . nec munus, quodcumque sit, etiam qualitercumque of-

The last part of Canon 346 affirms that in regard to the expenses of the visitation the legitimate custom of the place is to be observed. A number of legitimate customs are possible. For example:

A. The visiting bishop may have the right merely to the *victualia* for himself and his party. The term *victualia* is understood to include food and lodging for the persons and formerly fodder and stabling for the horses.

B. The bishop may have the right to the *victualia* and traveling expenses.

C. The place visited may have the option to pay in money the equivalent of the expenditures that would be necessary for food and lodging.[86]

D. Besides paying this commutation fee the place visited may have the obligation of reimbursing the visitor for his traveling expenses.

E. The visiting bishop may have to bear all the expenses of the visitation.

Similarly it is custom which regulates the division of expenses when the bishop visits several places on one trip or one day. However, in the canon the word *vel (victualia . . . vel procurationes)* must be understood disjunctively and hence it would not be a legitimate custom to demand or receive food and lodging and also payment for the same.[87]

The old law did not permit any of the expenses of visitation to be laid upon small houses of regulars,[88] but as these houses are no longer subject to episcopal visitation, the question cannot arise to-

feratur, excipiant . . . " Sess. XXIV, *de ref.*, c. 3. *Cf.* Lardone, "Le Procurazioni nella Visita Pastorale," *Perfice Munus*, V (1930), 439, 440.

[86] In Canon 346 *procurationes* are distinguished from *victualia*. The former evidently means the pecuniary equivalent of the latter. *Cf.* Lardone, "Le Procurazioni nella Visita Pastorale," *Perfice Munus*, V (1930), 440. This use of the term *procuratio* was not unknown in the old law (*cf.* Lucidi, *De Visitatione*, I, cap. II, n. 53).

[87] Lardone, *op. cit.*, p. 440. The old law consistently denied the lawfulness of receiving both. *Cf.* Council of Trent, sess. XXIV, *de ref.*, c. 3; S. C. C. Marsicana (without date)—Lucidi, *De Visitatione*, I, cap. II, n. 53; S. C. C., S. Marci, 16 Ian. 1723, ad 2,—Ferraris, "Procuratio," n. 28.

[88] Ferraris, "Procuratio," n. 9.

day. Monasteries of nuns, the houses of lay institutes of simple vows, the churches of clerical congregations of pontifical right and the parishes entrusted to religious were never in the old law universally exempted from paying the expenses and each case is to be determined by custom, unless a special privilege of exemption from the procuration has been obtained.[89]

The Code is silent on the procurations to be given to religious visitors. While there will hardly be any question of their right to receive food and lodging during the actual time of visitation, the doubt may arise whether the traveling expenses are to be paid *pro rata* by each community that is visited, or whether these expenses will be drawn from some fund which is at the disposal of the provincial or general curia (or chapter). This point and likewise the number of companions which the religious visitor may take with him and the length of time he shall stay in each community are left to the determination of the constitutions and custom.

[89] *Cf.* Lucidi, *De Visitatione,* I, cap. II, nn. 48, 49, 56.

CHAPTER X

THE PENALTIES FOR INTERFERENCE WITH VISITATION

CANON 513, § 1, as has been seen, forbids superiors to obstruct the visitation by causing the religious to fail in their duty of answering the visitor truthfully or by infringing in any other manner upon the visitor's rights[1] As a further safeguard that visitation be not frustrated in its purpose the Code, in Canon 2413, provides penalties against certain obstructive acts.[2] Canon 2413 binds religious of both sexes in the same way. However, the legislator evidently deemed it advisable to frame this canon in a manner which emphasizes that religious women especially must refrain from actions which are inconsistent with, or detrimental to, the purposes of visitation.

The Visitor Who May Inflict the Penalties

The visitor spoken of in Canon 2413 may be either an external or an internal visitor. The former type includes both local ordinaries and delegated visitors of the Holy See. The internal visitor may be any major superior designated by the constitutions, whose visitation is made a canonical right and duty by virtue of Canon 511. That major superiors with only dominative power and also major superioresses are able to apply the penalties of this canon

[1] *Cf. supra*, p. 151.

[2] Canon 2413, § 1. "Antistitae quae post indictam visitationem religiosas in aliam domum, Visitatore non consentiente, transtulerint, itemque religiosae omnes, sive antistitae sive subditae, quae per se vel per alios, directe vel indirecte, religiosas induxerint ut interrogatae a Visitatore taceant vel veritatem quoque modo dissimulent aut non sincere exponant, vel eisdem, ob responsa quae Visitatori dederint, molestiam, sub quovis praetextu, attulerint, inhabiles ad officia assequenda, quae aliarum regimen secumferunt, a Visitatore declarentur et Antistitae officio quo funguntur, priventur.

§ 2. Quae in superiore paragrapho praescripta sunt, etiam virorum religionibus applicentur."

appears to be indisputable. The penalties which a religious may incur for interfering with the visitation are deposition from offices of the institute and a declaration of disability to hold office in the future. These penalties are strictly canonical and require jurisdiction for their infliction only when the delinquent is a member of an exempt clerical institute, for only within such religious institutes do offices in the strict sense exist.[3] The cases which would necessitate a religious visitor of a lay or non-exempt institute to apply these sanctions could only be offenses by a religious of the same institute, in which no offices in the strict sense can exist.[4] Major superiors with simply dominative power possess true governing authority and the right of control over the internal affairs of their institute. It certainly does not exceed the authority of these superiors to inflict such punishments as removal from office and a declaration of disability to hold offices within the institute when one of their subjects has committed offenses which according to their own particular laws or the canons of the Code, render such an action justifiable.[5]

The Offenses for Which the Penalties Are Incurred

The offenses for which the penalties are incurred (*ferendae sententiae*) are the following three:

1. Illicitly transferring a religious to another house.
2. Inducing a religious to equivocate or conceal the truth.
3. Molesting a religious for her answers to legitimate questions.

1. As the transfer of a religious can be effected only by superioresses and not by subjects, the former alone are mentioned in relation to this offense. To be liable to the penalties, the superioress must have made the transfer after the visitation has been announced. If no announcement has been made, but the superioress, aware that

[3] *Cf.* Canon 145.

[4] The first paragraph of Canon 2413 can only refer to offices in a broad sense.

[5] Augustine doubts that female visitors are included in this canon.—*Commentary*, VIII, 521. Yet since female visitors now have the same visitatorial powers as the male visitors of non-exempt or lay institutes, there is no basis for excluding them and Canon 490 should be applied.

a visitation will be held in the near future, sends a subject to another house, she does not incur the penalties.[6] Whether the transfer be a formal assignment to another house by a higher superioress or a temporary mission at the command of even the local superioress, makes no material difference.[7] Nor does it matter that the cause for the transfer is a purpose that at other times would be entirely reasonable and legitimate. After the announcement the right of superioresses to move their subjects is suspended, unless the consent of the visitor is obtained. Augustine speaks as though the transfer must be against the express will of the visitor.[8] But this appears to be an undue restriction of the law, for the case most liable to arise, if a superioress desired to prevent a religious from speaking to the visitor, would be a transfer effected, if possible, without the visitor's knowledge, in which circumstance it could not be against his express will. The phrase *visitatore non consentiente* must rather be interpreted to mean that the visitor must take affirmative action to approve of the transfer. However, if the visitor were notified of the necessity of an immediate transfer, it would be evidence of good faith and his consent could be reasonably presumed before his answer arrived.

2. The second offense is committed by either superiors or subjects who in any way, directly or indirectly, personally or through others induce religious, when questioned by the visitor, to remain silent or to answer untruthfully. The attempt to induce another religious to conceal the truth by silence or equivocation or falsehoods is not punishable by this canon if the attempt fails.[9] The religious interrogated must actually be led to violate her obligation to reply directly and truthfully. This also implies that the questions of the visitor must be legitimate, *i.e.*, on matters which fall within the scope of the visitation and according to the norms set forth in the preceding chapter.

[6] Smith, *The Penal Law for Religious,* p. 141.

[7] Blat, *Commentarium Textus Codicis Iuris Canonici* V *(De Delictis et Poenis)*, n. 259.

[8] *Commentary,* VIII, 518.

[9] Smith, *Penal Law for Religious,* p. 141.

3. The last offense consists in molesting a religious on account of the replies which she gave to the visitor. Both superioresses and subjects may be guilty of this offense. The term "molestation" is very broad: reproaches, annoyances, signs of displeasure, removal from active duty, and any other form of persecution, no matter what the pretext, would be embraced under this term. However, the cause of these actions must actually be the replies given to the visitor. Even if a religious has been lacking in charity and prudence in her answers, no form of molestation is justifiable. It is, of course, not forbidden for a religious, against whom false allegations have been made, to have recourse to the visitor or superioress, who may punish the one who has testified falsely.[10]

The penalties for these offenses are the same. Superioresses are to be deposed from office and superioresses and subjects are to be declared incapable of obtaining any office which bears with it the government of other religious. Such offices are those of supreme moderatrix, provincial or local superioress, prefect of religious students, or an assistant who succeeds to the government of the community in the absence of the superioress.

It is evident from the text that deposition from office is a penalty *ferendae sententiae*; despite the word *declarentur,* it is sufficiently clear that the penalty of disability to obtain office is of the same nature.[11] The visitor, when the offense is certain, is ordinarily obliged by the preceptive words of the canon to inflict the penalties. Yet, it is left to his conscience and prudence to defer the application of the penalties to avoid greater evils, or to moderate them if circumstances notably diminish the imputability of the offense, or even to refrain from punishment if the delinquent has entirely amended and repaired the scandal.[12] The penalties may be imposed extra-judicially by a particular decree.

[10] Smith, *Penal Law for Religious,* p. 142.

[11] *Cf.* Canon 2217, § 2. As Larraona points out, it is certain that the word *declarentur* refers to penalties *ferendae sententiae* in several other canons (*e.g.,* in Canons 2314, § 1, 2°; 2345; 2368, § 1).—"De Visitatorum potestate applicandi poenas in Can. 2413 statutas," *Cp.R,* X (1929), 369, note 3.

[12] Canon 2223, § 3.

The Subject of the Penalties

The chief difficulty of this canon is the question on whom the visitor may inflict the penalties. It is clear, as has been noted, that the canon refers to any and all types of canonical visitors. Do the terms superioress (and superior) and religious refer to any and all superioresses (and superiors) and religious, who interfere with the visitation in the several ways enumerated? For example, may the local ordinary depose the superioress general of a pontifical institute for making a transfer after his announced intention of visiting, or may he punish a religious of another diocese who molested a sister for the latter's answers to his questions during visitation? Similar questions arise in regard to other visitors. Larraona remarked some years ago that commentators had not treated this problem [13] and later proposed a solution.[14] The reasoning of Larraona is sound and results in conclusions which are not open to the grave objections which can be urged against other possible interpretations. The following is a condensed statement of his solution.

To inflict penalties, there is required not only a coercive power (proportionate to the penalties inflicted) but also a coercive power which is related to him who committed the crime and upon whom the penalty is to be inflicted. In some way the delinquent must be subject to the superior who imposes the penalty. The visitor accordingly may inflict the penalties of Canon 2413 on those who are his subjects—whether by reason of actual visitation or by some other reason—or upon those who become his subjects by reason of a crime committed in a place where he exercises authority, but not on those who are not in any way his subjects or who cannot become his subjects *ex delicto* (*e. g.*, because they dwell and act outside his territory or because they are independent of, or superiors of, the visitor). Thus, not only on the basis of actual visitation may one be the subject of a visitor, but also on the basis of the habitual visitatorial jurisdiction which a visitor has as a superior (*e. g.*, a provincial or general). A superior with habitual authority, even when not visiting in person, has the powers which are his as visitor; such

[13] "Commentarium Codicis," *CpR*, IX (1928), 31.

[14] "De Visitatorum potestate applicandi poenas in Can. 2413 statutas," *CpR*, X (1929), 368-377.

a superior may do personally whatever his delegated visitor may do. *Ex delicto* a person becomes a subject according to Canon 1566; this refers directly (in so far as it pertains to the matter under consideration) to cases in which the visitor proceeds judicially.

Applying this principle to concrete cases the following conclusions are reached:

1. An apostolic visitor of the whole institute can inflict the penalties of the canon on all superiors and subjects, even on the supreme moderator, though in the latter case, in practice, the visitor would hardly fail to get in touch with the Sacred Congregation of Religious. However it appears probable that the Sacred Congregation does as a rule restrict this faculty in giving the general mandate of visitation.

2. An apostolic visitor of a house or province is limited in the exercise of his powers to the superiors and subjects of that house or province, unless he has greater powers by special delegation; but that is not to be presumed and must be proved.

3. The same principle is applicable to internal visitors. The general visitor may inflict the penalties of Canon 2413 upon all alike, whether superiors or subjects of the institute; the provincial visitor, upon the superiors and subjects of his province; the visitor of one house, upon the superior and subjects of that house.[15]

After stating these conclusions, Larraona then proceeds to deal with the objections which may be brought against this interpretation. First of all it is objected, the text of the canon does not indicate any such restrictions. It simply states that interference in the ways mentioned renders a superior or subject liable to the specified penalties which are to be inflicted by the visitor. In other words, *ex delicto* any superior or subject becomes the subject of the visitor and may be punished. Moreover the text of the canon, which seems to affirm this without limitation, is apparently confirmed by the fact that the portion of the canon dealing with illicit transfer by a superioress *(antistita)*, cannot refer to a superioress in a monastery

[15] It may be added that any superior or subject within the territory of a particular local ordinary and subject to his visitation by virtue of Canon 512 is liable to the penalties of this canon.

of nuns and hardly to other local superioresses as the latter do not usually have the power of transferring religious.

However, to insist upon the literal text is to adopt an interpretation which (a) is unnecessary and (b) leads to contradictions of legal principles and (c) results in conclusions legally incongruous.

(a) It is unnecessary both because the canon has a sufficiently broad application in the conclusions outlined above and because it cannot be conclusively proved that the word *antistita* must embrace major superioresses in every case for the term *antistita* when used elsewhere in the Code without qualification more often refers simply to the local superioresses.

(b) It involves contradictions of clear and established principles of penal and procedural law, for a lower superior cannot judge or punish a higher superior.

(c) It would result in conclusions legally incongruous. Thus according to the literal interpretation a visitor deputed to visit one house could depose a provincial or general and punish religious who are in no way subject to the visitation; a delegated visitor could punish the superior who sent him if that superior made a transfer after the visitation had been announced. Further, any visitor in order that he might not act rashly could summon before himself any and every superior against whom there was evidence of violations of the canon and call upon them to show cause why the penalty should not be inflicted.

The sound legal basis of Larraona's solution is difficult to overthrow and it provides an interpretation which there is very reason to accept as correct. However, from one application of Larraona's view it seems necessary to dissent. He has maintained that major superiors of diocesan institutes, which are spread through several dioceses, are not subject to the visitation of the local ordinary within whose territory they reside. Accordingly he concludes that they cannot be subject to the penalties of Canon 2413 for interference with the local ordinary's visitation.[16] The reasons for holding with D'Ambrosio[17] that the local ordinary may visit any major

[16] "De Visitatorum potestate applicandi poenas in Can. 2413 statutas," *CpR*, X (1929), 373-377.

[17] "De Domo Generalitia Instituti Polydiocesani quoad Canonicam Visita-

superior of a diocesan institute whose residence is within his territory, have already been set forth at considerable length.[18] From this premise, as D'Ambrosio states, the conclusion is inescapable, that the local ordinary for interference with his visitation may inflict the penalties of Canon 2413 upon any major superior, even the supreme moderator of a diocesan institute whose residence is within his territory.

Cases in which impediments are placed in the way of visitation by those who are not subject to the powers which a visitor possesses by virtue of Canon 2413, may be dealt with in other ways. Thus a local ordinary could give a major superior of a non-exempt pontifical institute residing in his territory a precept under threat of penalties commanding him to refrain from any and all forms of interference with the local ordinary's visitation. Visitors who cannot eliminate interference in some such way always have the remedy of referring the matter to the Holy See.

tionem Can. 512, § 1, n. 2 praescriptam et quoad poenas Can. 2413 sancitas," *Ap*, I (1928), 417-422.

[18] *Cf. supra*, pp. 93-97.

CONCLUSION

THE greater portion of the foregoing pages has been devoted to the laws on the local ordinary's visitation. However, an effort has been made to trace the development of systematic visitation by religious superiors up to the time when such visitation became an established practice regulated by the constitutions of the various institutes. Thenceforth only the occasional conciliar laws and the statement of the Code (Canon 511) on religious visitors were considered and these briefly since visitation by religious officials was and is governed almost entirely by the particular laws of each order and congregation. The common law of the Church has gone into much greater detail on the rights and duties of the local ordinary as the external visitor of the religious within his territory. In treating this topic it has been necessary to consider separately diocesan congregations, pontifical congregations and orders, and even to make subdivisions of these groups since the extent of the local ordinary's visitation depends upon the different legal status of the several types of religious. The local ordinary's visitation of parishes has also been considered and at some length for in certain points the law on this subject is rather involved. With respect to the question of the procedure on visitation the Code is decidedly brief; hence an endeavor has been made to supplement the prescriptions of Canon 513 by drawing upon the writings of the older canonists.

It is evident from the legislation in the Code that canonical visitation of religious is esteemed as a highly important method for maintaining good observance in religious communities. Almost inevitably every human society, not excepting religious orders and congregations, is in the course of its history endangered by internal disorders and threatened with decay. The laws on the visitation of religious aim to ward off this peril from religious institutes and a clear understanding and a faithful observance of these laws cannot fail to provide a valuable safeguard to the religious life.

BIBLIOGRAPHY

Sources

Acta Apostolicae Sedis, Romae, 1909.

Acta Sanctae Sedis, 41 vols., Romae, 1865-1908.

Bullarium Diplomatum et Privilegiorum Sanctorum Pontificum Taurinensis editio, auspicante Cardinali Francisco Gaude, 25 vols., Augustae Taurinorum, 1857-1872.

Canones et Decreta Sacrosancti Oecumenici Concilii Tridentini, Editio Novissima ad Fidem Optimorum Exemplarium castigate Impressa, Taurini, 1913.

Codex Iuris Canonici, Pii X Pontificis Maximi jussu digestus, Benedicti Papae XV auctoritate promulgatus, Romae, 1917.

Codicis Iuris Canonici Fontes, cura Emi. Petri Card. Gasparri editi, 7 vols., Romae, 1923-1935.

Collectanea in Usum Secretariae Sacrae Congregationis Episcoporum et Regularium, Ed. A. Bizzarri, Romae, 1885.

Concilii Plenarii Baltimorensis III (1884), Acta et Decreta, Baltimorae, 1886.

Corpus Iuris Canonici, Editio Lipsiensis II (Richter-Friedberg), 2 vols., Lipsiae, 1922.

Corpus Iuris Civilis, Vol. I, *Institutiones*—recognovit P. Krueger; *Digesta*—recognovit Theodorus Mommsen, retractavit P. Krueger; Vol. II, Codex *Justinianus*—recognovit et retractavit P. Krueger; Vol. III, *Novellae Constitutiones*—R. Schoell; opus Schoelli morte interceptum absolvit G. Kroll, Berolini, 1928-1929.

Mansi, Joannes Dominicus, *Sacrorum Conciliorum Nova et Amplissima Collectio,* 53 vols., Parisiis, 1901-1919.

Migne, Jacques Paul, *Patrologiae Cursus Completus—Series Graeca,* 161 vols., Parisiis, 1857-1866.

Migne, Jacques Paul, *Patrologiae Cursus Completus—Series Latina,* 221 vols., Parisiis, 1844-1855.

Monumenta Germaniae Historica, Gregorii I Papae registrum epistolarum, Tom. I, pars I, libri i-iv, edidit Paulus Ewald, 1887; Tom. I, pars II, libri v-vii, post Pauli Ewaldi obitum edidit L. M. Hartmann, 1889; Tom. II, libri viii-xiv, post Pauli Ewaldi obitum edidit L. M. Hartmann, 1893-1899.

Monumenta Germaniae Historica, Legum Sectio II, Capitularia Regum Francorum, Tom. I, Ed. A. Boretius, Hannoverae, 1883; Tom. II, Edd. A. Boretius et V. Krause, Hannoverae, 1897.

Monumenta Germaniae Historica, Scriptores, Tom. XV, *Vitae aliaeque historiae minores,* Edidit Societas Aperiendis Fontibus Rerum Germanicarum Medii Aevi, Hannoverae, 1887, 1888.

Pallottini, Salvator, *Collectio Omnium Conclusionum et Resolutionum quae in causis propositis apud S. Cong. Cardinalium S. Concilii Tridentini Interpretum prodierunt ab anno 1564 ad annum 1860,* 17 vols., Romae, 1868-1893.

AUTHORS

Acta Congressus Iuridici Internationalis, 2 vols., Romae, 1935, 1936.

[Bachofen], Charles Augustine, *A Commentary on the New Code of Canon Law,* 8 vols., St. Louis: Herder, 1926.

Barker, Ernest, *The Dominican Order and Convocation,* Oxford, 1913.

Bastien, Pierre, *Directoire Canonique à l'usage des Congrégations à voeux simples,* 3 ed., Bruges: Beyaert, 1923.

Bastnagel, Clement V., *The Appointment of Parochial Adjutants and Assistants,* The Catholic University of America, Canon Law Studies, n. 58, Washington: The Catholic University of America, 1930.

Benedict XIV, *De Synodo Dioecesana,* 4 vols., Lovanii, 1763.

——— *Institutiones Ecclesiasticae,* Venetiis, 1788.

Blat, A., *Commentarium Textus Codicis Iuris Canonici,* Vol. II: *De Personis,* Romae: Ferrari, 1921; Vol. V: *De Delicits et Poenis,* 1924.

Bouix, D., *Tractatus de Iure Regularium,* 2 ed., 2 vols., Parisiis, 1867.

——— *Tractatus de Capitulis,* Parisiis, 1882.

Butler, Cuthbert, *Benedictine Monachism,* New York, 1919.

——— *The Lausiac History of Palladius,* Texts and Studies, VI, 2 vols., Cambridge, 1898-1904.

Cabrol, Fernand, *St. Benedict,* London, 1934.

Cabrol, Fernand, et Leclercq, Henri, *Dictionaire d'Archéologie Chrétienne et de Liturgie,* 12 vols., Paris: Librairie Letouzey et Ané, 1924-1936.

Cambridge Medieval History, The, 8 vols., New York: Macmillan, 1936.

Cappello, Felix M., *De Visitatione SS. Liminum et Dioeceseon,* 2 vols., Romae: Pustet, 1912.

Conte, Matthaeus, a Coronata, *Institutiones Iuris Canonici,* 4 vols., Taurini: Marietti, 1928-1935.

Creusen, J., *Religieux et Religieuses d'apres le Droit Ecclesiastique,* 3 ed., Bruxelles: Dewit, 1924.

De Janua, Gaudentius, *De Visitatione cuiuscumque Praelatis Ecclesiastici et Regularis,* 2 vols., Romae, 1753.

De Peyrinis, F. Laurentius, *Religiosus subditus et Praelatus,* Placentiae, 1639.

Dudden, F. Homes, *Gregory the Great, His Place in History and Thought,* 2 vols., London, 1905.

Fagnanus, P., *Commentaria in Libros Decretalium,* 4 vols., Venetiis, 1696.

Fanfani, L., *De Iure Religiosorum,* 2 ed., Taurini: Marietti, 1925.

Ferraris, F. Lucius, *Bibliotheca Canonica, Iuridica, Moralis, Theologica, necnon Ascetica, Polemica, Rubricistica, Historica,* 9 vols., Romae, 1885-1892.

Galbraith, G. R., *The Constitution of the Dominican Order, 1216 to 1360,* Manchester: University Press, 1925.

Gasquet, F. A., *English Monastic Life,* 3 ed., New York, 1905.

Gougaud, Louis, *Gaelic Pioneers of Christianity, the Work and Influence of Irish Monks and Saints in Continental Europe,* Dublin, 1923.

Graham, Rose, *English Ecclesiastical Studies,* London, 1929.

Hannan, Jerome D., *The Canon Law of Wills,* The Catholic University of America, Canon Law Studies, n. 87, Washington: The Catholic University of America, 1934.

Hannay, James, *The Spirit and Origin of Christian Monasticism,* London, 1903.

Hastings, James, *Encyclopedia of Religion and Ethics,* 12 vols., New York: Scribner, 1908-1922.

Hilpisch, Stephanus, *Die Doppelklöster, Entstehung und Organisation,* Beiträge zur Geschichte des Alten Mönchtums und des Benediktinerordens, Heft. 15, Münster: Aschendorffsche Verlagsbuchhandlung, 1928.

Hinschius, Paul, *Das Kirchenrecht der Katholiken und Protestanten in Deutschland,* 6 vols., Berlin, 1869-1897.

Holzapfel, H., *Manuale Historiae Ordinis Fratrum Minorum,* Fribourg, 1909.

Holstenius, Lucas et Brockie, Marianus, *Codex Regularum Monasticarum et Canonicarum,* 6 vols., Augustae Vindelicorum, 1759.

Joannes Andreae, *In Quinque Decretalium Libros Novella Commentaria,* Venetiis, 1631.

Kozman, François, *Textes Législatifs Touchant Le Cénobitisme Égyptien,* Codificazione Canonica Orientale, Fonti, Serie II—Fasc. I, [Civitate Vaticane:] Typographie Polyglotte Vaticane, 1935.

Ladeuze, Paulin, *Étude sur le cénobitisme Pakhomien,* Louvain, 1898.

Lavisse, Ernest, *Histoire de France depuis les originies jusqu'à la Révolution,* 8 vols., Paris, 1900.

Leipoldt, Johannes, *Schenute von Atripe und die Entstehung des National-Aegyptischen Christentums,* Texte und Untersuchungen zur Geschichte der Altchristlichen Literatur, N. F., Bd. X., Heft. I, Leipzig, 1903.

Lucidi, Angelus, *De Visitatione Sacrorum Liminum,* 3 ed., 3 vols., Romae, 1883.

MacKean, W. H., *Christian Monasticism in Egypt,* New York, 1920.

Maroto, P., *Institutiones Iuris Canonici,* 3 ed., 2 vols., Romae, 1921.

Martène, Edmond, *De Antiquis Ecclesiae Ritibus,* 4 vols., Antwerpiae, 1739.

Mocchegiani, Petrus, *Iurisprudentia Ecclesiastica ad usum et commoditatem utriusque cleri,* 3 vols., Ad Claras Aquas, 1904-1905.

Molitor, Raphael, *Aus der Rechtsgeschichte benediktinischer Verbände,* 3 vols., Münster, 1928-1934.

Montalembert, Comte de, *Monks of the West,* with an Introduction by F. A. Gasquet, 6 vols., New York, 1896.

Morison, E. F., *St. Basil and His Rule,* London, 1912.

Mothon, *Institutions Canoniques,* 3 vols., Paris, 1922.

Münter, D. Frederick, *Statutenbuch des Ordens der Tempelherren,* Berlin, 1794.

Pastor, L., *History of the Popes,* 18 vols., St. Louis: Herder, 1923-1929.

Pejska, J., *Jus Canonicum Religiosorum,* 3 ed., Friburgi Brisgoviae: Herder, 1927.

Piatus Montensis, F., *Praelectiontes Iuris Regularis,* 3 ed., 2 vols., Tornaci: Casterman, 1906.

Piatus Montensis, F., et Appeltern, Victorius ab, *Compendium Praelectionum Iuris Regularis,* 2 ed., Tornaci: Casterman, 1913.

Prümmer, D., *Manuale Iuris Canonici,* 4 et 5 ed., Friburgi Brisgoviae: Herder, 1927.

Reiffenstuel, Anacletus, *Ius Canonicum Universum,* edidit V. Pelletier, 5 vols., Parisiis, 1868.

Rodericus, Emmanuel, *Quaestiones Regulares et Canonicae,* 2 vols., Turnoni, 1609.

Schaaf, Valentine, T., *The Cloister,* The Catholic University of America, Canon Law Studies, n. 13, Cincinnati: St. Anthony Messenger, 1921.

Schäfer, Timotheus, *Compendium De Religiosis,* Münster: Aschendorff, 1927.

Schreiber, Georg, *Kurie und Kloster im 12 Jahrhundert,* Kirchenrechtliche Abhandlungen, Heft. 65-68, Stuttgart, 1910.

Smith, L. M., *The Early History of Cluny,* London: Oxford University Press, 1920.

——— *Cluny in the Eleventh and Twelfth Centuries,* London: Allen, 1930.

Smith, Mariner, *The Penal Law for Religious,* The Catholic University of America, Canon Law Studies, n. 98, Washington: The Catholic University of America, 1935.

Thomassinus, Ludovicus, *Vetus et Nova Ecclesiae Disciplina,* 3 vols., Venetiis, 1730.

Vermeersch, A., *De Religiosis Personis et Institutis tractatus canonico-moralis,* 2 ed., 2 vols., Brugis, 1902-1904.

Vermeersch, A., et Creusen, J., *Epitome Iuris Canonici,* 3 ed., 3 vols., Romae: Dessain, 1927.

Vromant, G., *De Bonis Ecclesiae Temporalibus,* Louvain: Desbarax, 1927.

——— *Ius Missionariorum,* Vol. II: *De Personis,* Louvain: Desbarax, 1929.

Wernz, F., et Vidal, P., *Ius Canonicum ad Codicis normam exactaum,* Vol. II: *De Personis,* 2 ed., Romae: Universitas Gregoriana, 1928, Vol. III: *De Religiosis,* 1933.

Workman, Herbert B., *The Evolution of the Monastic Ideal,* London, 1913.

Periodicals

American Historical Review, The, New York, 1895—

Apollinaris, Romae, 1928—

Archiv für Katholisches Kirchenrecht, Innsbruck, 1857-1861; Mainz, 1862—

Byzantinische Zeitschrift, Leipzig, 1905—

Clergy Review, The, London, 1931—

Commentarium pro Religiosis, Romae, 1920—

Homiletic and Pastoral Review, The, New York, 1900—

Journal of Theological Studies, The, London, 1899—
Jus Pontificium, Romae, 1921—
Novelle Revue Théologique, Louvain, 1869—
Perfice Munus, Turin, 1926—
Periodica de re canonica et morali, Brugis, 1905—; ab anno 1927: *Periodica de re canonica, morali, liturgica.*
Studien und Mitteilungen zur Geschichte des Benediktiner-Ordens, München, 1882—
Theologisch-praktische Quartalschrift, Linz, 1832—

ALPHABETICAL INDEX

BIOGRAPHICAL NOTE

Thomas Francis Reilly was born at Dorchester, Massachusetts, December 20, 1908. He attended Boston Latin School and St. Mary's College, in North East, Pennsylvania. He entered the Redemptorist Novitiate, Ilchester, Maryland, in 1927 and was professed the following year. His seminary course was made at Mount St. Alphonsus, New York, where he was ordained on June 10, 1933. In September 1934, he entered the School of Canon Law at the Catholic University of America, from which he obtained the degrees of J.C.B. and J.C.L. in the years 1935 and 1936 respectively.

CANON LAW STUDIES

1. Freriks, Rev. Celestine A., C.PP.S., J.C.D., Religious Congregations in Their External Relations, 121 pp., 1916.
2. Gallither, Rev. Daniel M., O.P., J.C.D., Canonical Elections, 117 pp., 1917.
3. Borkowski, Rev. Aurelius L., O.F.M., J.C.D., De Confraternitatibus Ecclesiasticis, 136 pp., 1918.
4. Castillo, Rev. Cayo, J.C.D., Disertacion Historico-Canonica sobre la Potestad del Cabildo en Sede Vacante o Impedida del Vicario Capitular, 99 pp., 1919 (1918).
5. Kubelbeck, Rev. William J., S.T.B., J.C.D., The Sacred Penitentiaria and Its Relation to Faculties of Ordinaries and Priests, 129 pp., 1918.
6. Petrovits, Rev. Joseph, J.C., S.T.D., J.C.D., The New Church Law on Matrimony, X-461 pp., 1919.
7. Hickey, Rev. John J., S.T.B., J.C.D., Irregularities and Simple Impediments in the New Code of Canon Law, 100 pp., 1920.
8. Klekotka, Rev. Peter J., S.T.B., J.C.D., Diocesan Consultors, 179 pp., 1920.
9. Wanenmacher, Rev. Francis, J.C.D., The Evidence in Ecclesiastical Procedure Affecting the Marriage Bond, 1920 (Printed 1935).
10. Golden, Rev. Henry Francis, J.C.D., Parochial Benefices in the New Code, IV-119 pp., 1921 (Printed 1925).
11. Koudelka, Rev. Charles J., J.C.D., Pastors, Their Rights and Duties According to the New Code of Canon Law, 211 pp., 1921.
12. Melo, Rev. Antonius, O.F.M., J.C.D., De Exemptione Regularium, X-188 pp., 1921.
13. Schaaf, Rev. Valentine Theodore, O.F.M., S.T.B., J.C.D., The Cloister, X-180 pp., 1921.
14. Burke, Rev. Thomas Joseph, S.T.D., J.C.D., Competence in Ecclesiastical Tribunals, IV-117 pp., 1922.
15. Leech, Rev. George Leo, J.C.D., A Comparative Study of the Constitution "Apostolicae Sedis" and the "Codex Juris Canonici," 179 pp., 1922.
16. Motry, Rev. Hubert Louis, S.T.D., J.C.D., Diocesan Faculties According to the Code of Canon Law, II-167 pp., 1922.
17. Murphy, Rev. George Lawrence, J.C.D., Delinquencies and Penalties in the Administration and the reception of the Sacraments, IV-121 pp., 1923.
18. O'Reilly, Rev. John Anthony, S.T.B., J.C.D., Ecclesiastical Sepulture in the New Code of Canon Law, II-129 pp., 1923.
19. Michalicka, Rev. Wenceslas Cyrill, O.S.B., J.C.D., Judicial Procedure in Dismissal of Clerical Exempt Religious, 107 pp., 1923.

20. DARGIN, REV. EDWARD VINCENT, S.T.B., J.C.D., Reserved Cases According to the Code of Canon Law, IV-103 pp., 1924.
21. GODFREY, REV. JOHN A., S.T.B., J.C.D., The Right of Patronage According to the Code of Canon Law, 153 pp., 1924.
22. HAGEDORN, REV. FRANCIS EDWARD, J.C.D., General Legislation on Indulgences, II-154 pp., 1924.
23. KING, REV. JAMES IGNATIUS, J.C.D., The Administration of the Sacraments to Dying Non-Catholics, V-141 pp., 1924.
24. WINSLOW, REV. FRANCIS JOSEPH, O.F.M., J.C.D., Vicars and Prefects Apostolic, IV-149 pp., 1924.
25. CORREA, REV. JOSE SERVELION, S.T.L., J.C.D., La Potestad Legislativa de la Iglesia Catolica, IV-127 pp., 1925.
26. DUGAN, REV. HENRY FRANCIS, A.M., J.C.D., The Judiciary Department of the Diocesan Curia, 87 pp., 1925.
27. KELLER, Rev. CHARLES FREDERICK, S.T.B., J.C.D., Mass Stipends, 167 pp., 1925.
28. PASCHANG, REV. JOHN LINUS, J.C.D., The Sacramentals According to the Code of Canon Law, 129 pp., 1925.
29. POINTEK, REV. CYRILLUS, O.F.M., S.T.B., J.C.D., De Indulto Exclaustrationis necnon Saecularizationis, XIII-289 pp., 1925.
30. KEARNEY, REV. RICHARD JOSEPH, S.T.B., J.C.D., Sponsors at Baptism According to the Code of Canon Law, IV-127 pp., 1925.
31. BARTLETT, REV. CHESTER JOSEPH, A.M., LL.B., J.C.D., The Tenure of Parochial Property in the United States of America, V-108 pp., 1926.
32. KILKER, REV. ADRIAN JEROME, J.C.D., Extreme Unction, V-425 pp., 1926.
33. MCCORMICK, REV. ROBERT EMMETT, J.C.D., Confessors of Religious, VIII-266 pp., 1926.
34. MILLER, REV. NEWTON THOMAS, J.C.D., Founded Masses According to the Code of Canon Law, VII-93 pp., 1926.
35. ROELKER, REV. EDWARD G., S.T.D., J.C.D., Principles of Privilege According to the Code of Canon Law, XI-166 pp., 1926.
36. BAKALARCZYK, REV. RICHARDUS, M.I.C., J.U.D., De Novitiatu, VIII-208 pp., 1927.
37. PIZZUTI, REV. LAWRENCE, O.F.M., J.U.L., De Parochis Religiosis, 1927. (Not Printed.)
38. BLILEY, REV. NICHOLAS MARTIN, O.S.B., J.C.D., Altars According to the Code of Canon Law, XIX-132 pp., 1927.
39. BROWN, MR. BRENDAN FRANCIS, A.B., LL.M., J.U.D., The Canonical Juristic Personality with Special Reference to its Status in the United States of America, V-212 pp., 1927.
40. CAVANAUGH, REV. WILLIAM THOMAS, C.P., J.U.D., The Reservation of the Blessed Sacrament, VIII-101 pp., 1927.
41. DOHENY, REV. WILLIAM J., C.S.C., A.B., J.U.D., Church Property: Modes of Acquisition, X-118 pp., 1927.

42. FELDHAUS, REV. ALOYSIUS H., C.PP.S., J.C.D., Oratories, IX-141 pp., 1927.
43. KELLY, REV. JAMES PATRICK, A.B., J.C.D., The Jurisdiction of the Simple Confessor, X-208 pp., 1927.
44. NEUBERGER, REV. NICHOLAS J., J.C.D., Canon 6 or the Relation of the Codex Juris Canonici to the Preceding Legislation, V-95 pp. 1927.
45. O'KEEFE, REV. GERALD MICHAEL, J.C.D., Matrimonial Dispensations, Powers of Bishops, Priests, and Confessors, VIII-232 pp., 1927.
46. QUIGLEY, REV. JOSEPH A. M., A.B., J.C.D., Condemned Societies, 139 pp., 1927.
47. ZAPLOTNIK, REV. JOHANNES LEO, J.C.D., De Vicariis Foraneis, X-142 pp., 1927.
48. DUSKIE, REV. JOHN ALOYSIUS, A.B., J.C.D., The Canonical Status of the Orientals in the United States, VIII-196 pp., 1928.
49. HYLAND, REV. FRANCIS EDWARD, J.C.D., Excommunication, Its Nature, Historical Development and Effects, VIII-181 pp., 1928.
50. REINMANN, REV. GERALD JOSEPH, O.M.C., J.C.D., The Third Order Secular of Saint Francis, 201 pp., 1928.
51. SCHENK, REV. FRANCIS J., J.C.D., The Matrimonial Impediments of Mixed Religion and Disparity of Cult, XVI-318 pp., 1929.
52. COADY, REV. JOHN JOSEPH, S.T.D., J.U.D., A.M., The Appointment of Pastors, VIII-150 pp., 1929.
53. KAY, REV. THOMAS HENRY, J.C.D., Competence in Matrimonial Procedure, VIII-164 pp., 1929.
54. TURNER, REV. SIDNEY JOSEPH, C.P., J.U.D., The Vow of Poverty, XLIX-217 pp., 1929.
55. KEARNEY, REV. RAYMOND A., A.B., S.T.D., J.C.D., The Principles of Delegation, VII-149 pp., 1929.
56. CONRAN, REV. EDWARD JAMES, A.B., J.C.D., The Interdict, V-163 pp., 1930.
57. O'NEIL, REV. WILLIAM H., J.C.D., Papal Rescripts of Favor, VII-218 pp., 1930.
58. BASTNAGEL, REV. CLEMENT VINCENT, J.U.D., The Appointment of Parochial Adjutants and Assistants, XV-257 pp., 1930.
59. FERRY, REV. WILLIAM A., A.B., J.C.D., Stole Fees, V-136 pp., 1930.
60. COSTELLO, REV. JOHN MICHAEL, A.B., J.C.D., Domicile and Quasi-Domicile, VII-201 pp., 1930.
61. KREMER, REV. MICHAEL NICHOLAS, A.B., S.T.B., J.C.D., Church Support in the United States, VI-136 pp., 1930.
62. ANGULO, REV. LUIS, C.M., J.C.D., Legislation de la Iglesia sobre la intencion en la application de la Santa Misa, VII-104 pp., 1931.
63. FREY, REV. WOLFGANG NORBERT, O.S.B., A.B., J.C.D., The Act of Religious Profession, VIII-174 pp., 1931.
64. ROBERTS, REV. JAMES BRENDAN, A.B., J.C.D., The Banns of Marriage, XIV-140 pp., 1931.

65. Ryder, Rev. Raymond Aloysius, A.B., J.C.D., Simony, IX-151 pp., 1931.
66. Campagna, Rev. Angelo, Ph.D., J.U.D., Il Vicario Generale del Vescovo, VII-205 pp., 1931.
67. Cox, Rev. Joseph Godfrey, A.B., J.C.D., The Administration of Seminaries, VI-124 pp., 1931.
68. Gregory, Rev. Donald J., J.U.D., The Pauline Privilege, XV-165 pp., 1931.
69. Donohue, Rev. John F., J.C.D., The Impediment of Crime, VII-110 pp., 1931.
70. Dooley, Rev. Eugene A., O.M.I., J.C.D., Church Law on Sacred Relics, IX-143 pp., 1931.
71. Orth, Rev. Clement Raymond, O.M.C., J.C.D., The Approbation of Religious Institutes, 171 pp., 1931.
72. Pernicone, Rev. Joseph M., A.B., J.C.D., The Ecclesiastical Prohibition of Books, XII-267 pp., 1932.
73. Clinton, Rev. Connell, A.B., J.C.D., The Paschal Precept, IX-108 pp., 1932.
74. Donnelly, Rev. Francis B., A.M., S.T.L., J.C.D., The Diocesan Synod, VIII-125 pp., 1932.
75. Torrente, Rev. Camilo, C.M.F., J.C.D., Las Processiones Sagradas, V-145 pp., 1932.
76. Murphy, Rev. Edwin J., C.PP.S., J.C.D., Suspension Ex Informata Conscientia, XI-122 pp., 1932.
77. Mackenzie, Rev. Eric F., A.M., S.T.L., J.C.D., The Delict of Heresy in Its Commission, Penalization, Absolution, VII-124 pp., 1932.
78. Lyons, Rev. Avitus E., S.T.B., J.C.D., The Collegiate Tribunal of First Instance, XI-147 pp., 1932.
79. Connolly, Rev. Thomas A., J.C.D., Appeals, XI-195 pp., 1932.
80. Sangmeister, Rev. Joseph V., A.B., J.C.D., Force and Fear as Precluding Matrimonial Consent, V-211 pp., 1932.
81. Jaeger, Rev. Leo A., A.B., J.C.D., The Administration of Vacant and Quasi-Vacant Episcopal Sees in the United States, IX-229 pp., 1932.
82. Rimlinger, Rev. Herbert T., J.C.D., Error Invalidating Matrimonial Consent, VII-79 pp., 1932.
83. Barrett, Rev. John D. M., S.S., J.C.D., A Comparative Study of the Third Plenary Council of Baltimore and the Code, IX-221 pp., 1932.
84. Carberry, Rev. John J., Ph.D., S.T.D., J.C.D., The Juridical Form of Marriage, X-177 pp., 1934.
85. Dolan, Rev. John L., A.B., J.C.D., The Defensor Vinculi, XII-157 pp., 1934.
86. Hannan, Rev. Jerome D., A.M., S.T.D., LL.B., J.C.D. The Canon Law of Wills, IX-517 pp., 1934.
87. Lemieux, Rev. Delisle A., A.M., J.C.D., The Sentence in Ecclesiastical Procedure, IX-131 pp., 1934.
88. O'Rourke, Rev. James J., A.B., J.C.D. Paris Registers, VII-109 pp., 1934.

89. Timlin, Rev. Bartholomew, O.F.M., A.M., J.C.D., Conditional Matrimonial Consent, X-381 pp., 1934.
90. Wahl, Rev. Francis X., A.B., J.C.D., The Matrimonial Impediments of Consanguinity and Affinity, VI-125 pp., 1934.
91. White, Rev. Robert J., A.B., LL.B., S.T.B., J.C.D., Canonical Ante-Nuptial Promises and the Civil Law, VI-152 pp., 1934.
92. Herrera, Rev. Antonio Parra, O.C.D., J.C.D., Legislacion Ecclesiastica sobra el Ayuno y la Abstinencia, XI-191 pp., 1935.
93. Kennedy, Rev. Edwin J., J.C.D., The Special Matrimonial Process in Cases of Evident Nullity, X-165 pp., 1935.
94. Manning, Rev. John J., A.B., J.C.D., Presumption of Law in Matrimonial Procedure, XI-111 pp., 1935.
95. Moeder, Rev. John M., J.C.D., The Proper Bishop for Ordination and Dimissorial Letters, VII-135 pp., 1935.
96. O'Mara, Rev. William A., A.B., J.C.D., Canonical Causes for Matrimonial Dispensations, IX-155 pp., 1935.
97. Reilly, Rev. Peter, J.C.D., Residence of Pastors, IX-81 pp., 1935.
98. Smith, Rev. Mariner T., O.P., S.T.Lr., J.C.D., The Penal Law for Religious, VII-169 pp., 1935.
99. Whalen, Rev. Donald W., A.M., J.C.D., The Value of Testimonial Evidence in Matrimonial Procedure, XIII-297 pp., 1935.
100. Cleary, Rev. Joseph F., J.C.D., Canonical Limitations on the Alienation of Church Property, VIII-141 pp., 1936.
101. Glynn, Rev. John C., J.C.D., The Promoter of Justice, XX-337 pp., 1936.
102. Brennan, Rev. James H., S.S., M.A., S.T.B., J.C.D., The Simple Convalidation of Marriage, VI-135 pp., 1937.
103. Brunini, Rev. Joseph Bernard, J.C.D., The Clerical Obligations of Canons 139 and 142, X-121 pp., 1937.
104. Connor, Rev. Maurice, A.B., J.C.D., The Administrative Removal of Pastors, VIII-159 pp., 1937.
105. Guilfoyle, Rev. Merlin Joseph, J.C.D., Custom, XI-144 pp., 1937.
106. Hughes, Rev. James Austin, A.B., A.M., J.C.D., Witnesses in Criminal Trials of Clerics, IX-140 pp., 1937.
107. Jansen, Rev. Raymond J., A.B., S.T.L., J.C.D., Canonical Provisions for Catechetical Instruction, VII-153 pp., 1937.
108. Kealy, Rev. John James, A.B., J.C.D., The Introductory Libellus in Church Court Procedure, XI-121 pp., 1937.
109. McManus, Rev. James Edward, C.SS.R., J.C.D., The Administration of Temporal Goods in Religious Institutes, XVI-196 pp., 1937.
110. Moriarity, Rev. Eugene James, J.C.D., Oaths in Ecclesiastical Courts, X-115 pp., 1937.
111. Rainer, Rev. Eligius George, C.SS.R., J.C.D., Suspension of Clerics, XVII-249 pp., 1937.
112. Reilly, Rev. Thomas F., C.SS.R., J.C.L., Visitation of Religious.

CPSIA information can be obtained
at www.ICGtesting.com
Printed in the USA
BVHW07*2244110918
527223BV00004B/79/P